Three-Note Voicings and Beyond

by Randy Vincent

Music Engraving - Chuck Gee
Cover Design & Artwork - Attila Nagy
Photos - Kathy Vincent

ISBN 1-883217-66-0

Table of Contents

Page

Author's Introduction i

About the Author ii

Chapter 1 - Three-Note "Shell" Voicings 1
    Cycles 1
    II-V-I Progressions 4
    Adding notes to "shell" voicings 6
    Modified "shell" voicings 8

Chapter 2 - Three-Note Comping Derived From "Shells" 11
    Cycles 11
    II-V-I Progressions (Part A) 13
    II-V-I Progressions (Part B) 20
    Playing the voicings on other sets of strings 29
    Practicing and using the rootless voicings 32

Chapter 3 - Basic Triad Review **33**
    Close triad voicings 33
    Open triad voicings 37

Chapter 4 - "Walking" Guitar 44
    The basic concept 44
    Long II-V-I 45
    Short II-V-I 51
    Long cycles 56
    Short cycles 62
    Turnarounds 64
    Twelve-bar blues 72
    Rhythm changes 76

Chapter 5 - Using Triads In "Slash" Chords And Upper Structure Voicings 81
    Triadic "slash" chords 81
    Upper structure voicings 91

Chapter 6 - Triad Pairs 104
    Major triad pairs 104
    Minor triad pairs 106
    Combining major and minor whole-step pairs to harmonize major modes 108
    Combining minor and diminished whole-step pairs to harmonize melodic minor modes 110
    More tricks with triad pairs 112

Chapter 7 - Dominant Cycles Revisited plus Diminished and Wholetone Scales 124
    A fresh look at dominant cycles 124
    A fresh look at diminished scales 133
    A fresh look at wholetone scales 138

Chapter 8 - Quartal Harmony and Secundal Harmony 142
    Quartal harmony 143
    Secundal harmony 150
    Using hexatonic seconds to harmonize melodies 152

Chapter 9 - Drop 2 Reductions 155
    Top-three-note drop 2 reductions 156
    Bottom-three-note drop 2 reductions 157
    Mixing the top and bottom drop 2 reductions 158
    Modal drop 2 reductions 159
    Some miscellaneous drop 2 reductions 164

Chapter 10 - Deriving Simulated Shearing-Style Block Chords From Drop 2 Reductions 166
    Bebop scale Shearing-style voicings 167
    Shearing-style extension voicings 170
    Simulated Shearing reductions 172

Chapter 11 - Comping Revisited 174
    Blues comping 174
    II-V-I comp melodies 178

Chapter 12 - Melodies Revisited 185
    Harmonizing melodies with chromatic parallel voicings 185
    Free three-note combinations 187
    A melody in similated Shearing-style voicings 192

Author's Introduction

This book is primarily about three-note voicings for jazz guitar, but also deals with some four and five note voicings that are a neccessary consequence of some of the three-note ones. For example, triads are three-notes by themselves, but are used in "slash" chords and Upper Structure voicings as well as some triad-pair hybrid voicings, so we'll check those out too.

To use this book you should at least have the basics of playing the guitar and enough knowledge of standard music notation to be able to interpret the examples. The book proceeds in a logical fashion so beginners to jazz guitar can start at the beginning of the book and proceed as far as they'd like to go, while more advanced players can skip sections they're already familiar with and jump in anywhere they find interesting. The material covers a range from quite basic to very advanced.

Many of the examples are fragments from standard tunes, so a good approach to application would be to study the tune fragment, practice the suggested exercises, then work out the rest of the tune using the concept demonstrated. You can find all of the tunes in the New Real Book series available from Sher Music Co.

Three-note voicings are especially suited to a "dynamic" concept where harmony is derived from three independent moving voices. Since the voices may have independent rhythms, it makes the chord diagrams a little tricky. In general the diagrams are standard guitar "grids" with dots showing where the fingers go and fret numbers along the side. For multiple moving lines with independent rhythms we generally use hollow dots for sustaining notes and solid dots for voices in motion. In some cases it is neccessary to have a new diagram with one or two notes sustaining from the previous diagram. These will be shown by hollow or solid dots in parenthesis.

I have found the studies in this book to be a great source of material for practical use in comping, melody playing, and for jazz improvization, and I am still working on much of it, so it should provide years of fun stuff to practice.

SPECIAL THANKS:
To Chuck Sher, who not only made this book possible, but without his encouragement it never would have happened.
To Chuck Gee for his patience and expertise.
To Erik Lindquist for his assistance with proofreading and contact information.

Dedicated to the memory of my father Ralph L. Vincent 1919-2010

Randy Vincent

About the Author

Randy Vincent has had a long and illustrious career in jazz. He has performed, toured and/or recorded with Dizzy Gillespie, Joe Henderson, Bobby Hutcherson, Bebop And Beyond, The Turtle Island String Quartet, and many others.

Randy has taught jazz guitar at Sonoma State University since 1981 and has conducted clinics throughout the US and overseas. Some of his more well-known former students include Julian Lage, Dave MacNab, Chris Pimentel, and Liberty Ellmen. He currently teaches at Sonoma State University and privately.

He is the author of a previous Sher Music Co. book, "Jazz Guitar Voicings, Vol.1 - The Drop 2 Book."

He has performed at numerous jazz festivals including the Monterey Jazz Festival and Dizzy Gillespie's 75th birthday celebration at the Hollywood Bowl, as well as performing regularly with the Santa Rosa Symphony's Pops Concerts.

A selected discography of Randy's recordings:
    Randy Vincent - "Nisha's Dream" and "Mirror Image"
    Bobby Hutcherson - "Ambos Mundos"
    Bebop And Beyond - "Bebop And Beyond Plays Dizzy Gillespie" (featuring Dizzy)
            and "Bebop And Beyond Plays Thelonious Monk" (featuring Joe Henderson)
    Stephanie Ozer - "O Comeco" (featuring Leny Andrade)
    Larry Baskett Trio - "Chalice" and "Poor Boy Blue"
    Mel Graves - "Emotion In Motion"
    Turtle Island String Quartet - "Spider Dreams"
    Peter Welker - "Para Peachy" and "We'll Be Together Again
    Welker/Oster Jazz Alliance - "Shining Hour" and "Detour Ahead"
    Vern Thompson - "Passions Of The Heart", "Sea Of Dreams" and "Convergence"
            (featuring Bob Sheppard, Akira Tana, Tony Dumas and Billy Childs)
    Mike Vax Big Band - "Alternate Route"
    Dave Eshelman's Garden Big Band - "Milagro's Journey"

Chapter 1 - Three-Note "Shell" Voicings

CYCLES

Play Ex. 1-1, the first four measures of the bridge to Duke Jordan's "Jordu." This is the sound of what many musicians refer to as "shell" voicings, which are 3-note voicings for seventh chords consisting of the root, 3rd and 7th of each chord. Notice the clear uncluttered sound and streamlined voice leading, as well as the ease with which they can be played on the guitar. This makes them a practical foundation for creating a system of generic voicings for jazz guitar.

Ex. 1-1

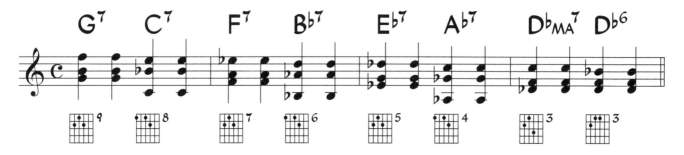

Now play Ex. 1-2, a "jazzed-up" (literally) version of the first couple of bars of the same progression using a device called tritone substitution to create a more interesting bass line. More on this later.

Ex. 1-2

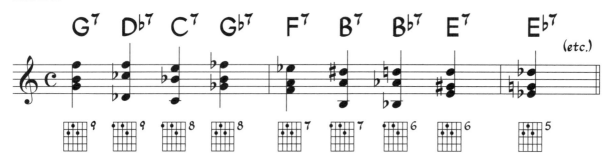

ROOT MOVEMENT

Let's do a bit of analysis on the first example. The chords are moving counter-clockwise around the circle of 5ths. This means, in theory, that each new chord root is a 5th lower than the previous chord root. If we tried to do this literally, we'd very quickly "run out of guitar". Fortunately there's an easy solution. The inversion of down-a-5th is up-a-4th, so we merely alternate down-a-5th from the fifth string to the sixth string with up-a-4th from the sixth string back to the fifth string. This is shown in Ex. 1-3.

Ex. 1-3

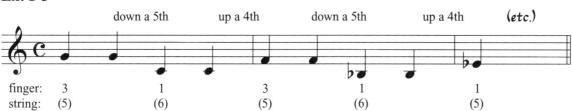

ADDING THE 3RDS AND 7THS

Now we have used the bottom two strings, leaving the middle two, the third and fourth strings, for the 3rds and 7ths. The best way to voice the 3rds and 7ths is not to have them follow the down-5-up-4 cycle, but to create a smooth melodic voice leading by having the 3rds and 7ths invert and swap places with each chord change. This is shown in example 1-4.

Ex. 1-4

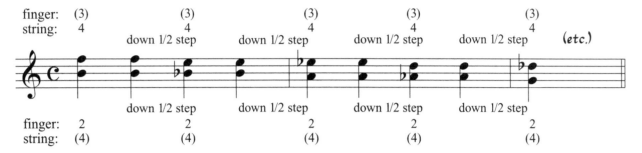

Notice that the 3rd of G7, the note B, is on the fourth string, while the 7th, the note F, is on the third string. When we change to C7, the B note drops by a half step to the 7th of C, the note Bb, and the F note drops by a half step to the note E, the 3rd of C. Notice that the shape on the fingerboard remains unchanged as the chords change. This is because all the chords in the first three bars are dominant 7 chords whose 3rds and 7ths are a tritone apart, and the tritone is the only interval that inverts into itself (an augmented 4th is enharmonic, or sounds the same as, its inversion, a diminished 5th).

Ex. 1-5 shows the bass line for Ex. 1-2. The line always drops by a half step after alternately going down or up by a tritone.

Ex. 1-5

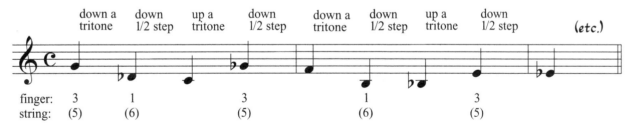

A DYNAMIC CONCEPT OF HARMONY

By the way, let's talk about an important point. Most guitar players learn chords by looking at the inevitable chord grid diagrams and memorizing the "grip" that their fingers make in matching the shape on the diagram. This is what I call a "static" concept. The spelling of each vertical chord is correct but the horizontal voice-leading may be distorted by the fact that what comes before and after gets ignored. In the method we are using here the melodic lines are creating the chords so the horizontal voice-leading is automatically correct. This is what I call a "dynamic" concept. The chord shapes are there, but are actually created by the individual moving lines.

ALTERNATE FINGERINGS

The shapes themselves can be fingered in several different ways. Ex. 1-6 shows several possible fingerings for our first chord shape, followed by three sets of practical fingerings to use for playing the cycle in Ex. 1-1 and 1-2. The first set of fingerings uses the same fingers to play the same notes that were used in Ex. 1-3, 1-4, and 1-5. This fingering has the greatest economy of hand motion, so why the other two sets of fingerings? The second set leaves the first finger free to possibly add notes on higher strings later on, while the third set leaves the fourth finger free for the same purpose. Therefore you should practice the cycles with all three fingerings, so that when the time comes you'll be ready.

Ex. 1-6

Alternate fingerings

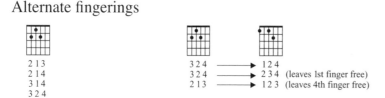

MAJOR 7 AND MINOR 7 CYCLES

Look at Ex. 1-7A, which shows the voice leading for the 3rds and 7ths of major7 chords going around the cycle of 5ths. The interval between the 3rd on the fourth string and 7th on the third string in this case is a perfect 5th. When the chord changes we again swap the 3rd and 7th, which places the 7th on the fourth string and 3rd on the third string. This changes the 5th into its inversion, a perfect 4th. The note B is a common tone between the first two chords. It's the 3rd of G and also the 7th of C, so the note doesn't move at the first change of chords. The note F# drops by a whole step to change from the 7th in the first chord into the 3rd of the second chord. On the next movement in the cycle the process is reversed. Now the E becomes the common tone while the F# moves down a whole step, and so on. Ex. 1-7B is identical except a half-step lower, creating the voice leading for the 3rds and 7ths of minor7 chords going around the cycle of 5ths.

Ex. 1-7

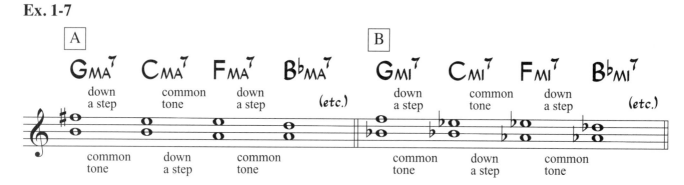

Play Ex. 1-8, which shows the first two bars of maj7 chords going around the cycle and the first two bars of m7 chords going around the cycle. Be sure to start high on the fingerboard and extend the cycles as long as you can until you "run out of guitar".

Ex. 1-8

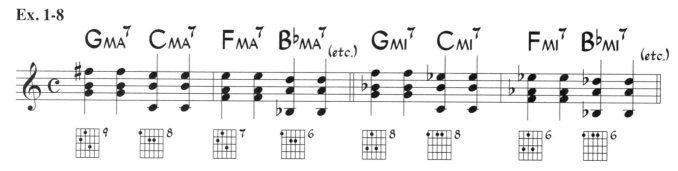

3

Ex. 1-9 shows two practical sets of fingerings to use to play the cycles. Feel free to experiment and find more if you can.

Ex. 1-9

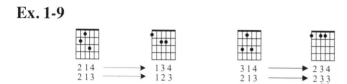

II-V-I PROGRESSIONS

DIATONIC CHORDS

Now we have forms available for dom7, maj7, and m7 chords with roots on both the fifth and sixth strings, so we have everything we need to play II-V-I progressions in any key with great voice leading. As you probably already know, any II-V-I goes counter-clockwise around the circle of 5ths, just like the cycles we've been working on. However, the traditional II-V-I is diatonic, meaning all the notes of all the chords belong inside the scale of the I chord. This causes the qualities of the chords to change as they progress through the cycle, making the II chord a m7, the V chord a dom7, and the I chord a maj7. The roots of the first three chords in the cycles we've seen so far are G, C, and F, so they could be converted into a II-V-I in the key of F by selecting the qualities IIm7-Vdom7-Imaj7, making the three chords Gm7-C7-Fmaj7. Ex. 1-10 shows the voice leading of the 3rds and 7ths for this progression.

Ex. 1-10

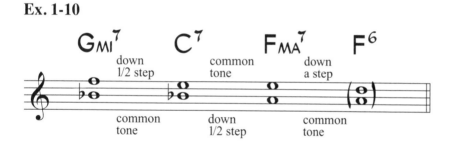

The 3rds and 7ths still swap and the upper and lower lines continue to take turns between being common tones and stepping down the scale. The notes in parenthesis shows what happens if we continue that process, which is exactly what my ear wants to hear, so the Fmaj7 changes into F6, which is completely compatible with the Fmaj7 I chord function. The Imaj7 to I6 movement is very commonly used to create a feeling of motion when the progression has gone "static" on the I chord (notice this was used in Ex. 1-1 on the Db chord).

Play Ex. 1-11, the II-V-I in F in three-note "shell" voicings. The root of the II chord and the I chord are located on the fifth string, while the root of the V chord is on the sixth string.

Ex. 1-11

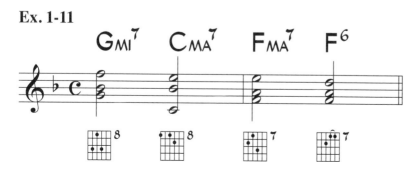

PLAYING II-V-I IN ALL KEYS

In order to facilitate the ability to play II-V-Is in all keys, we'll need to work out the progression with the roots of the II and I chords on the sixth string, and the root of the V chord on the fifth string, so let's start the cycle at C, located on the sixth string, and play Cm7-F7-Bbmaj7-Bb6, the II-V-I in the key of Bb, shown in Ex. 1-12. Practice II-V-I progressions in all keys, going around the circle of 5ths at first. Later on try going through the keys up and down in half steps, whole steps, minor 3rds and major 3rds.

Ex. 1-12

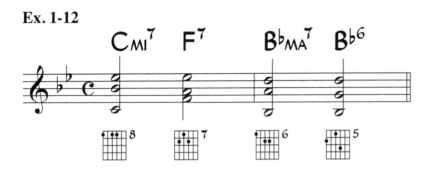

CHORDS WITH FLATTED FIFTHS

You might be wondering about chords with a flatted 5th since these "shell" voicings don't have a 5th. In some contexts this is not a problem because the tonality may have implied the b5th of the chord in question. For example, when playing "Autumn Leaves" in G minor, the Am7b5 doesn't require the 5th because the note Eb has been well established in the Cm7, F7, and Ebmaj7 chords.

In diminished 7th and m7b5 chords the b5 is a color tone, so you may want to try replacing either the 3rd or 7th with the b5th. Another possible solution is to use the b5 replacement voicing first before swiching to the standard "shell" voicing to keep the pure voice leading intact. Ex. 1-13 and Ex. 1-14 demonstrate this with II-V-I progressions in F minor and in Bb minor respectively. These examples also introduce some new chord qualities and forms, the m-maj7 and the m6 in addition to addressing the m7b5. Work out some practical fingerings with alternates and play in all keys.

Ex. 1-13

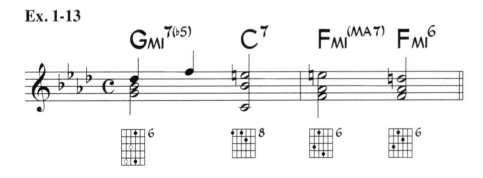

Ex. 1-14

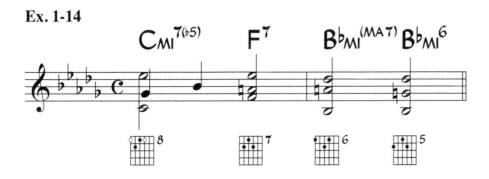

"SHELL" VOICING VARIATIONS

These three-note "shell" voicings are ideal for playing Freddie Green-style rhythm guitar, as well as being the foundation of many other practical jazz guitar voicings. Many solo guitar voicings add notes on the second string to the basic "shell" voicing, and frequently the first string as well. These chords are also usful for accompanying when there's no bass player (both with and without the added notes). Many of the great jazz players also use slightly modified "shell" chords where all the notes are on strings three, four, and six, or on strings two, three, and five. This is done by using 5ths in the bass voice instead of roots on some of the chords to smooth out the bass line voice leading (more on this later). The basic three-note "shell" voicings are also the main resolution or "target" chords for what we could call "walking guitar voicings," which we'll also get to in a while. For now, let's try adding a few notes to some cycles and II-V-I progressions.

ADDING NOTES TO "SHELL" VOICINGS

Play Ex. 1-15, the first four measures of the bridge to "Jordu". It is identical to Ex. 1-1 except we have added notes on the second string making the dominant chords cycle between dom9th chords and dom13th chords, and adding a 9th to both the Dbmaj7 and the Db6. The basic "shell" part of the dominant chords must be played with the first three fingers since the 9ths and 13ths must be played with the fourth finger (although the 9ths could be barred by the third finger). The 9th on the Dbmaj9 chord should be played with the third finger.

Ex. 1-15

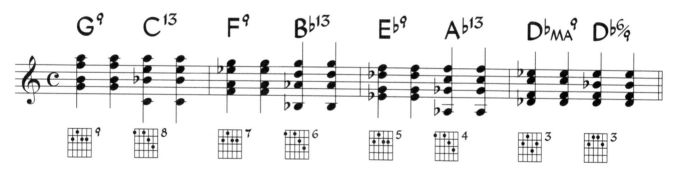

Ex. 1-16 shows the most commonly added notes on the second string for our dominant voicings with the root on the fifth string (G7 in the example) and the root on the sixth string (C7 in the example). On the C7 chord, the Gb could be spelled F# with the chord now named C7#11, and the G# could be spelled Ab with the chord named C7b13.

Ex. 1-16

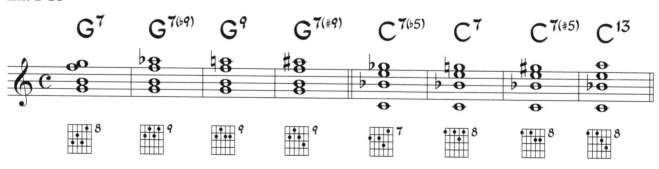

Ex. 1-17 shows the most commonly added notes on the second string for the II-V-I starting with the root on the fifth string, while Ex. 1-18 shows them for the II-V-I starting with the root on the sixth string. Ex.s 1-19 and 1-20 are variations of the same progressions using alt. dominant chords and new alternates for the 6th chords.

Ex. 1-17

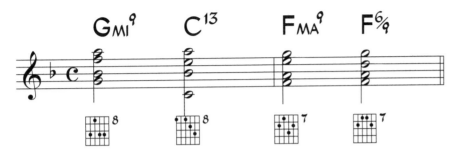

Ex. 1-18

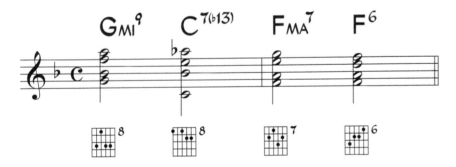

Ex. 1-19

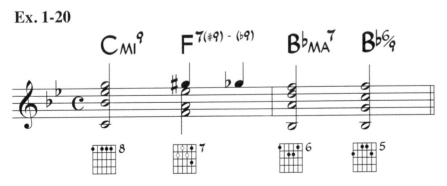

Ex. 1-20

You should experiment with finding other second-string added-notes and combining with notes found on the first string as well, but I'm going to leave that up to you because this book is primarily about three-note voicings and we have a lot of terrain to cover, so let's get to it.

MODIFIED "SHELL" VOICINGS

Play Ex. 1-21, the first four bars of "Perdido", and Ex. 1-22, the first eight bars of "All The Things You Are". These are examples of modified "shell" voicings as shown to me many years ago by my teacher, Park Hill, who had done a lot of big band work and had studied the rhythm guitar style of Freddie Green. They are essentially the same as the chords we've already done except the bass voice does not go root to root, but stays on the same string, swapping between roots and 5ths as the chords cycle, producing a very smooth voice leading.

Ex. 1-21

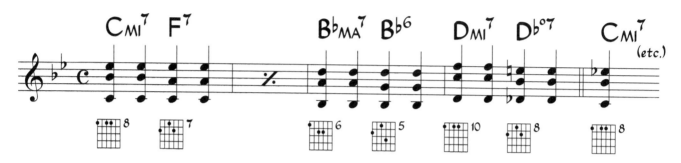

Ex. 1-22

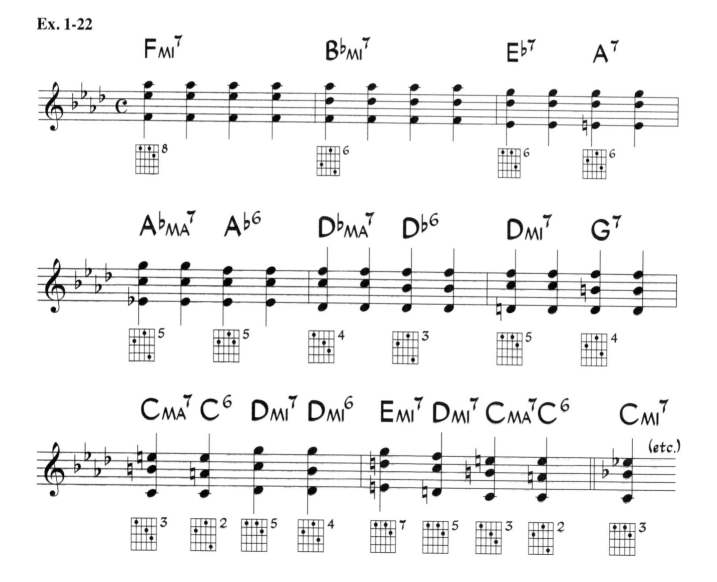

Notice that the voicings for Ex. 1-22 are on a different set of strings as well. These modified "shells" lend themselves better to the higher strings than the original "shells" (although Freddie still preferred to stay on the lower set). They also take on the same added notes that the original ones do, keeping in mind that the notes added on the second string will be located on the first string when we're using the higher string set. The modified chords are used frequently by many great jazz players and by many great Brazilian guitarists as well.

VAN EPS EXERCISES

Check out Ex. 1-23, the first in a series of exercises given to me by Park that were inspired by George Van Eps, another of Park's heroes. Instead of strumming quarter notes like Freddie, notice that the outer voices sustain while the middle voice keeps moving. The outer voices are "walking tenths". Tenths are 3rds that have been opened by an octave. The 10ths must be played by the second and fourth fingers sliding up and down the fifth and second strings, while the quarter notes are played by the third and first fingers. Be careful to make sure that the half notes keep ringing (without restriking) while changing the quarter notes. This can be done finger-style, but also with a pick (Park played all these exercises beautifully using a pick). Pick-style requires that the left hand carefully mutes all the strings not involved in the voicings. In each chord the 7th drops to the diatonic 6th, resulting in Cmaj7 to C6, Dm7 to Dm6, Em7 to a first inversion C major triad (instead of Em6, which contains the non-diatonic note C#), and Fmaj7 to F6.

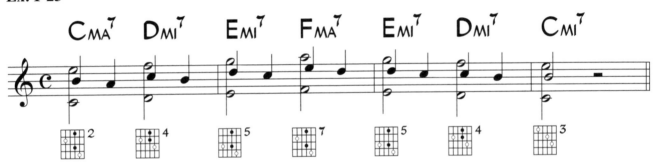

Ex. 1-24 shows the same idea transposed to the key of F while remaining on the same set of strings. This places the quarter note melody on top of the voicing on the second string, with "walking sixths" below. Sixths are inverted 3rds. None of the chords contain the root, but have the 5th on the bottom instead.

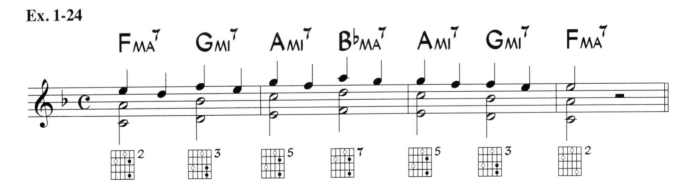

Ex. 1-25 is based on Ex. 1-23 with the quarter note melody changed into a chromatically elaborated 8th note line using lower neighbor tones and various approach tones.

Ex. 1-25

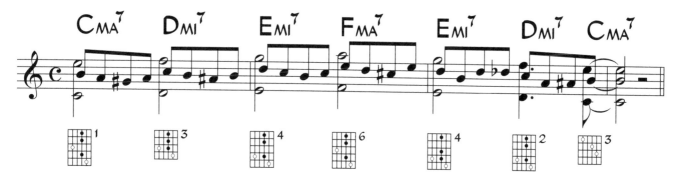

Ex. 1-26 shows the same idea based on Ex. 1-24.

Ex. 1-26

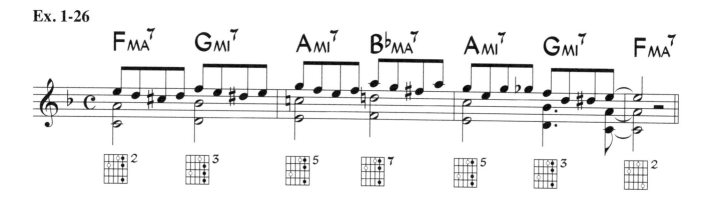

ANALYZING THESE VOICINGS

This would be a good time to take another look at what many of these voicings really are. Look at Ex. 1-23. After Cmaj7 changes into C6, the three notes actually spell out an inverted A minor triad. The Dm6 is an inverted B diminished triad, etc. In Ex. 1-24 the Fmaj7 voicing is literally the inverted A minor triad again, while the Gm7 is literally an inverted Bb major triad. Many of the modified "shells" are actually open-voiced triad inversions. When we get to "walking" guitar chords most of the connecting chords will prove to be triads, so we'll have to check out triads before we get there (triads are three notes, after all). But first let's take a look at some three-note comping ideas that can be derived directly from our "shell" voicings.

Chapter 2
Three-Note Comping Derived From "Shells"

ROOTLESS COMPING

Play Ex. 2-1. This is a rootless comp for the first four bars of the bridge to "Jordu." To understand how this is derived from "shell" voicings, please refer to Ex. 1-15. Notice that the voicings in Ex. 2-1 are the same but with the roots left out and the rhythm changed from four-to-the-bar Freddie Green-style to a style designed to compliment a soloist. If the melody of "Jordu" was being played, a different rhythm that compliments that would be used.

Ex. 2-1

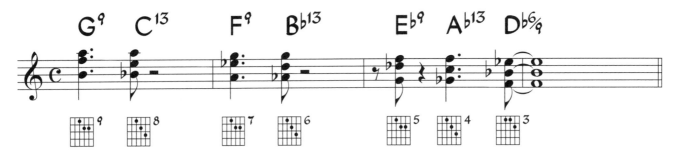

CHROMATIC APPROACH CHORDS

Ex. 2-2 is a slight variation using some chromatic approach chords. The chords whose symbols are in parenthesis, the Gb9 and the C6/9, are really just half step slides into the main chords used for embellishment. Notice that anytime a chord falls on the "and" of 4 or the "and" of 2 without a new attack on the following beats (1 and 3), it is the chord that belongs on that following downbeat. This is a form of rhythmic anticipation that is very common in jazz. These basic comp voicings are added-note "shell" voicings with the roots omitted.

Ex. 2-2

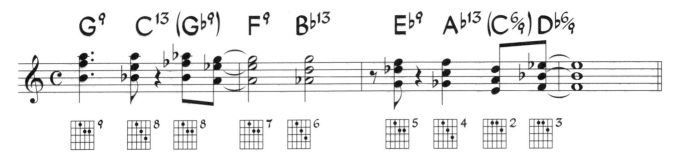

PARALLEL MOTION

On the next four examples we'll use parallel motion to form specific dominant cycles. In each example the fingerboard shape and fingering remains constant. In Ex. 2-3, by starting with the root used as the added note and using exact parallel motion we create the progression G7-C7b5-F7-Bb7b5 etc. (I'm leaving out comp rhythms for now so we can concentrate on the voicings.)

Ex. 2-3

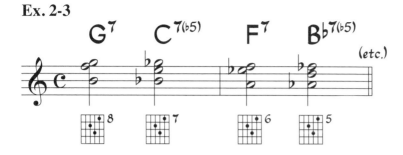

Ex. 2-4 starts with the b9 added note to create G7b9-C7-F7b9-Bb7, etc.

Ex. 2-4

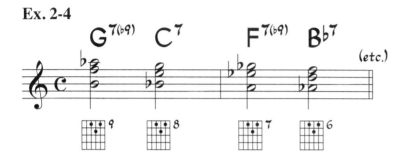

Ex. 2-5 adds the natural 9th to start, yielding G9-C7#5-F9-Bb7#5, etc.

Ex. 2-5

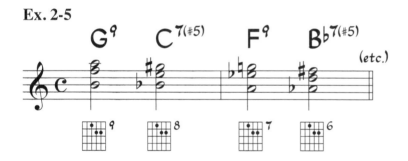

Ex. 2-6 starts with the added #9 to form the progression G7#9-C13-F7#9-Bb13, etc. All these cycles are easily playable with the root bass notes added on the bottom two strings, and I advise practicing them that way first so your ear can really hear what's happening harmonically.

Ex. 2-6

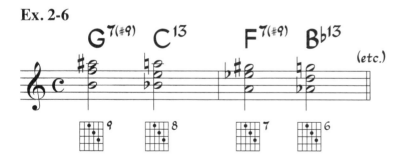

OBLIQUE MOTION

Ex. 2-7 uses a different device, a common tone, to create oblique motion, which is one or more voices moving in similar motion while one or more voices remains motionless. In this example we fix G as the unmoving note, making it a common tone in the four chords in the cycle. The G is the root of G7, becoming the 5th of C7, then becoming the 9th of F9, and finally the 13th of Bb13.

Ex. 2-7

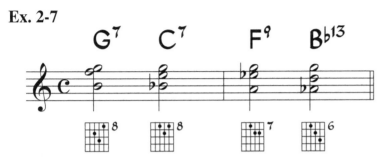

There's a lot more intense stuff we can do with these 3-note dominant cycles, but it's really more appropriate for chord melody, chord solo improvisation, intros, endings and cadenzas, so it will have to be in a later chapter so we can focus on comping for now. It's time to check out some II-V-I progressions.

II-V-I PROGRESSIONS (Part A)

Play Ex. 2-8 (it's the same as Ex. 1-17), II-V-I in "shell" voicings with added notes.

Ex. 2-8

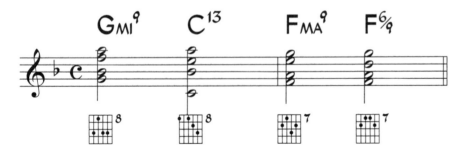

Now play Ex. 2-9, the same thing with the roots omitted.

Ex. 2-9

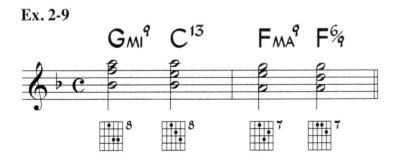

Ex. 2-10 is the altered version, the same as Ex. 1-19 with the roots omitted.

Ex. 2-10

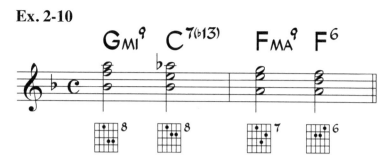

ADDING MOTION TO ROOTLESS II-V-I

Let's see what we can do with the three-note versions now that we've freed up a finger. Ex. 2-11 is a simple unaltered variation.

Ex. 2-11

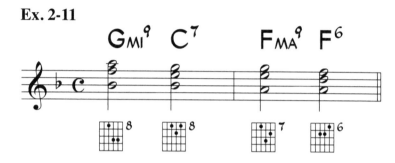

Ex. 2-12 features the 13th on the V chord changing to a b13th to create a passing tone to the 9th of the I chord.

Ex. 2-12

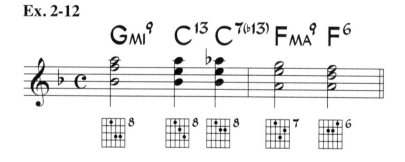

Ex. 2-13 uses the #11 on the V chord as a lower neighbor tone to the 5th, and goes to the root on the I chord.

Ex. 2-13

Ex. 2-14 uses the b13th going to the #11 on the V chord to form a chromatic enclosure surrounding and targeting the 9th of the I chord.

Ex. 2-14

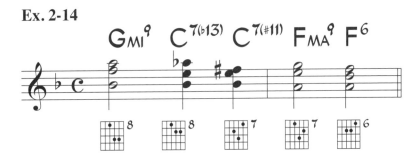

Ex. 2-15 reverses the order of the enclosure notes.

Ex. 2-15

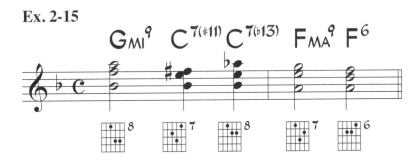

Play Ex. 2-16 and Ex. 2-17. These are sample comps on our basic II-V-I using upper and lower chromatic approach chords and rhythmic anticipations.

Ex. 2-16

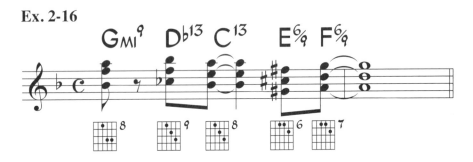

Ex. 2-17

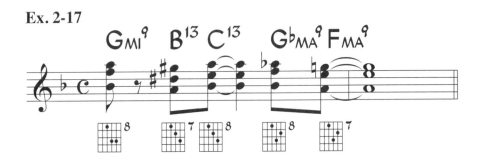

SUSTAINING NOTES

Another useful way to play these progressions is demonstrated in Ex. 2-18. This is the same as Ex. 2-9 except any note that doesn't move is sustained without restriking. This is a great way to practice all these three-note variations because it helps you hear which lines are moving and which are motionless (it separates the parts), and it helps you develop more control with both the left and right hands.

Ex. 2-18

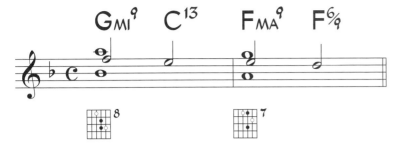

Ex. 2-19 applies this same method to the progression from Ex. 2-11. Notice you'll sometimes have to use a different fingering on some chords to make it work. Take the Fmaj9, for instance. In Ex. 2-18 it can be played with the first three fingers, lifting the third finger to get the D note on F6 with a partial barre by the first finger. In Ex. 2-19, however, it must be played by the second, third, and fourth fingers so the note A, played by the second finger, can sustain while the other fingers exchange to play D and F with the third and first fingers.

Ex. 2-19

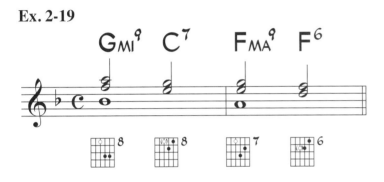

Examples 2-20 and 2-21 apply the technique to the progressions from examples 2-14 and 2-13 respectively. The following examples will not be written this way (for clarity), but remember to try using the sustaining technique as an alternate way to practice these II-V-I voicings (including those in part B ahead).

Ex. 2-20

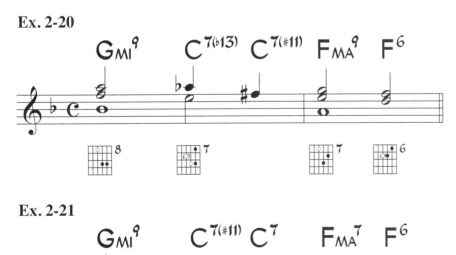

Ex. 2-21

16

II-V-I IN MINOR

Ex. 2-22 shows one possible way to convert our "rootless" three-note II-V-I into a minor key. For convenience we'll use the parallel minor key, F minor.

Ex. 2-22

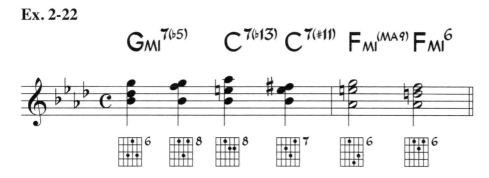

INVERTING ROOTLESS II-V-I

These rootless three-note II-V-Is sound great on the second, third and fourth strings, not too high and not too low. But we can get more use out of these three strings by finding the inversions of the voicings we've been playing. Lets take the first chord from Ex. 2-9, Gm9. It contains the notes Bb, F, and A. By lowering the Bb to A, the F to Bb, and the A to F, keeping them on the same strings, we get the voicing in Ex. 2-23, an inversion of our original Gm9 chord.

Ex. 2-23

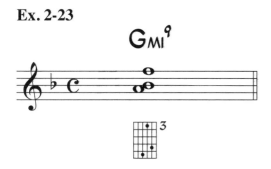

If we move the same notes the same way we did in our previous examples, the complete inverted II-V-I forms emerge automatically, as if by magic (but it isn't magic, it requires the work we're about to do). To complete the inverted form of Ex. 2-9 we have to first move the F down a half step to E, forming C13, then move A and Bb down the F scale to G and A respectively, forming Fmaj9, followed by E dropping to D, forming the F6/9. The result is shown in Ex. 2-24.

Ex. 2-24

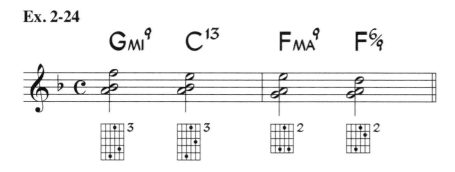

Examples 2-25, 2-26, and 2-27 are derived from examples 2-11, 2-14, and 2-13 respectively, while Ex. 2-28 is in F minor, derived from Ex. 2-22.

Ex. 2-25

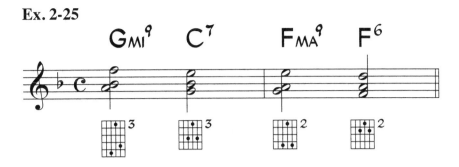

Ex. 2-26

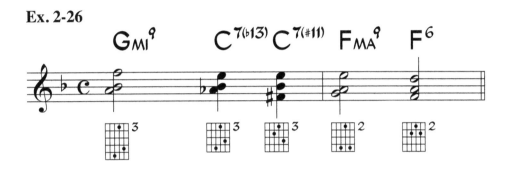

Ex. 2-27

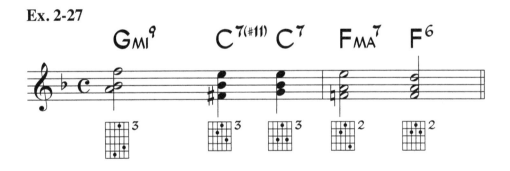

Ex. 2-28

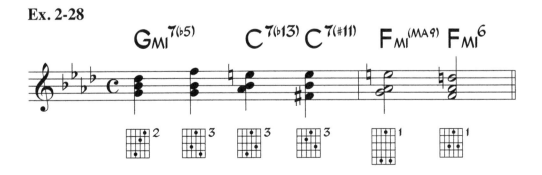

ANOTHER INVERSION WITH VARIATIONS

Being three-note chords, there has to be one more inversion to go. Looking at our original Gm9 (Ex. 2-9), let's raise the Bb to F, the F to A, and the A to Bb, keeping them on the same strings to produce the last inversion of our first chord, the Gm9 shown in Ex. 2-29. Using the same process we used on the previous inversion, we can derive the II-V-I voicings shown in examples 2-30, 2-31, 2-32, 2-33, and (in F minor) 2-34.

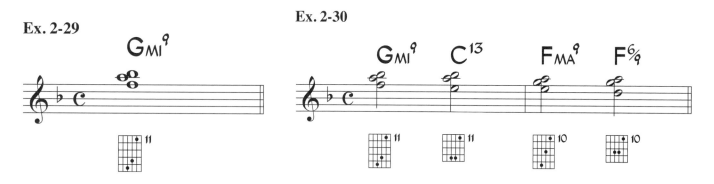

Ex. 2-29
Ex. 2-30

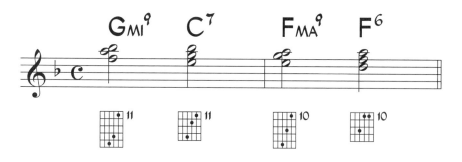

Ex. 2-31

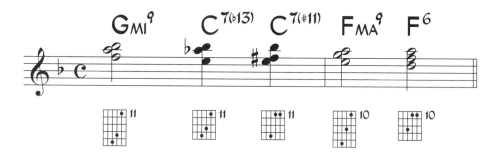

Ex. 2-32

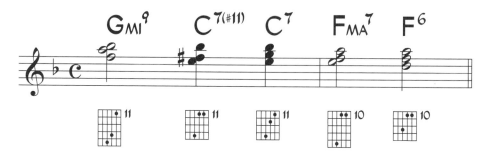

Ex. 2-33

Ex. 2-34

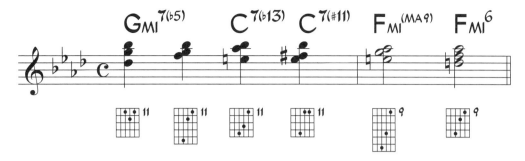

II-V-I PROGRESSIONS (Part B)

All the II-V-I variations we've just done were all derived from one set of "shell" voicings. As you recall, there are two sets of "shell" voicings, so to be complete we have to work out rootless comp voicings with inversions and variations based on the other set. Play Ex. 2-35 (it's the same as Ex. 1-18), II-V-I using this other set of "shell" voicings with added notes.

Ex. 2-35

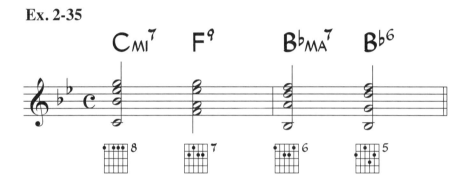

Now play Ex. 2-36, the same thing with the roots omitted. Ex. 2-37 is the altered version, the same as Ex. 1-20 with the roots omitted.

Ex. 2-36

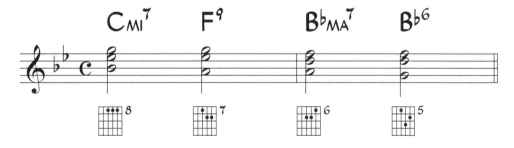

Ex. 2-37

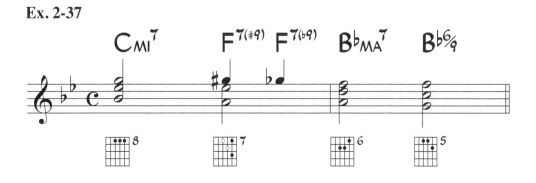

BASIC VARIATIONS

Once again, leaving out the bass note gives us a lot of flexibility to create variations and to add motion to the basic forms. Ex. 2-38 is the same as 2-37, the basic altered version, but uses the #9 and b9 on the V chord to enclose the 13th on the I chord as a target tone. This makes both the Bbmaj13 and the Bb6/9 three-note parallel fourth chords. Fourth chords will get their own chapter later on.

Ex. 2-38

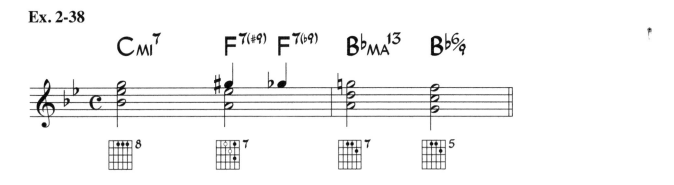

Ex. 2-39 replaces the 5th of the II chord with the 11th, which voice-leads nicely to a reversed version of the altered enclosure of the 13th on the I chord, with the b9 first, followed by the #9 on the V chord.

Ex. 2-39

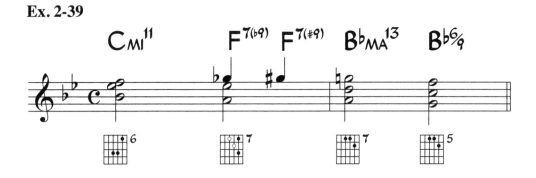

MINOR II-V-I

Ex. 2-40 shows one possible variation in Bb minor, the parallel minor key.

Ex. 2-40

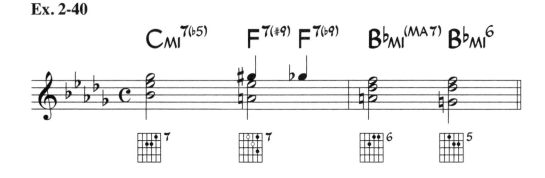

ADDING SCALE LINES TO THE PROGRESSIONS

This set of voicings lends itself to adding scale lines that descend from the 9th on the on the I chord. This type of movement can be heard in the playing of Barney Kessel, Jim Hall, ingly) Jimi Hendrix (!), among many others, including my teacher, Park Hill.

Ex. 2-41 shows a basic version that is similar to an exercise that I found in Mickey Baker's *Complete Course in Jazz Guitar Book 2*, many years ago (I refuse to say how many). It's based on Ex. 2-36, with the added descending scale lines.

Ex. 2-41

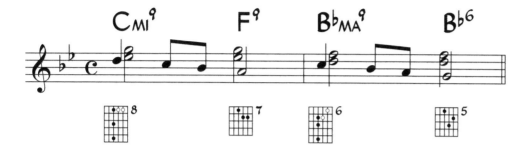

Ex. 2-42 is the basic altered version based on Ex. 2-37, with the added scale lines.

Ex. 2-42

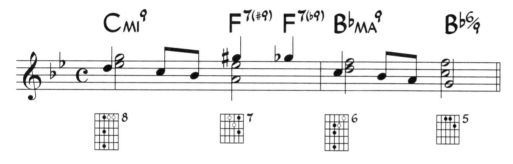

Ex. 2-43 is based on Ex. 2-38.

Ex. 2-43

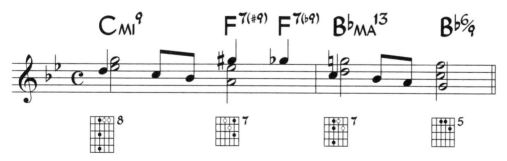

Try Ex. 2-44 (see next page). It's based on Ex. 2-39. The 11th combined with the 9th results in a very long stretch of the left hand fingers. If this is very uncomfortable or painful for you, please skip this example. Never try to force something that causes pain since you need to avoid injury in order to continue practicing and playing.

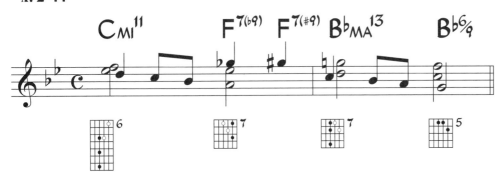

Ex. 2-45 is based on Ex. 2-40, II-V-I in Bb minor. The use of the natural 9 on the IIm7b5 chord comes from the locrian#2 scale (the sixth mode of melodic minor - see *The Jazz Theory Book* by Mark Levine). If this sounds too weird in context, you can simply omit that first note from the added scale line. This is demonstrated in Ex. 2-46, along with a variation on the I chord, creating a Bbm-maj13 chord.

Ex. 2-45

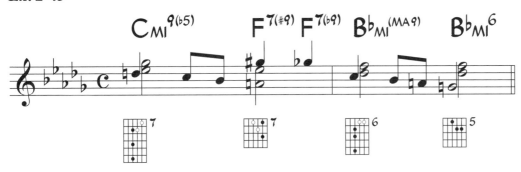

Ex. 2-46

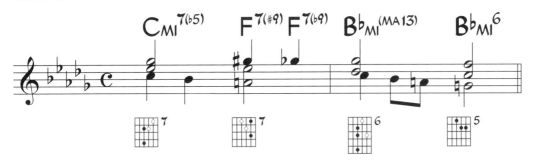

These voicings with moving scale lines lend themselves well to the technique of sustaining the non-moving tones without re-striking while playing the descending lines.

INVERTING AND TRANSPOSING THE PART B VOICINGS

It's time to start inverting our new set of voicings. Look at the first chord in Ex. 2-36, Cm7. The three notes, from the top down, are G, the 5th, Eb, the min3rd, and Bb, the min7th. This collection of pitches literally happens to be a second inversion Eb major triad, so it should be easy for you to invert (if not, it will be after you read the chapter reviewing basic triads!). Let's invert the triad back to root position by raising the G to Bb, the Eb to G, and the Bb to Eb, staying on the same set of strings. This gives us the voicing in Ex. 2-47.

Ex. 2-47

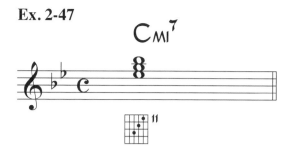

C_{MI}^7

By the way, we might as well start transposing keys since we want to eventually play everything in every key. All these forms are movable so the easiest way to transpose is to slide the forms up or down the fingerboard. If we slide the root position Eb triad down to the eighth fret, we get a root position C triad. From the bottom up we have the root, C, the 3rd, E, and the 5th, G, which also can function as the min3rd, 5th, and min7th of Am7, shown in Ex. 2-48.

Ex. 2-48

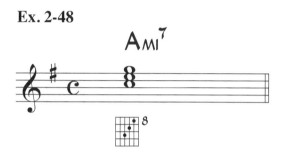

A_{MI}^7

CREATING II-V-I VARIATIONS FROM THE TRANSPOSED INVERSION

Once again we'll create II-V-I by moving the same chord tones in the same way we have been doing on the part B progressions, but this time we have the added challenge of thinking in a different key, so the actual notes are different. In II going to V (see Ex. 2-36) the 7th of the II chord moves down a half step, becoming the 3rd of the V chord. Then when V goes to I the 7th of the V chord moves down a half step, becoming the 3rd of the I chord, while the 9th of the V chord moves down a whole step, becoming the 5th of the I chord, followed by the 7th going down a whole step to become the 6th. Applying the same procedure to the voicing from Ex. 2-48, we get the progression shown in Ex. 2-49, II-V-I in the key of G.

Ex. 2-49

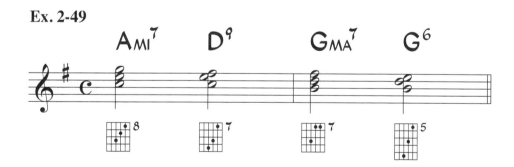

A_{MI}^7 D^9 G_{MA}^7 G^6

I'm not going to show every possible variation, but I'll show you enough so if you want, you can work out more yourself.

Ex. 2-50 shows an altered version of our basic example.

Ex. 2-50

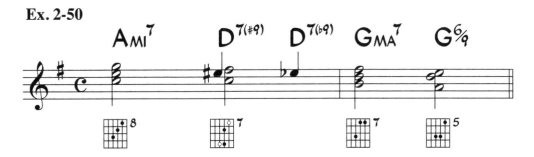

Ex. 2-51 is another altered version with more variations on the II chord and on the I chord.

Ex. 2-51

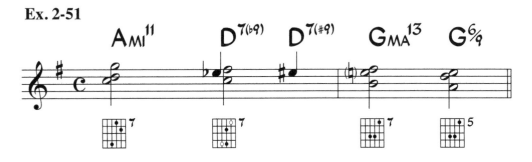

Ex. 2-52 shows II-V-I in G minor, the parallel minor key.

Ex. 2-52

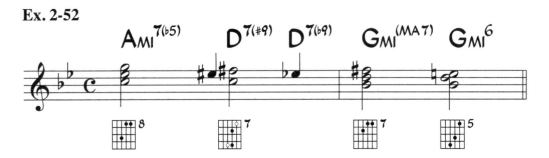

ADDING SCALE LINES TO THE TRANSPOSED INVERSIONS

Now let's add the same scale lines descending from the 9ths of the II chord and the I chord to our transposed inversions. Play Ex. 2-53, the basic unaltered II-V-I in G with the added scale motion (it's based on Ex.2-49). Notice that the descending lines are now the top voice, rather than being on the bottom of the voicings like they were before.

Ex. 2-53

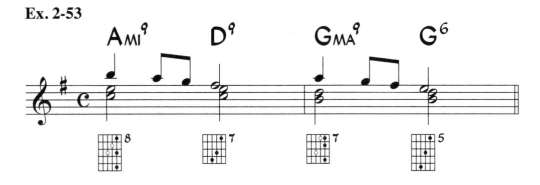

Ex. 2-54 is based on Ex. 2-50 with the added lines.

Ex. 2-54

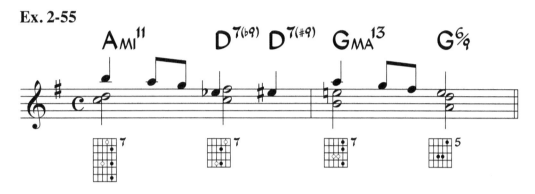

Ex. 2-55 is based on Ex. 2-51 with the added lines.

Ex. 2-55

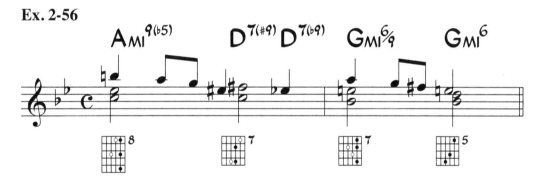

Ex. 2-56 is in G minor, based on Ex. 2-52 with the added lines.

Ex. 2-56

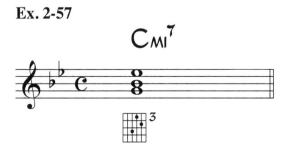

ANOTHER TRANSPOSED INVERSION

If you guessed that, being three-note voicings, we still have one more inversion to go, you are correct. Looking back again to Ex. 2-36, let's take the Eb triad that represesnts Cm7 and find the next lower inversion this time. We lower the G to Eb, the Eb to Bb, and theBb to G, keeping them on the same strings. This forms a first inversion Eb triad, used to represent Cm7 as shown in Ex. 2-57.

Ex. 2-57

Let's transpose it by moving it up two frets, making it Dm7, the II chord in the key of C, shown in Ex. 2-58.

Ex. 2-58

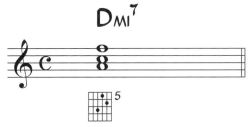

Now we apply the same procedure as before, moving the appropriate voices to create the basic unaltered II-V-I shown in Ex. 2-59.

Ex. 2-59

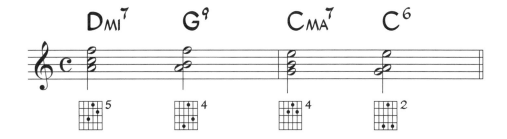

Ex. 2-60 is an altered version.

Ex. 2-60

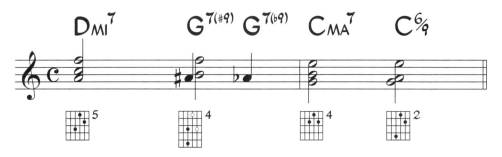

Ex. 2-61 has more variations.

Ex. 2-61

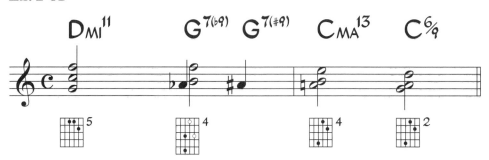

Ex. 2-62 is in C minor, the parallel minor key.

Ex. 2-62

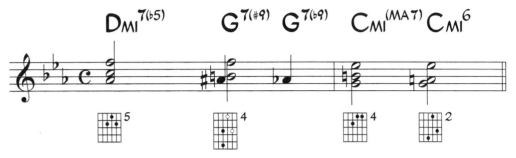

MORE SCALE LINES

When we add the same scale lines descending from the 9ths of the II chord and the I chord, we now find that the moving lines are in the middle voice this time, rather than on the bottom or top as before. Ex. 2-63 is based on Ex. 2-59 with the added lines.

Ex. 2-63

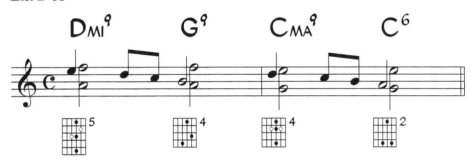

Ex. 2-64 is based on Ex. 2-60 with the added lines.

Ex. 2-64

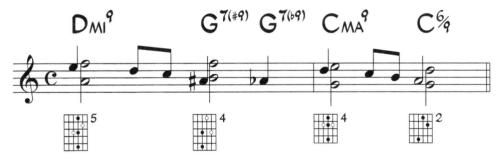

Ex. 2-65 is based on Ex. 2-61 with the added lines.

Ex. 2-65

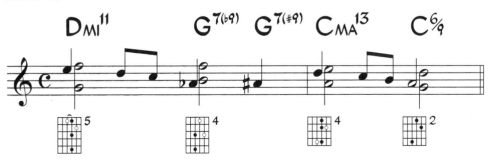

Ex. 2-66 is in C minor, based on Ex. 2-62 with the added lines. Incidently, perhaps you've noticed that all of the part B m-maj7 voicings have the exact same shape on the fingerboard no matter which inversion we're in. This is because we're actually using an augmented triad voicing, which, being symmetrical, has the same intervallic structure in every inversion. There are many other triads being used in these voicings as well, including major, minor, and diminished. If you haven't seen that already, you will after the triad review chapter.

Ex. 2-66

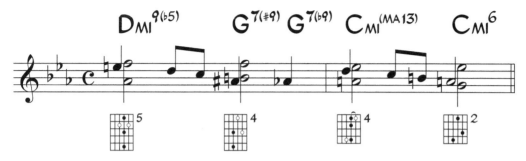

PLAYING THE VOICINGS ON OTHER SETS OF STRINGS

Another way to transpose keys and to increase the playable range of these voicings is to place them on other sets of three consecutive strings. I generally prefer the sound on the set we've been using, but the top three strings (by "top" I mean the highest-pitched strings, not the closest to the ceiling!) and the lower middle set (strings three, four, and five) are very useful and therefore important to learn (the bottom set of three is too "muddy" for these voicings). I'm not going to show the alterations and variations on these new sets because we have much other material to cover, and also because it will help your playing more if you work them out for yourself. I will, however, show you the initial basic unaltered II-V-I in major, using both part A and part B voicings, on both new sets of strings to get you started.

PART A, II-V-I VOICINGS ON THE TOP THREE STRINGS

Ex. 2-67 shows the basic unaltered part A, II-V-I voicings in the key of Bb on the top three strings.

Ex. 2-67

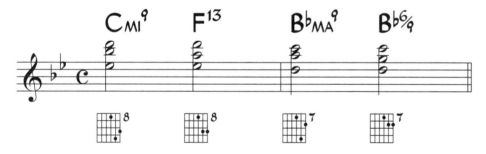

Ex. 2-68 shows an inversion of the basic unaltered part A, II-V-I voicings in the key of Db on the top three strings.

Ex. 2-68

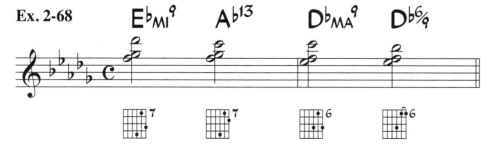

Ex. 2-69 shows the other inversion of these voicings in the key of G on the top three strings.

Ex. 2-69

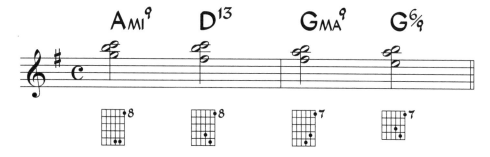

PART A, II-V-I VOICINGS ON THE LOWER MIDDLE SET OF THREE STRINGS

Ex. 2-70 shows the basic unaltered part A, II-V-I voicings in the key of Bb on the lower middle set of three consecutive strings.

Ex. 2-70

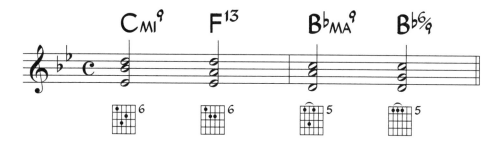

Ex. 2-71 shows an inversion of these voicings in the key of Eb on the lower middle set of three strings.

Ex. 2-71

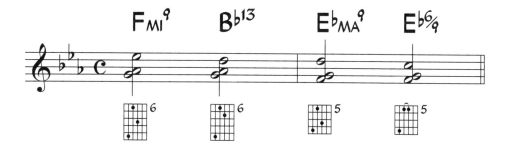

Ex. 2-72 shows the other inversion of these voicings in the key of G on the lower middle set of strings.

Ex. 2-72

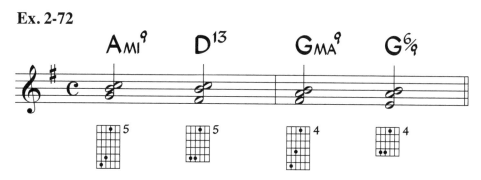

PART B, II-V-I VOICINGS ON THE TOP THREE STRINGS

Ex. 2-73 shows the basic unaltered part B, II-V-I voicings in the key of Eb on the top three strings.

Ex. 2-73

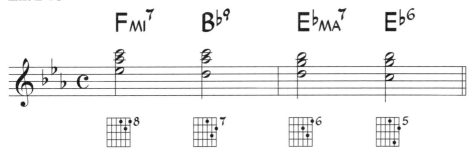

Ex. 2-74 shows an inversion of these voicings in the key of C on the top three strings.

Ex. 2-74

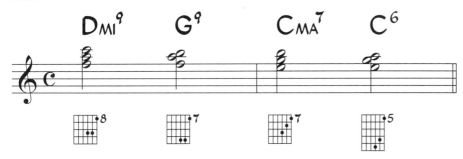

Ex. 2-75 shows the other inversion of these voicings in the key of G on the top three strings.

Ex. 2-75

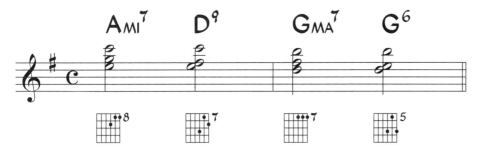

PART B, II-V-I VOICINGS ON THE LOWER MIDDLE SET OF THREE STRINGS

Ex. 2-76 shows the basic unaltered part B II-V-I voicings in the key of F on the lower middle set of three consecutive strings.

Ex. 2-76

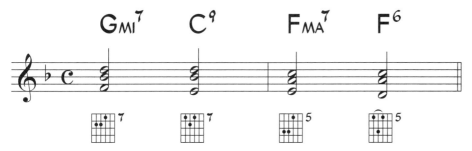

Ex. 2-77 shows an inversion of these voicings in the key of D on the lower middle set of three strings.

Ex. 2-77

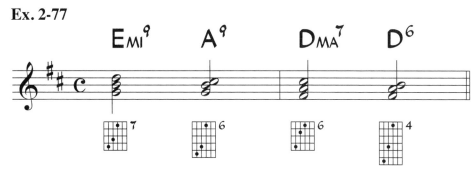

Ex. 2-78 shows the last inversion of these voicings in the key of Ab on the lower middle set of strings.

Ex. 2-78

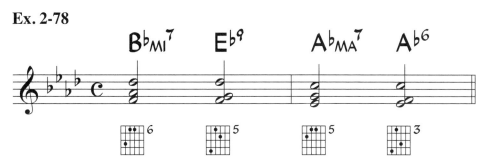

Please note that the terms "part A" and "part B" are not universal names for these voicing types, but are just a reference to their presentation in this book.

PRACTICING AND USING THE ROOTLESS VOICINGS

Of course you should practice all the progressions in every key and on the three sets of three consecutive strings that I've shown you, as far as range will allow. Let me remind you that any version that has a finger stretch that causes pain should be skipped. Sometimes a long stretch will be reachable in the upper positions but may become impracticle on the lower frets. I'm sure Allan Holdsworth can play all of them in all positions. I can do most in all positions and a few in mid-to-upper positions, but if you find that, for you, a particular example is painful in all positions, please don't do it. There's plenty of useful material to do without risking injury.

When the time comes to start using the voicings to comp for other musicians, keep in mind that, as always, you must be listening at all times and play just what's appropriate for the situation. Many of our examples, coming from the dynamic concept of harmony as mutiple melodies, may be great to hear by themselves and fun to practice, but very possibly too busy in a given context for good comping. Many of the added scale line versions, for instance, might be great "fill-ins" behind a sustained melody note on a ballad, or great for intros or improvised chord solos. Much of the time it will suffice to use simpler unalterd and altered variations, applying comp rhythms with anticipations and and a few chromatic approach embellishments now and then. Now it's time to review triads.

Chapter 3 - Basic Triad Review

For those who already know everything about three-note triad voicings on the guitar (shouldn't everybody?), you may skip this chapter and jump ahead to the chapter on "walking" guitar voicings. But I advise at least glancing through the chapter to be sure. If you see anything unfamiliar, please take time to check it out. It could only help you with what's still to come.

As you probably already know, there are four possible types of tertian triads (triads built from 3rds): major, minor, diminished, and augmented (see Ex. 3-1).

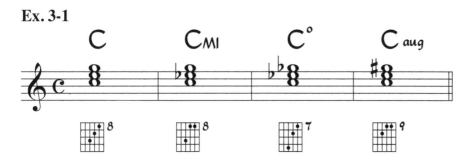

Ex. 3-1

I use this order, instead of the traditional maj-min-aug-dim order, because it makes sense to me to derive the diminished triads from the minor ones (while they're still fresh) by lowering their 5ths.

Close voicings have the notes packed closely together, spanning less than the range of an octave (see Ex. 3-2). Open voicings take the middle note of a close triad and move it up or down by an octave, spreading the voicing out (see Ex. 3-3). First let's review the close voicings.

Ex. 3-2

Ex. 3-3

CLOSE TRIAD VOICINGS

All the practical movable close-voiced triads on the guitar lie on three consecutive strings. The sets are the top three, the upper-middle three, the lower-middle three, and the bottom three (top and bottom refer to pitch, not to the relationship to the floor or ceiling).

The triads have a root-position and two inversions (first and second), as shown in Ex. 3-4, plus as many octave duplications as the range of your guitar allows.

Ex. 3-4

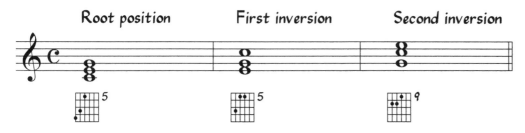

A good way to review them is to play two inversions on each set of three consecutive strings before playing the next two inversions on the next set, etc., which forms a long harmonized arpeggio covering the full range of the guitar. I'll demonstrate three keys for each chord because this will show every form on every set of strings. Of course you should continue on your own and review them in every key.

CLOSE-VOICED MAJOR TRIADS

Ex. 3-5 shows the close voiced C major triads.

Ex. 3-5

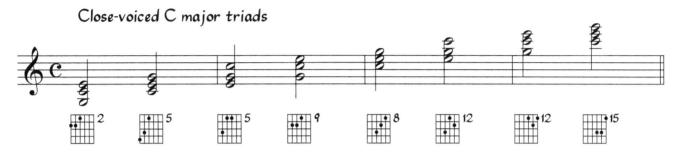

Ex. 3-6 shows the close-voiced F major triads.

Ex. 3-6

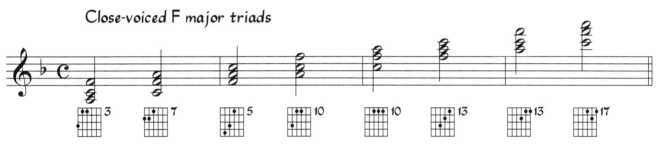

Ex. 3-7 shows the close-voiced Bb major triads.

Ex. 3-7

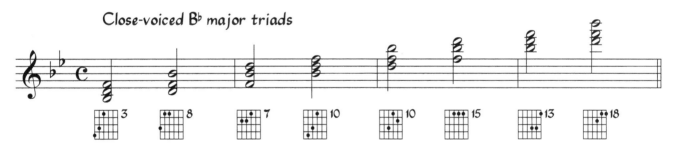

CLOSE-VOICED MINOR TRIADS

Ex. 3-8 shows the close-voiced C minor triads.

Ex. 3-8

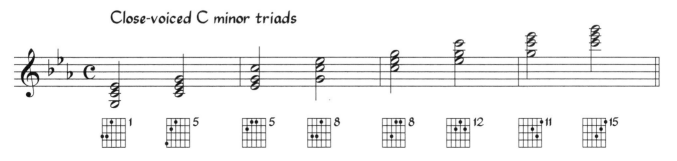

Ex. 3-9 shows the close-voiced F minor triads.

Ex. 3-9

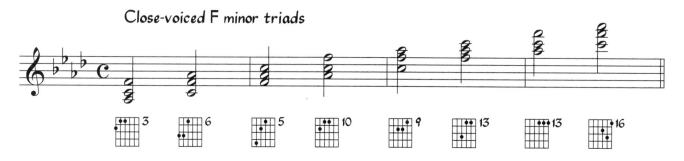

Close-voiced F minor triads

Ex. 3-10 shows the close-voiced Bb minor triads.

Ex. 3-10

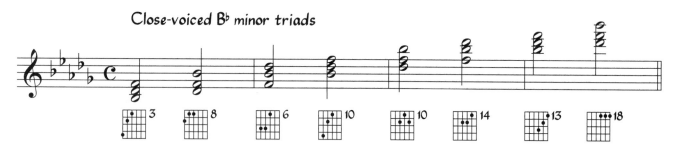

Close-voiced B♭ minor triads

CLOSE-VOICED DIMINISHED TRIADS

Ex. 3-11 shows the close-voiced C diminished triads.

Ex. 3-11

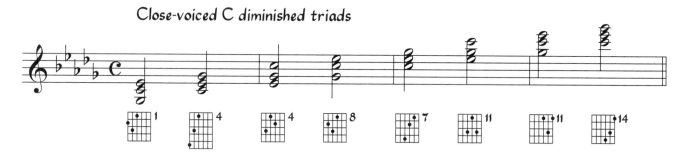

Close-voiced C diminished triads

Ex. 3-12 shows the close-voiced F diminished triads.

Ex. 3-12

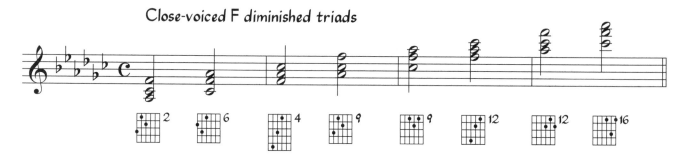

Close-voiced F diminished triads

Ex. 3-13 shows the close-voiced Bb diminished triads.

Ex. 3-13

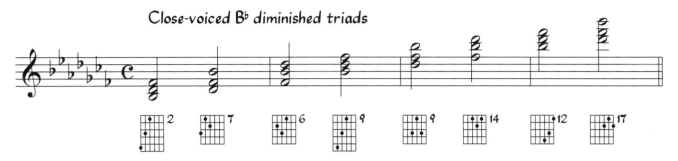

Close-voiced B♭ diminished triads

CLOSE-VOICED AUGMENTED TRIADS

Ex. 3-14 shows the close-voiced C augmented triads. Being symmetrical (the major 3rd intervals divide an octave into three equal parts), the inversions keep the same fingerboard shapes and fingerings when they move up on the same set of strings. In fact, since all the inversions are the same, the forms and fingerings will be identical in all keys. I'll show you the next key anyway just to prove the point.

Ex. 3-14

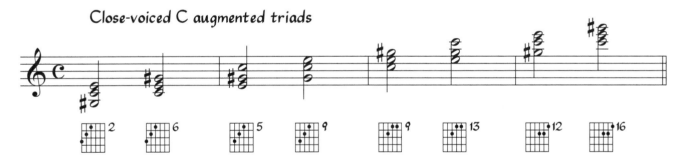

Close-voiced C augmented triads

Ex. 3-15 shows the close-voiced F augmented triads.

Ex. 3-15

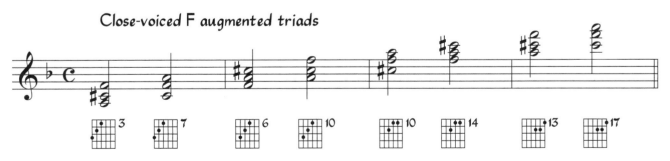

Close-voiced F augmented triads

As I'm sure you probably already know, Caug=Eaug=Abaug, Faug=Aaug=Dbaug, Bbaug=Daug=F#aug, and Ebaug=Gaug=Baug. That's all twelve, so there are really only four "keys" for the augmented triad.

OPEN TRIAD VOICINGS

To open the triad voicings we'll start by using the voicings we just reviewed and we'll raise the middle by one octave, using the same string configurations the we used for the modified "shell" voicings (as was demonstrated in Ex. 3-3).

OPEN-VOICED MAJOR TRIADS

Ex. 3-16 shows the open-voiced C major triads.

Ex. 3-16

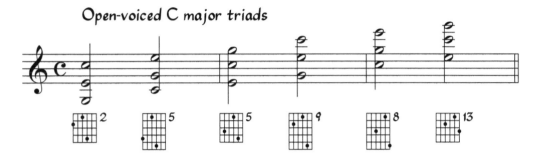

Ex. 3-17 shows the open-voiced F major triads.

Ex. 3-17

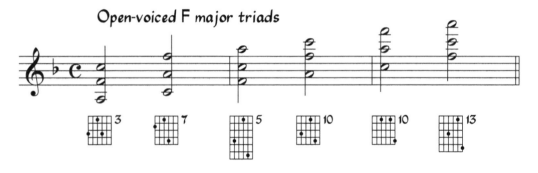

Ex. 3-18 shows the open-voiced Bb major triads.

Ex. 3-18

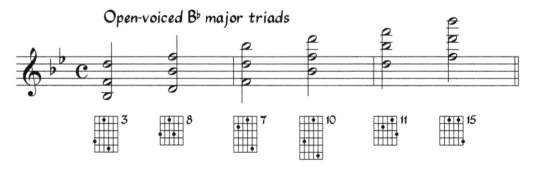

OPEN-VOICED MINOR TRIADS

Ex. 3-19 shows the open-voiced C minor triads.

Ex. 3-19

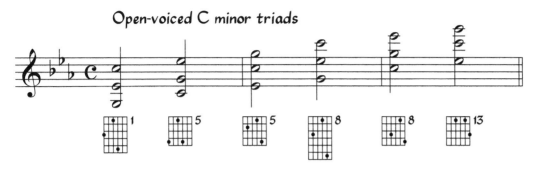

Ex. 3-20 shows the open-voiced F minor triads.

Ex. 3-20

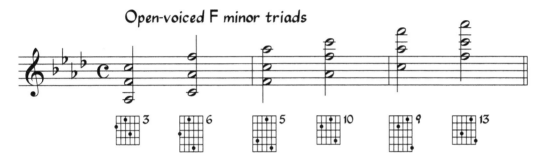

Ex. 3-21 shows the open-voiced Bb minor triads.

Ex. 3-21

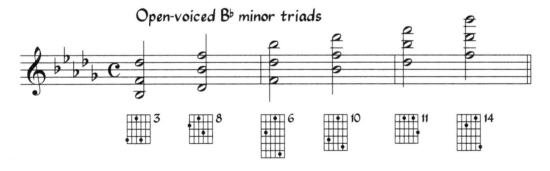

OPEN-VOICED DIMINISHED TRIADS

Ex. 3-22 shows the open-voiced C diminished triads.

Ex. 3-22

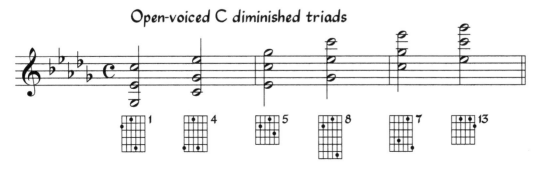

Ex. 3-23 shows the open-voiced F diminished triads.

Ex. 3-23

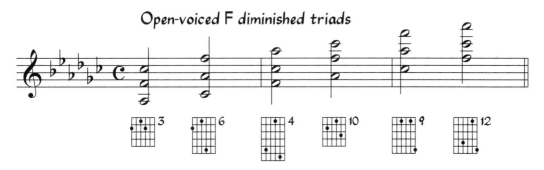

Ex. 3-24 shows the open-voiced Bb diminished triads.

Ex. 3-24

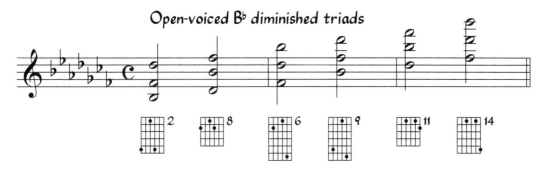

OPEN-VOICED AUGMENTED TRIADS

Once again, being symmetrical, I only need to show the augmented triads in one key. You use the same forms to work them out in the other keys.

Ex. 3-25 shows the open-voiced C augmented triads.

Ex. 3-25

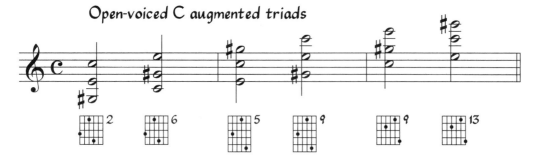

THE NEED FOR ALTERNATE FORMS AND FINGERINGS

The open-voiced triads will eventually have notes added inside the voicing. Ex. 3-26 demonstrates this by adding a D note inside an open-voiced C triad. But what if we want to insert the note F instead? There's no practical way to do it using the form we're using. By moving the E note from the third string to the fourth string, we free the third string and can now easily add the F note as demonstrated in Ex. 3-27. Let's be properly prepared by reviewing the alternate forms and fingerings for all the open triads.

Ex. 3-26   **Ex. 3-27**

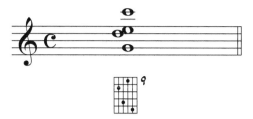   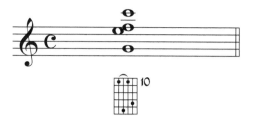

ALTERNATE FORM OPEN-VOICED MAJOR TRIADS

Ex. 3-28 shows the alternate forms for open-voiced C major triads.

Ex. 3-28

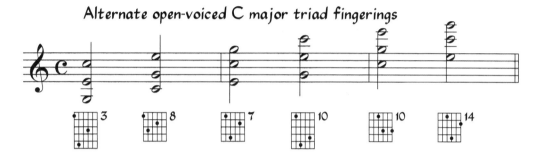

Alternate open-voiced C major triad fingerings

Ex. 3-29 shows them for F major triads.

Ex. 3-29

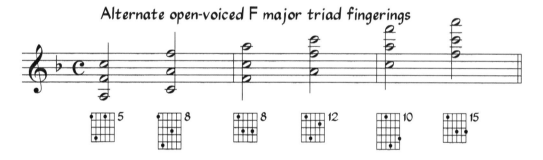

Alternate open-voiced F major triad fingerings

Ex. 3-30 shows them for Bb major triads.

Ex. 3-30

Alternate open-voiced B♭ major triad fingerings

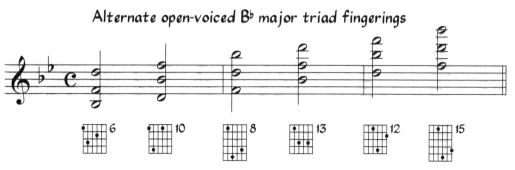

ALTERNATE FORM OPEN-VOICED MINOR TRIADS

Ex. 3-31 shows the alternate forms for open-voiced C minor triads.

Ex. 3-31

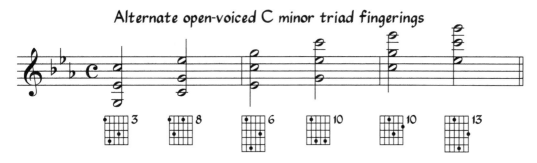

Alternate open-voiced C minor triad fingerings

Ex. 3-32 shows them for F minor triads.

Ex. 3-32

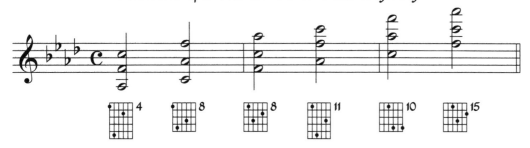

Alternate open-voiced F minor triad fingerings

Ex. 3-33 shows them for Bb minor triads.

Ex. 3-33

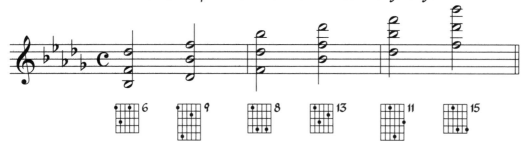

Alternate open-voiced B♭ minor triad fingerings

ALTERNATE FORM OPEN-VOICED DIMINISHED TRIADS

Ex. 3-34 shows the alternate forms for open-voiced C diminished triads.

Ex. 3-34

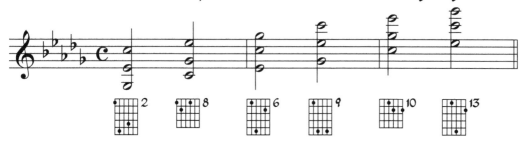

Alternate open-voiced C diminished triad fingerings

Ex. 3-35 shows them for F diminished triads.

Ex. 3-35

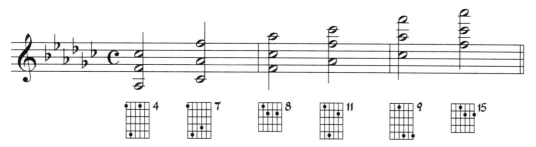

Alternate open-voiced F diminished triad fingerings

Ex. 3-36 shows them for Bb diminished triads.

Ex. 3-36

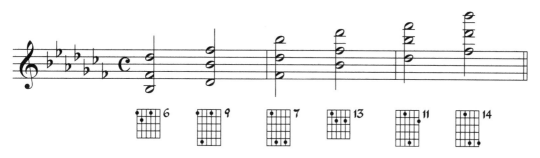

Alternate open-voiced Bb diminished triad fingerings

ALTERNATE FORM OPEN-VOICED AUGMENTED TRIADS

Ex. 3-37 shows the alternate forms for open-voiced augmented triads.

Ex. 3-37

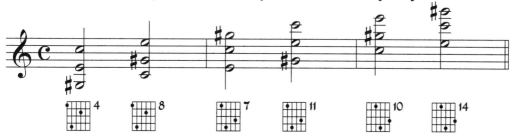

Alternate open-voiced C augmented triad fingerings

ONE MORE ALTERNATE FORM

I'll show you one last alternate form for a second inversion open-voiced major triad that we'll be using very soon. The form turns out to be the same no matter which set of strings you place it on. Ex. 3-38 demonstrates it using a C triad in two different octaves, and on different sets of strings.

Ex. 3-38

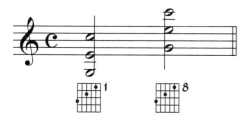

OPEN TRIADS ACROSS THE FINGERBOARD

Now we have enough forms to play the following study, which moves the open inversions across the fingerboard while staying in the same area. Play Ex. 3-39. Notice that the triads are going around the cycle after doing the inversions across the fingerboard and back. All the forms are at the fifth or sixth frets. To continue around the cycle use the same forms for Db, the next chord in the cycle, that started the study on the C chord, only at the sixth fret instead of the fifth, and continue the same sequence.

Ex. 3-39

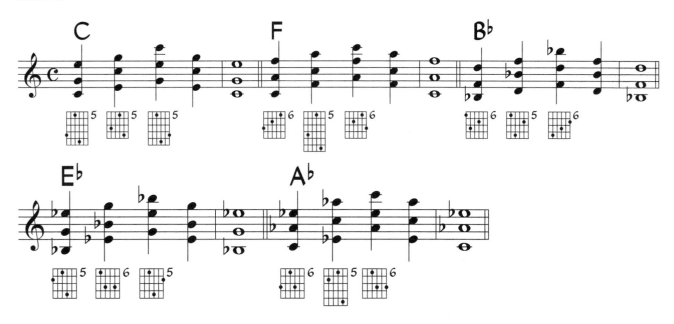

In addition to working out the rest of the cycle on your own, you should also work it out using all minor triads.

Now we're ready to tackle "walking" guitar chords.

Chapter 4 - "Walking" Guitar

THE BASIC CONCEPT

Try Ex. 4-1. It's a demonstration of "walking" guitar chords based on the first four bars oꓸ a twelve-bar blues in the key of F. It resembles a walking bass line in three-part harmony. This can be very useful when accompanying without a bass player or any other chord playing instrument. This could be playing duo with a vocalist or horn player, or another guitar player who is playing single-note lines (or even a pianist playing single-note lines---check out Jim Hall and Bill Evans playing "My Funny Valentine" on the classic recording *Undercurrent*, a most amazing example of walking guitar behind portions of Bill's solo).

Ex. 4-1

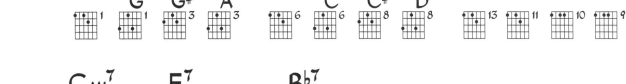

Let's take a closer look at what's going on in the example. The first chord is a basic three-note "shell" voicing for F7. The second chord is a first inversion Eb major triad harmonizing the bass note G. The third chord is a first inversion F diminished triad harmonizing the bass note Ab (I usually think "G#" when the line is ascending, but calling it Ab fits the Fdim chord spelling). The fourth chord is a first inversion F major triad harmonizing the bass note A natural.

The second measure is the same as the first except starting from Bb, so it's Bb7-Ab/C-Bbdim/Db-Bb/Dnatural.

The third measure begins with our "shell" F7, up an octave this time. Next is Eb7, down a whole step and leading to Dm7 followed by Dbm7. This forms a descending chromatic line leading to the Cm7 in the next bar.

The fourth measure begins with the Cm7 followed by a first inversion Bb diminished triad harmonizing the bass note Db. Next is a second inversion F major triad harmonizing the bass note C followed by a basic "shell" B7, which is a tritone substitution for F7. This B7 creates chromatic motion leading smoothly target chord Bb7 on the first beat of the fifth measure.

This is all really just a basic blues. It's one bar of F7, one bar of Bb7, one bar of F7 and one bar of Cm7 to F7. All the other chords are passing chords used to create movement between the basic "target" chords.

In order to become fluent at improvising these type of walking chord lines on tunes, we'll need a vocabulary of walking chord lines for various common situations, such as II-V and II-V-I, various turn-arounds, and cycles.

LONG II-V-I

First let's try some II-V-I progressions where the II chord lasts for four beats and the V chord lasts for four beats before resolving to the I chord. We'll stay in the key of F for the time being.

BASIC MAJOR II-V-I

Look at Ex. 4-2. There are eight chords walking over Gm7-C7, the II-V, before resolving to Fmaj7, the I chord. The basic changes, Gm7-C7-Fmaj7, are written in over the music notation. Under the notation, above each chord diagram, are the literal names of each voicing analyzed like we did on the blues we just looked at. These literal names are for analysis and to demonstrate the application of triads only. Don't try to think this way when playing. Keep your thinking simple and try to see the harmonies as movement within the basic chords.

Ex. 4-2

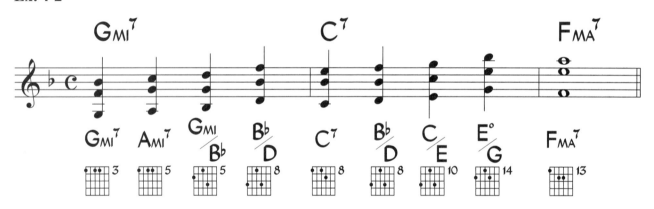

Ex. 4-3 is a variation of 4-2. The B7 is a lower chromatic approach chord leading up to the C7.

Ex. 4-3

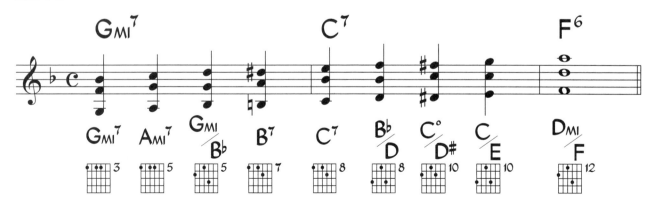

Ex. 4-4 is a descending version (starting an octave higher). Here we have some connecting chords which are not triads, the E7b5no3 and the C7no3/Bb. Sometimes these occur to keep the voice-leading and melodies (especially the outer voices) strong.

Ex. 4-4

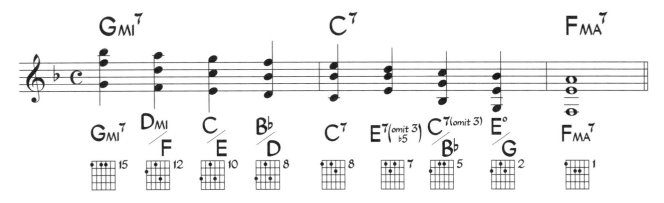

Ex. 4-5 is a variation of 4-4 using some lower chromatic approach chords. Notice that the chromatic approach chords are on the weaker beat two, leading into the stronger beat three.

Ex. 4-5

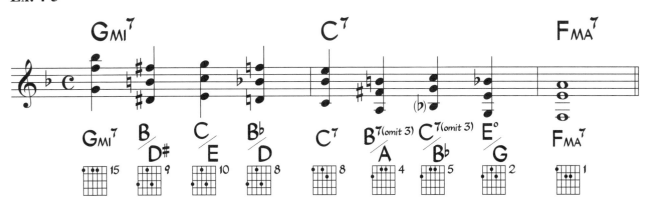

You can create more II-V-Is that are combinations of the ones I'm showing you. For example, you can combine measure one of Ex. 4-2 with measure two and three of Ex. 4-4 (and vice-versa). You should experiment with as many of these combinations as you can find.

II-V-I WITH SIMPLE SUBSTITUTIONS

Look at Ex. 4-6. The basic changes above the music are Gm7-Am7-Bb6-C7 (two beats each)-F. This is a simple substitution for II-V-I. This example uses a pattern in 3rds and resolves into an inverted I chord, F with A, the 3rd, in the bass.

Ex. 4-6

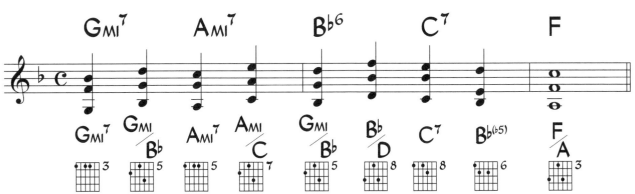

Ex. 4-7 is a variation of 4-6 using some lower chromatic approach chords and an alteration. Notice that the basic chord symbols above the notation call for a C7b9, so we use a Bbdim triad before resolving to the inverted F chord. Actually, you could use this C7b9 right before resolving to the F anytime, even when not called for in the given chord symbol.

Ex. 4-7

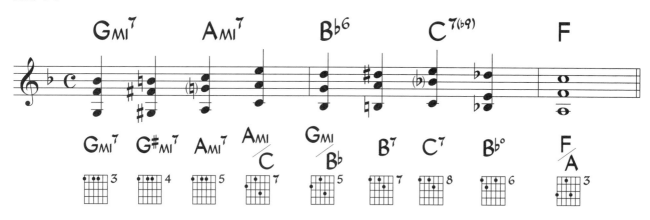

MORE VARIATIONS

In the examples we've seen so far, the first voicing on each chord change has literally been the chord called for in the basic changes written above the music, with the other voicings acting as passing chords in between. Now we'll look at some variations where a triad inversion replaces one of the basic changes.

Ex. 4-8 uses a C/G on the first beat of C7, as well as chromatics and substitutes, including Gb7, the tritone substitute for C7.

Ex. 4-8

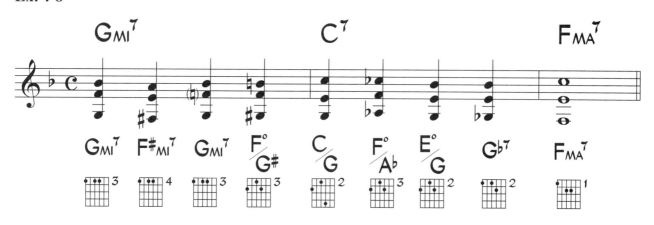

Ex. 4-9 uses Bb/D on the first beat of Gm7, along with some chromatic approach chords. The C#m/E could be thought of as E6, a chromatic approach to the F6. It could also be analyzed as the 3rd, b9th, and #5th (or b13th) of a C7alt chord.

Ex. 4-9

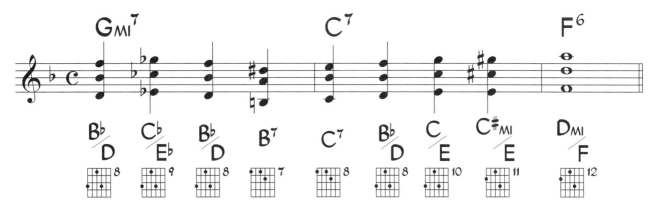

THE IMPORTANCE OF MELODIC VOICE-LEADING

Ex. 4-10 shows how melodic voice-leading can generate new forms and string combinations. First play just the top note of each voicing. This is the melody I wanted to hear, starting with a Bb major 1-2-3-5 pattern over the Gm7, which leads from the 3rd of the Gm7 to the 3rd of C7, the note E. The D# is a chromatic lower neighbor that returns to the E. Then the melody goes back to the first Bb note, which needs to be resolved, so it moves to A, the 3rd of the Fmaj7.

Ex. 4-10

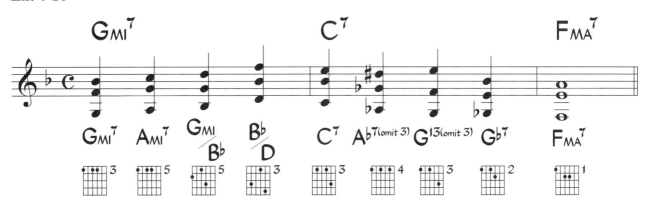

Next play just the bottom note of each voicing, forming the bass line melody I wanted to hear. It starts with 1-2-3-5 pattern in G minor (which results in diatonic parallel 10ths with the top melody line), followed by the root of the C7. Then it uses a descending chromatic line that targets the root of the Fmaj7.

The middle voice is chosen to create the strongest harmonies. The outer melodies are the ones the ear most easily identifies. The middle voice forms parallel 7ths with the descending chromatic portion of the bass line, which along with the top melody results in the unusual chord names Ab7no3 and G13no3.

This concept of a top melody with a bass line and one inner harmony part is actually the basis of all our "walking" guitar examples.

BASIC II-V-I IN MINOR

Ex. 4-11 is based on Ex. 4-2, but changed from the key of F major to the key of F minor, the parallel minor key, making the II chord Gm7b5, the V chord C7b9, and the I chord Fm6. Please remember that the literal chord names are for analysis only. Never think "Ddim/F" (never when actually playing, but only when practicing), think "Fm6".

Ex. 4-11

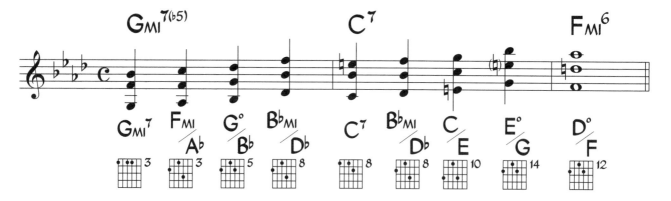

Ex. 4-12 is based on Ex. 4-3, also changed from Fmajor to Fminor.

Ex. 4-12

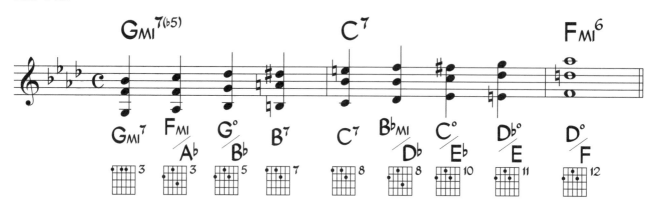

Ex. 4-13 is based on Ex. 4-4, changed to minor.

Ex. 4-13

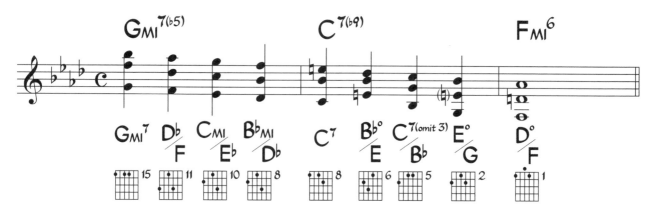

Ex. 4-14 is based on Ex. 4-5, once again changed to minor.

Ex. 4-14

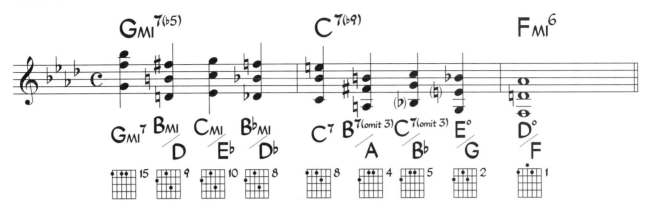

Don't forget to try combinations swapping measures from the different examples.

Ex. 4-15 is based on Ex. 4-6, changed to minor.

Ex. 4-15

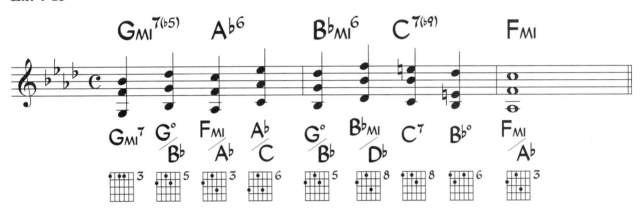

No, I'm not going to convert them all for you. Some you should work out for yourself. I will say that you can convert Ex. 4-8 to minor by simply replacing the final Fmaj7 chord with an Fm6 chord. The rest of the example works in both major and minor.

OK, I'll do one more. Ex. 4-16 is a converted version of Ex. 4-10, our melodic voice-leading model. Notice that the second measure required no conversion since it too works in both major and minor.

Ex. 4-16

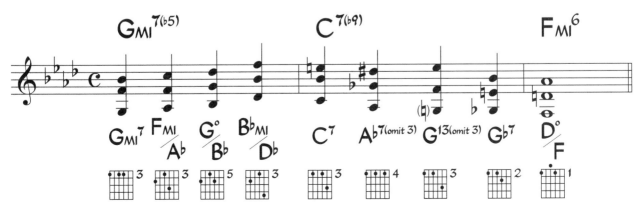

SHORT II-V-I

Now let's try some II-V-Is where the II chord and the V chord last for two beats each before resolving to the I chord. This is also a good time to change the key for a while, so we'll go to the key of Bb.

SHORT II-V-I IN MAJOR

Ex. 4-17 is a basic "shell" II-V-I with tritone substitutions added to create the "up-a-tritone-down-a-half-step-down-a-tritone-down-a-half-step" bass line similar to one we looked at early on in chapter 1. The Gb7 could also be analyzed as a descending chromatic approach chord to the F7.

Ex. 4-17

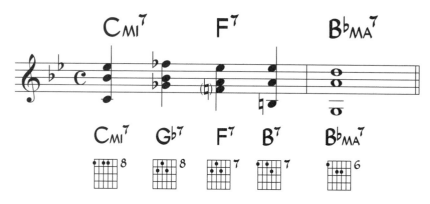

Ex. 4-18 uses modified "shells" to smooth out the bass line. Now the lack of melodic motion in the top voice on beats three and four of the first measure may call for a variation.

Ex. 4-18

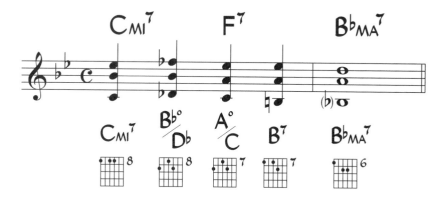

Ex. 4-19 keeps the top voice moving by using F/C on the third beat.

Ex. 4-19

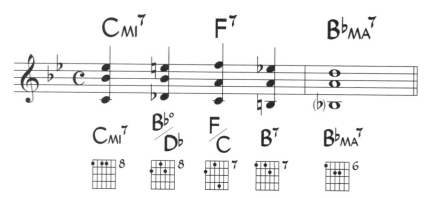

Ex. 4-20 is the same as Ex. 4-19 except the F/C is played with an alternate form. Try playing the entire example keeping the second finger on the fouth string (the middle voice) while exchanging and sliding the other fingers around the second finger as needed.

Ex. 4-20

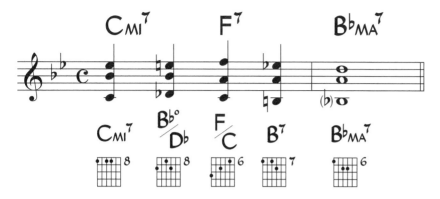

Ex. 4-21 uses a Gb/Db, an upper chromatic approach chord targeting the F/C.

Ex. 4-21

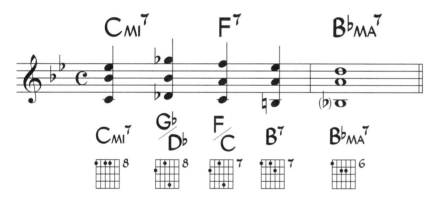

Ex. 4-22 is the same as 4-21 except this time both the Gb/Db and the F/C are played with the alternate forms. Try the second finger playing the middle voice through the entire example again.

Ex. 4-22

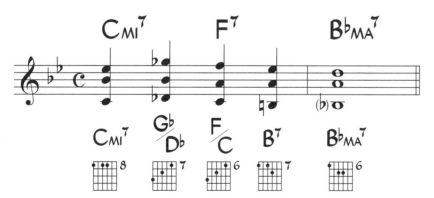

SOME NEW TRICKS

Ex. 4-23 demonstrates a new trick. The fourth beat uses a lower chromatic approach note in the top voice, while the lower two voices are upper chromatic approach notes, creating contrary motion when the B6/9 resolves to the Bb6. (See next page.)

Ex. 4-23

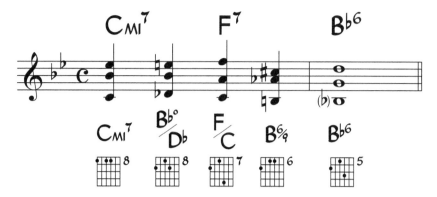

Ex. 4-24 shows another new trick. This time a more angular melody is created by having the top line and bass line switching between portions of two different guide-tone lines.

Ex. 4-24

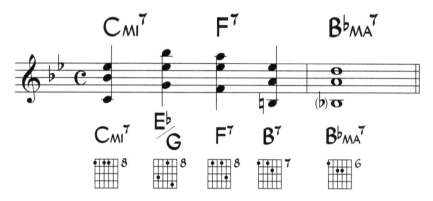

SHORT II-V-I IN PARALLEL MINOR

Ex. 4-25 is based on Ex. 4-24, but converted into the key of Bb minor, the parallel minor key.

Ex. 4-25

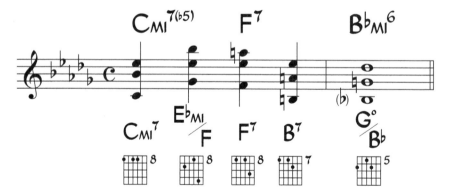

I'm not going to show you all the examples converted to minor because it is just too easy to do. If you take Ex. 4-17 through Ex. 4-22 and change the final Bbmaj7 to Bbm6, your conversions are done. This is because the II-V portions of the examples fit both the major and the minor tonalities (the II chord form has no 5th, so it works for Cm7, the II chord in Bb major, and it works for Cm7b5, the II chord in Bb minor).

SHORT II-V-I USING THE "OTHER" FORM

As you recall, there are two forms for each "shell" voicing. All the short II-V-Is we've looked at so far have been based on just one form, so we need to check out the other form in order to facilitate playing them in all keys. This time let's use the key of C.

Ex. 4-26 is similar to Ex. 4-17, a basic "shell" II-V-I with added tritone substitutions but using the "other" form this time.

Ex. 4-26

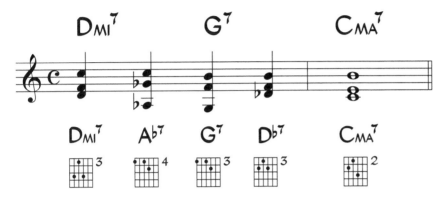

Ex. 4-27 starts with a modified "shell" and walks up the fingerboard, resolving to the I chord voicing we used in our earlier examples. The A#dim is a lower chromatic approach chord leading to Bdim, which functions as an inverted G7.

Ex. 4-27

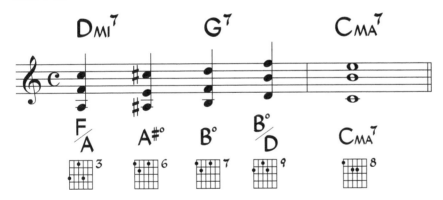

Ex. 4-28 also goes there but uses a couple of lower chromatic approach chords along the way, the F#7 leading to G7, and what amounts to a B6 leading to the C6.

Ex. 4-28

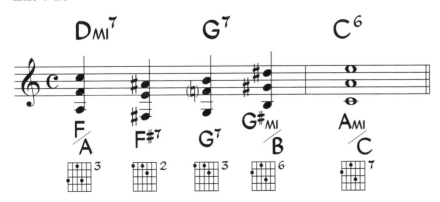

Ex. 4-29 is similar to Ex. 4-24, but with the forms and direction of interval leaps reversed.

Ex. 4-29

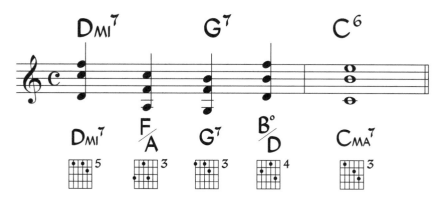

SHORT II-V-I IN MINOR USING THE "OTHER" FORM

Ex. 4-30 is based on Ex. 4-26 converted to the key of C minor, the parallel minor key.

Ex. 4-30

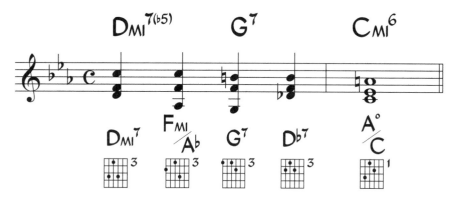

Ex. 4-31 is based on Ex. 4-27 converted to minor.

Ex. 4-31

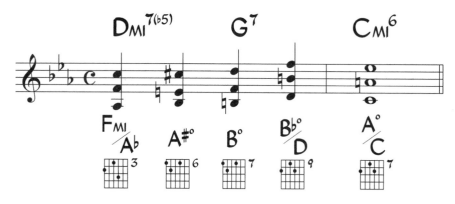

Ex. 4-32 is based on Ex. 4-28 converted to minor. (See next page.)

Ex. 4-32

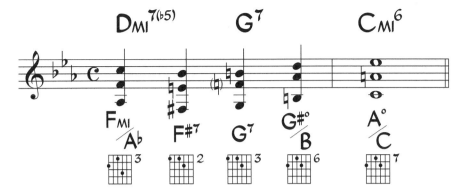

Ex. 4-33 is based on Ex. 4-29 converted to minor.

Ex. 4-33

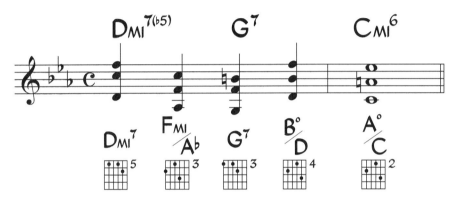

LONG CYCLES

For our purposes in this chapter, long cycles are chords of the same type moving counter-clockwise around the circle of 5ths, with each chord lasting for four beats.

LONG DOMINANT CYCLES

Ex. 4-34 shows the first two bars (plus the first beat of the third bar) of a long dominant cycle starting on G7, played on the lower strings. To continue the cycle "walk" the chords up from the F7 using the same forms used on the G7. Then walk up again from the Bb7, still using the same forms, followed by walking down from Eb7 using the same forms used on the C7. Each time you arrive at a new chord in the cycle choose to walk up or down as the range on the guitar permits. Follow this same procedure for all the long cycles.

Ex. 4-34

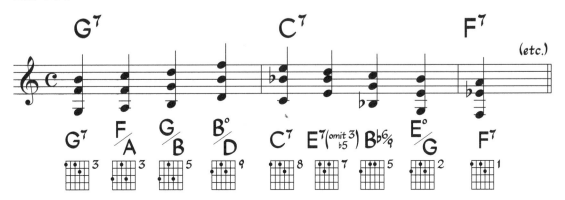

Ex. 4-35 shows the same voicings starting on C7, played on the middle strings. The top strings aren't generally used, so we won't go there now, although there will be a few here and there as you'll see in upcoming examples.

Ex. 4-35

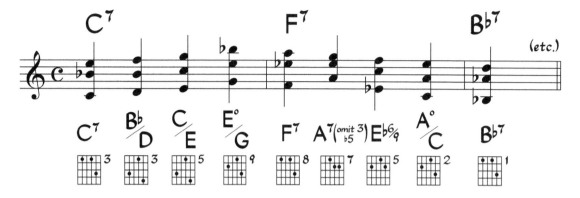

Ex. 4-36 is a variation of Ex. 4-34.

Ex. 4-36

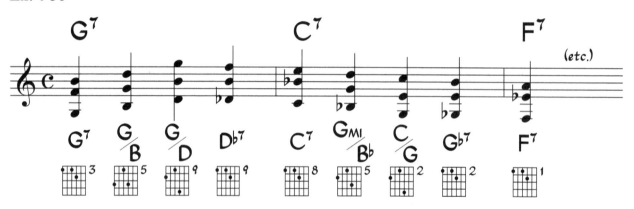

Ex. 4-37 is a variation of Ex. 4-35.

Ex. 4-37

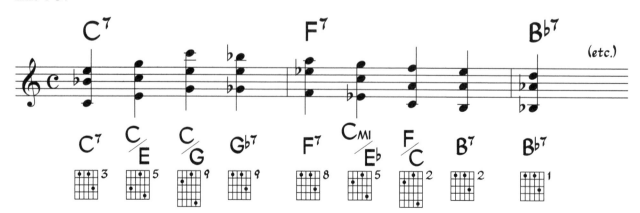

Ex. 4-38 is identical to Ex. 4-37 but is placed on different string groups, crossing all the string sets, and has some alternate forms.

Ex. 4-38

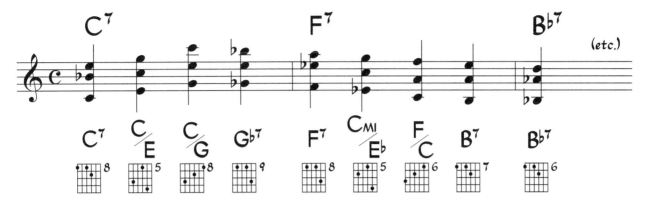

Ex. 4-39 is another variation starting on G7 on the lower strings.

Ex. 4-39

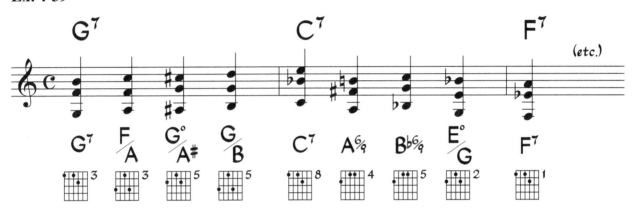

Ex. 4-40 shows the same voicings starting on C7 and played on the middle strings.

Ex. 4-40

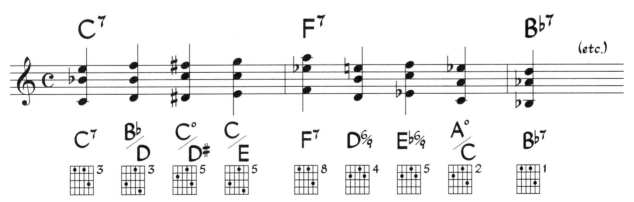

Ex. 4-41 walks up and down arpeggios and crosses all the string groups.

Ex. 4-41

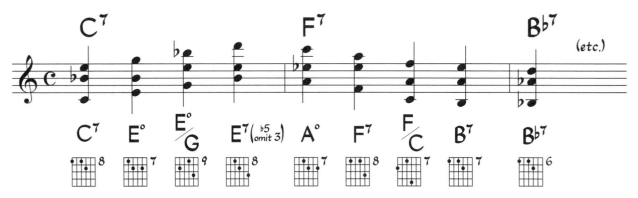

LONG MAJOR CYCLES

Ex. 4-42 shows the first two measures (plus a beat) of a long cycle of major7 chords on the lower set of strings starting on Gmaj7. The voicing on the second beat of the first measure combines a diatonic bass note with the upper two voices acting as part of a lower chromatic approach chord.

Ex. 4-42

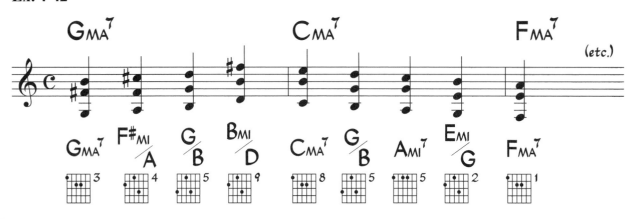

Ex. 4-43 shows the same voicings on the middle set of strings starting on Cmaj7.

Ex. 4-43

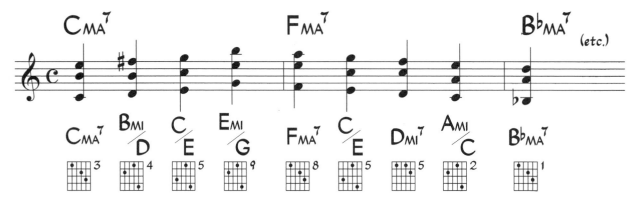

Ex. 4-44 shows a more chromaticised variation on the lower set starting from Gmaj7.

Ex. 4-44

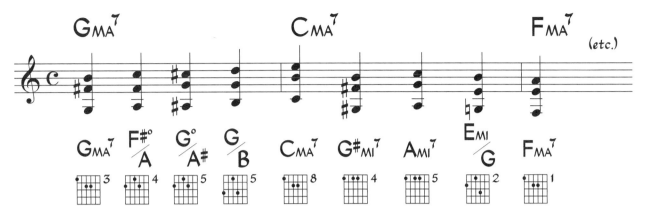

Ex. 4-45 shows the same variation on the middle set starting from Cmaj7.

Ex. 4-45

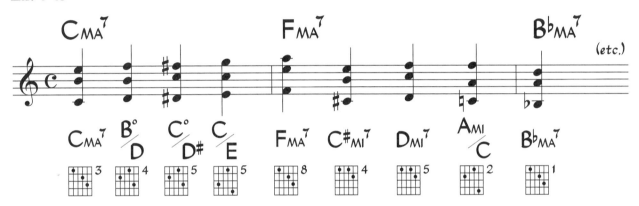

LONG MINOR CYCLES

Ex. 4-46 shows the first two measures (plus a beat) of a long cycle of minor7 chords on the lower set of strings starting on Gm7.

Ex. 4-46

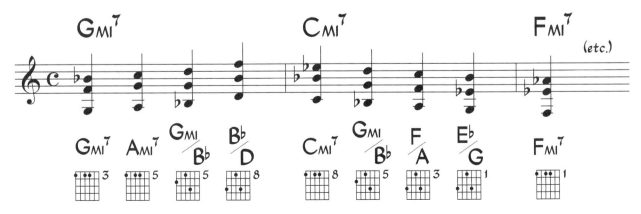

Ex. 4-47 shows the same voicings on the middle set of strings starting on Cm7.

Ex. 4-47

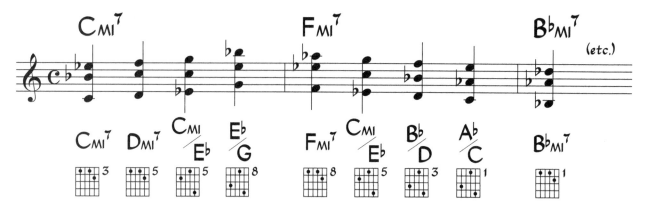

The last two examples are both entirely diatonic within each chord change. Ex. 4-48 and Ex. 4-49 are slightly chromaticised variations.

Ex. 4-48

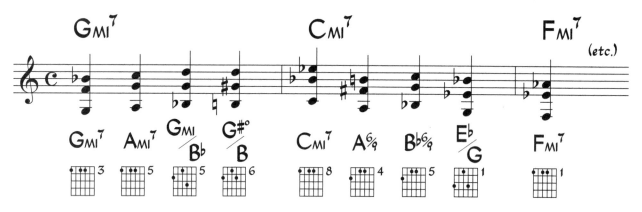

Ex. 4-49

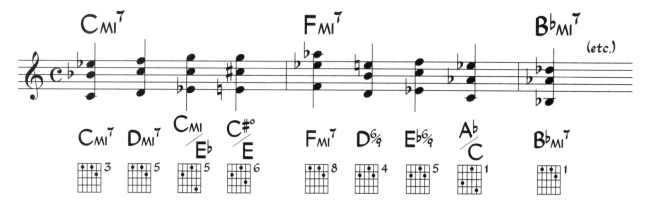

SHORT CYCLES

Short cycles are chords of the same type moving counter-clockwise around the circle of 5ths, with each chord lasting for only two beats.

SHORT DOMINANT CYCLES

Play Ex. 4-50. You may recognize it as being identical to Ex. 1-2 from early in the first chapter. As you recall, it's really just basic "shell" voicings for two beats each of G7-C7-F7 etc. that have tritone substitutions inserted in-between the main chords to give it that "walking" motion in the bass line. The top voice is relatively static, however, so let's try some variations.

Ex. 4-50

Ex. 4-51 keeps the outer voices in motion.

Ex. 4-51

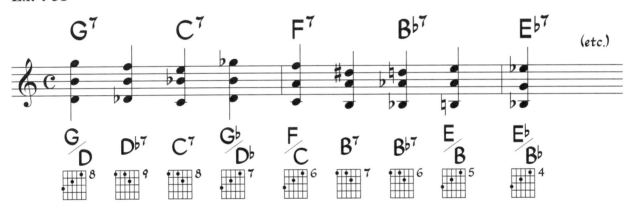

Ex. 4-52 applies the same trick we used in Ex. 2-24 to the short dominant cycle.

Ex. 4-52

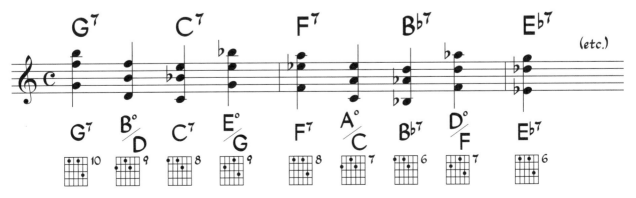

Ex. 4-53 uses something a bit unorthodox, starting on a third inversion dominant7 chord, the G7/F. It's use here is justified by the melodic lines it helps create.

Ex. 4-53

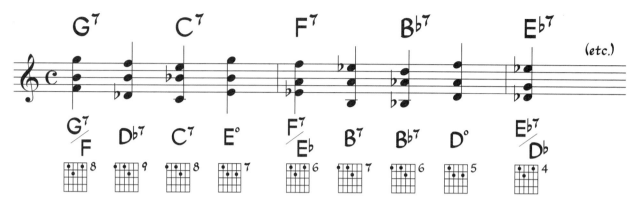

SHORT MAJOR CYCLES

Ex. 4-54 is a short cycle of major7 chords starting on Cmaj7.

Ex. 4-54

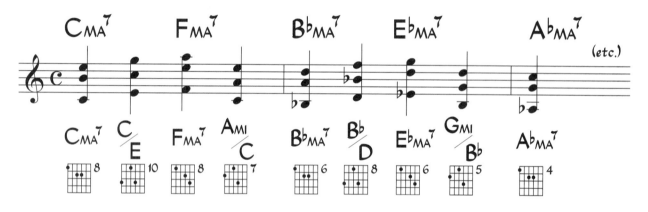

Ex. 4-55 is a slight variation.

Ex. 4-55

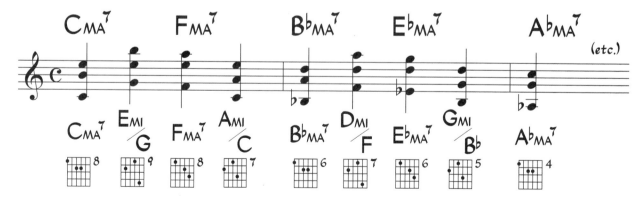

SHORT MINOR CYCLES

Ex. 4-56 is a short cycle of minor7 chords starting on Cm7.

Ex. 4-56

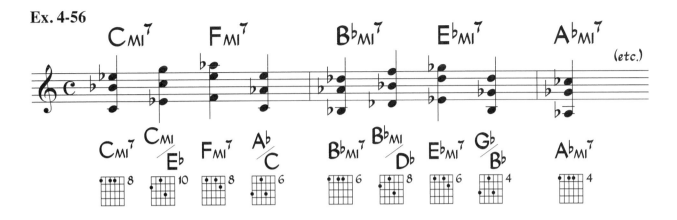

Ex. 4-57 is a slight variation.

Ex. 4-57

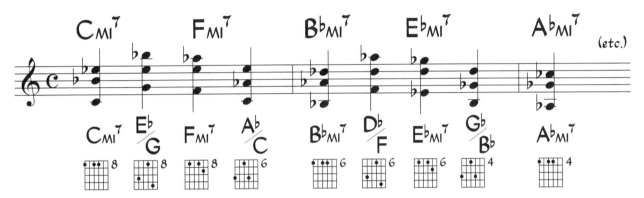

TURNAROUNDS

Turnarounds are short progressions used to move from a point of resolution to whatever chord is used to start the next section. The most common point of resolution is the I chord, so most turnarounds will start there or from its common substitution, the III chord. The most common chords used to start a new section are the I chord, the II chord, and the IV chord, so we'll check them out. Perhaps the most common starting chord is the I, so let's start there.

TURNAROUNDS TO THE I CHORD

The progression that most turnarounds to I are based on is the famous I-VI-II-V. Let's get right to "walking" chord lines with chromatics (I think we're past the need for "training wheels" by now). We'll use the key of F for the time being.

Ex. 4-58 is a basic I-VI-II-V turnaround to I in F using chromatics, inversions and tritone substitutions to create the "walking" chords.

Ex. 4-58

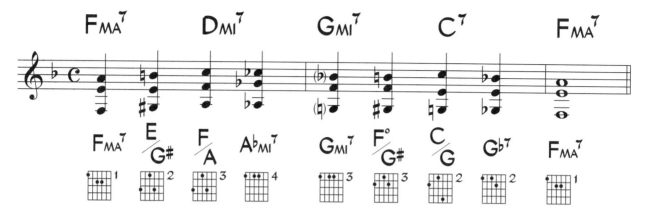

Ex. 4-59 is a variation starting on an inverted I chord, an Fmaj7/C.

Ex. 4-59

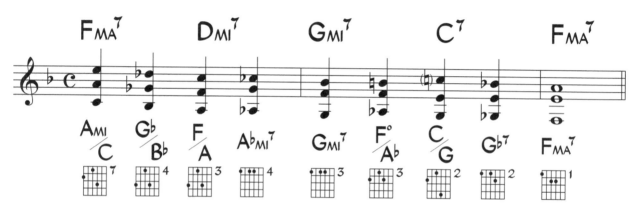

Ex. 4-60 alters the quality of the VI chord from minor7 to dominant7, making it a secondary dominant, the V of II (D7 is the V of Gm7, the II chord in the key of F).

Ex. 4-60

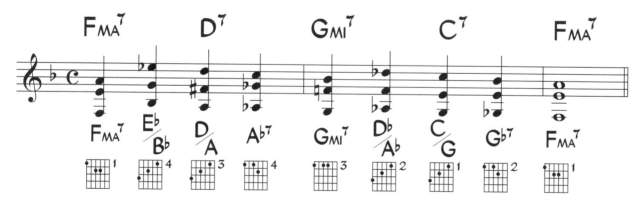

Ex. 4-61 uses a first inversion I chord, F/A, which is getting close to using the common substitute for I, the III chord. (See next page.)

Ex. 4-61

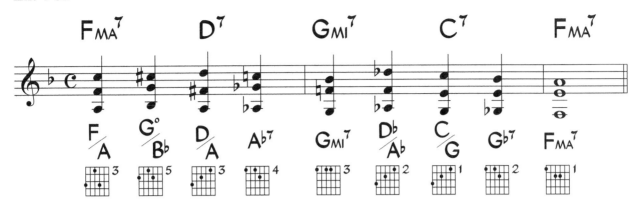

Ex. 4-62 uses the III-for-I sustitution, Am7 for Fmaj7. The Am7 could be thought of as a "pivot" chord. It is both the III-for-I substitute and the II part of a secondary II-V, the II-V of II (Am7-D7 is the II-V of the Gm7, the II chord in the key of F).

Ex. 4-62

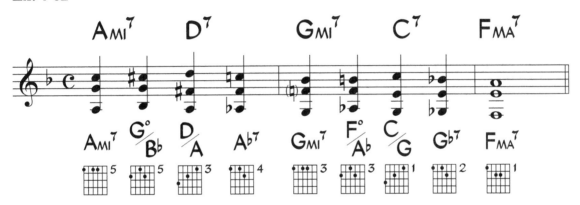

Ex. 4-63 starts on the second inversion I chord, the Fmaj7/C, which is also Am/C, which can function as the III chord inverted. This example uses some different forms than the last example to play some of the same harmonies. Try mixing up the various forms and fingerings, and try re-combining portions from different examples to create more variations.

Ex. 4-63

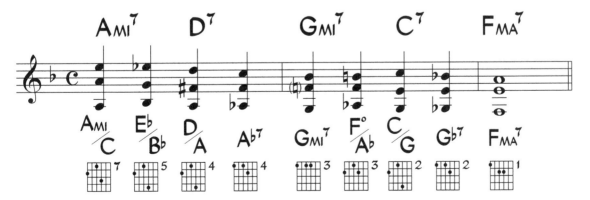

Ex. 4-64 starts on the high register root position I chord and works down the fingerboard, resolving to the III chord substituting for the I chord. (See next page.)

Ex. 4-64

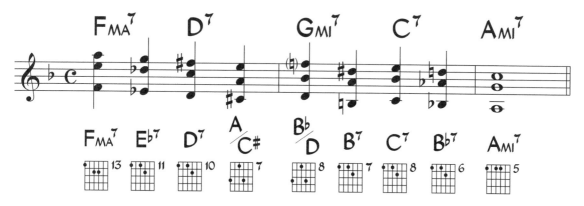

Ex. 4-65 is in the same location, but starts with a second inversion III chord and resolves to the high register I chord (on different strings this time).

Ex. 4-65

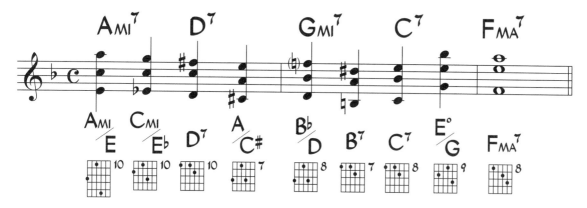

Since many blues and blues-influenced tunes use a dominant7-type chord for the I chord, you should try all the examples using dom7 chords instead of maj7 for the I chords.

TURNAROUNDS TO THE I CHORD IN MINOR

Turnarounds going from the I chord back to the I are very common in minor keys, so let's check out a few to get you started. We'll use the key of C minor this time.

I-VI-II-V going back to I in C minor would be Cm-Am7b5-Dm7b5-G7-Cm. Ex. 4-66 is very similar to the first part of the previously mentioned Jim Hall walking guitar accompaniment to Bill Evans' solo on "My Funny Valentine" from *Undercurrent*. The initial Cm6 is followed by a lower chromatic approach chord which returns to the Cm6, which is now actually the first inversion of Am7b5. The rest of the example uses the devices we've already been using.

Ex. 4-66

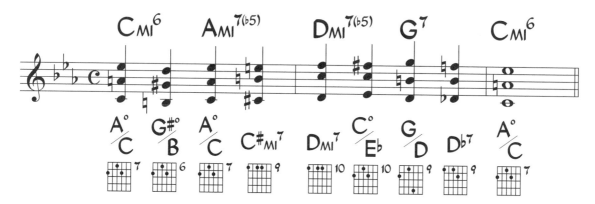

Ex. 4-67 shows a variation.

Ex. 4-67

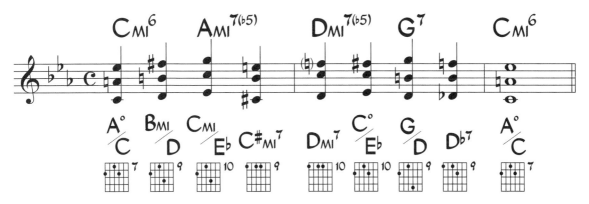

Ex. 4-68 is in a different location, using other forms and other sets of strings.

Ex. 4-68

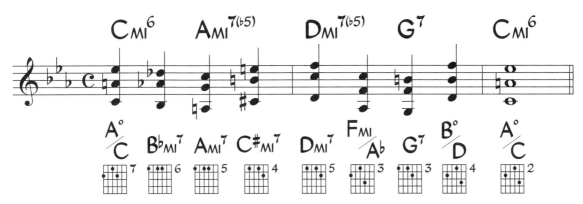

Ex. 4-69 is based on an alternate turnaround, I-bVII-bVI-V going back to I. In C minor this would be Cm-Bb7-Ab7-G7-Cm. Since the root movement is already step-wise, we use chromatic approach chords the create the walking motion. Here it's mostly lower approach chords.

Ex. 4-69

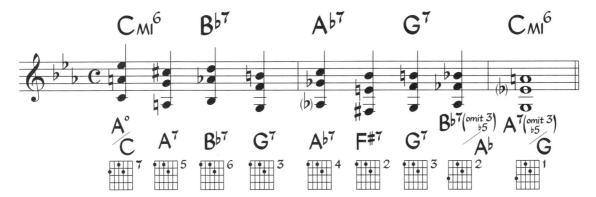

Ex. 4-70 uses mostly upper chromatic approach chords.

Ex. 4-70

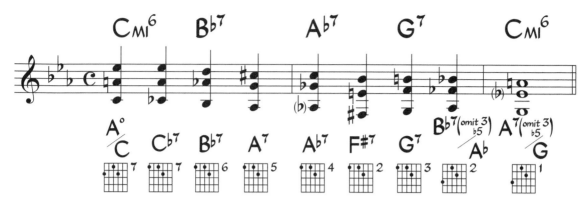

By the way, many tunes in major keys actually start out in their relative minor keys, so you should also practice turnarounds to VI (the relative minor). I'm not going to show any so you'll have to work them out yourself. Start by trying to combine the first measure of a simple I-VI-II-V turnaround in major with the second measure of any minor turnaround in the relative minor key.

Also keep in mind that in any given situation, you may want to replace the final Cm6 chord with Cm7 if it sounds better in context. Please feel free to do so. I used Cm6 in the examples for its more "tonic" minor sound. Try all the examples both ways, and try Cm-maj7 as well.

TURNAROUNDS TO THE II CHORD

Many turnarounds to the II chord start with step-wise diatonic movement up the scale to the III chord, which then becomes a pivot functioning as a II in a secondary II-V going back to the II in the home key. Let's use the key of F to demonstrate. The progression in F is Fmaj7-Gm7-Am7-D7-Gm7.

Ex. 4-71 uses inversions after the root position chords to form a melodic pattern in thirds out of the basic step-wise root movement.

Ex. 4-71

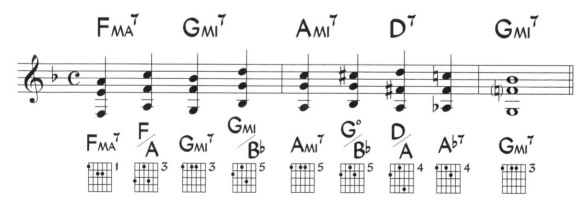

Ex. 4-72 uses lower chromatic approach chords to change the ascending diatonic scale into an ascending chromatic scale.

Ex. 4-72

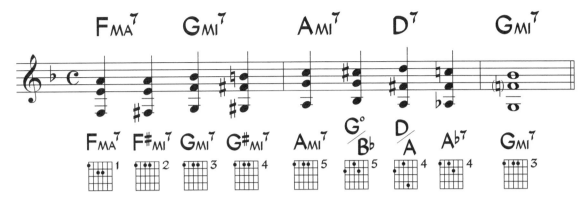

Another popular variation uses the IV chord (Bbmaj7 in the key of F) instead of the II (Gm7 in F). The two chords are relatives and can frequently substitute for each other. The next two examples will use the IV chord name, but could be used for either version.

Ex. 4-73 starts on the second inversion I chord (Fmaj7/C) and works its way down the fingerboard.

Ex. 4-73

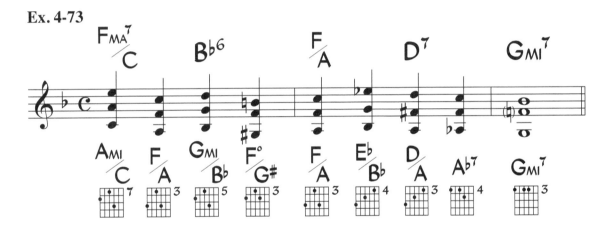

Ex. 4-74 starts on the root position in the higher register and works its way down.

Ex. 4-74

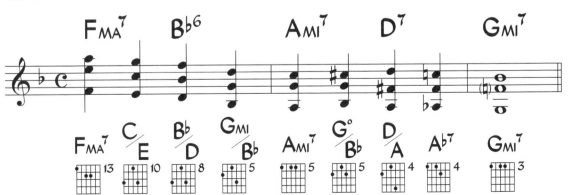

Ex. 4-75 starts on a higher register first inversion (F/A) on the middle strings and descends from there.

Ex. 4-75

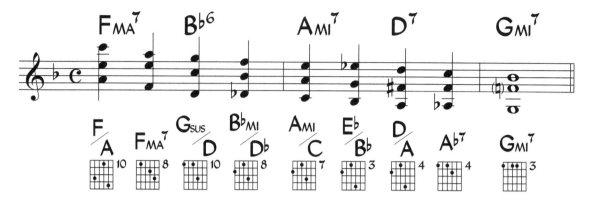

It would be a good idea to play a long or short II-V-I progression after the turnaround to II. You could create a practice loop (II-V-I-turnaround-to-II-V-I, etc.).

Incidently, sometimes tunes start on a II chord with a major 3rd (G7 instead of Gm7 in the key of F), so practice resolving the turnarounds to II (to G7 in the key of F). You could then continue with a long or short dominant cycle taking you back to the I, forming a loop. Of course, play them in all keys and other sets of strings when practical.

TURNAROUNDS TO THE IV CHORD

Turnarounds to IV can start out like turnarounds to I, but the second measure should use a secondary II-V, the II-V of IV. In the key of F this would be Fmaj7-Dm7-Cm7-F7 going to Bbmaj7.

Ex. 4-76 is a walking version of the turnaround to IV in the key of F.

Ex. 4-76

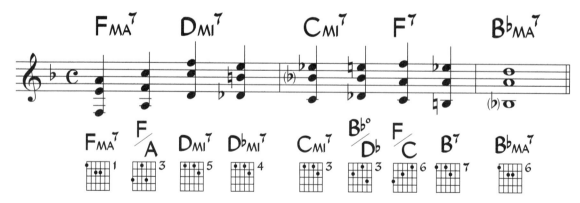

Ex. 4-77 is another version starting on the high register Fmaj7.

Ex. 4-77

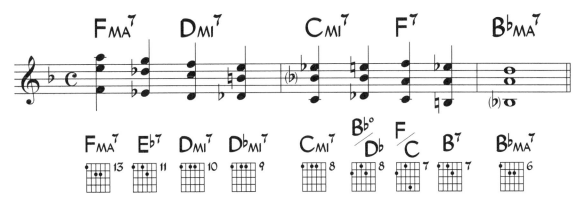

Ex. 4-78 is based on a slightly different harmonic scheme, Fmaj7-Gm7-Am7-F7. On the F7 we substitute Cm7-B7. Now the m7 chords can be connected with all chromatic approach chords, making most of the example easy to play by using one m7 form walking up the fingerboard, mostly in half steps.

Ex. 4-78

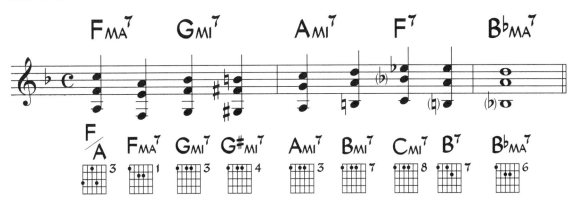

I'll leave it up to you to work out more variations, in addition to the other keys and other sets of strings. By now you should have enough vocabulary to play walking chords through twelve-bar blues, rhythm-changes, and other tunes as well. Let's check out the blues first.

TWELVE-BAR BLUES

TRADITIONAL BLUES BRIEFLY ANALYZED

The twelve-bar blues form can be thought of as three four-bar sections. The first is basically the I chord. The second is basically the IV chord going back to the I chord. The third section is basically the V chord going back to the I chord. In blues, all three of these chords are traditionally dominant7-type chords.

JAZZ BLUES

Most jazz versions will go to the IV in the second bar of the first section. In F this would be Bb7, introducing the all-important "blue" note Ab. Most jazz versions also relace the V chord in the third section with a II-V. To walk through the blues form we can use a long dominant cycle for the first two bars, followed by a turnaround to IV on the next two bars since the next section begins on the IV chord. The last two bars of the second section should use a turnaround to II. After the II-V in the third section the last two bars of the form are a turnaround to I. Let's give it a try.

WALKING THE BLUES

The first example of walking blues, Ex. 4-79, is a complete twelve-bar form that begins exactly like Ex. 4-1 at the begining of this chapter, but keeps on going to finish the form.

Ex. 4-79

The seventh and eighth bars are similar to turnarounds to II we've looked at, but starting on the second inversion I chord (that's where the melodic voice-leading on the IV chord took us). The ninth and tenth bars are the same as the long II-V-I from Ex. 4-8, only resolves into a dom7-type I chord. The last two bars are a turnaround to I that we haven't used in this way before, but it's based on the short dominant cycle from Ex. 4-50, so it should seem very familiar. The very end of the example shows the resolution chord, F7, which is the first chord of the next twelve-bar form. Since it's the same as the first chord, you can repeat the entire example, looping it for practice purposes. The upcoming blues examples also start with the same F7 voicing, so you can play the examples with each one leading right into the next.

Ex. 4-80 is a new variation. I'm not going to analyze every detail and tell where every cycle, II-V-I, and turaround comes from, but I encourage you to play the top line by itself, listening to the melody, then play the bass line by itself, listening to its melody. Then play just the top melody and bass line together. This process should give you real insight into where these walking progressions actually come from.

Ex. 4-80

Ex. 4-81 is another variation (this one uses a voice-leading that is similar to one Joe Diorio showed in his book *Fusion*, but Joe's version is in Bb and uses almost all four-note chords). In this example we replace the Gm7 from the II-V portion of the blues with G7, making it a secondary dominant, the V of the V chord, so in those two bars we use a modified long dominant cycle. The final turnaround also uses a short dominant cycle adapted to create the turnaround to the I chord.

Ex. 4-81

Once again, it is up to you to transpose into other keys and to work out on alternate sets of strings, as well as coming up with more variations. For more variations you can start by re-combining sections from different variations already given, wherever voice-leading allows.

RHYTHM CHANGES

"Rhythm changes" is the name for a 32-bar AABA form where the A sections are essentially strings of turnarounds to I and the B section is a very long dominant cycle (two bars on each chord) leading back to the I. Rhythm changes can be in any key, but the key of Bb is by far the most common, so our examples will be in Bb.

ANALYZING THE A SECTIONS

Let's break down the A sections into two-bar fragments. The first two bars are a turnaround to I. The second two bars are another turnaround to I, but in our examples this turnaround will use a short dominant cycle that "back-cycles" to the I chord. A back-cycle is worked out "backwards" from the target chord (the I in this case), but, of course, is played "forwards." The basic progression here will be Bb-G7-C7-F7 going back to Bb. The next two bars are I going to IV and returning to I (similar to the first two bars of twelve-bar blues). There are two common ways to get back to I from IV. One is to use a #IVdim7 (Eb-Edim7-Bb in Bb) and the other is to use a IVmin (Eb-Ebmin-Bb in Bb). The last two bars are another turnaround to I on the first A and the last A, but is shortened to a quicker resolution on the second A to set up the B section, also commonly called the "bridge".

WALKING THE A SECTIONS

Play Ex. 4-82, an eight-bar A section that could be the first eight or the last eight of a chorus of rhythm changes. The first two bars are based on a turnaround to I that we haven't looked at yet, I-bIIIdim7-II-V-I, or Bb-Dbdim7-Cm7-F7-Bb in the key of Bb. The second two bars is an example of the back-cycled dominants. The next two bars connect the IV back to I using the #IVdim7, and the last two are a familiar turnaround to I.

Ex. 4-82

Ex. 4-83 is designed to be a second eight going to the bridge because of the last two bars, but the rest of the example could be used for any A section. The first two bars are, once again, based on a turnaround we haven't previously seen, I-#Idim7-II-#IIdim7-I/III or III as a substitute for I (Bb-Bdim7-Cm7-C#dim7-Bb/D or Dm7 substituting for Bb). Since the root movement is already chromatic, we'll use some special devices to create walking lines. First, on the second beat, we use a lower chromatic neighbor chord, which must return to the Bbmaj7 chord before moving on. This creates a delay for the arrival of the Bdim7 chord, placing it on the fourth beat. In the second measure the same devices are applied to the Cm7 going to the C#dim7 and on to the Dm7 in the third measure. The result is continuous motion. The next two two-bar sections are variations of the same changes as in Ex. 4-82. The last two bars target the first chord of the B section, the D7, but you can replace these two bars with any turnaround to I as needed.

Ex. 4-83

Ex. 4-84 starts with the same basic two-bar ascending chromatic progression that was used in Ex. 4-83, but this time the walking motion is achieved by using a melodic pattern of 3rds. The second two bars are, once again, a short dominant cycle turnaround to I. This is followed by a I going to IV going back to I using the IVminor this time (the Dm7 is a III for I substitution). Finally, another turnaround to I.

Ex. 4-84

WALKING THE B SECTION

Ex. 4-85 demonstates one possible solution for walking through the rhythm changes bridge using a variety of devices to keep the melodies moving, including upper and lower chromatic nieghbors and tritone subtitutions. Try playing just the top voice of each chord as a melody, then the bottom voice as a melodic bass line. Do this same process when creating your own variations to make sure the melodies are strong.

Ex. 4-85

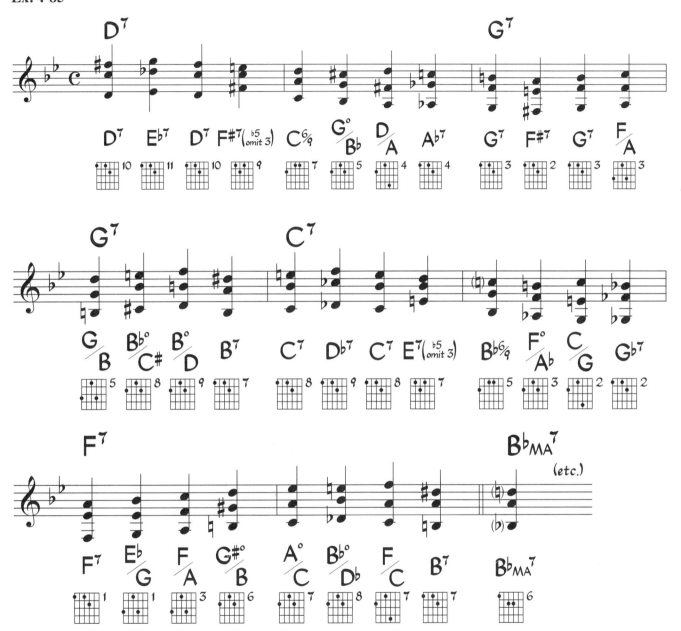

Now your assignment is to put together complete choruses using two A sections followed by a B section, and finally a last A section.

Remember to transpose to other keys, and try other sets of strings, and, of course, try creating variations on your own. I think that's enough walking for now. Let's move on.

Chapter 5 - Using Triads In "Slash" Chords And Upper Structure Voicings

TRIADIC "SLASH" CHORDS

Play Ex. 5-1, the vamp from the coda of Mike Nock's tune "Doors." This is an example of the sound of triadic slash chords.

Ex. 5-1

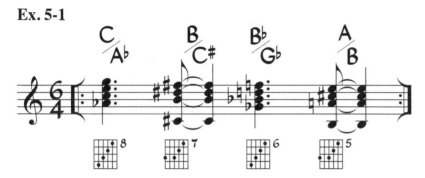

I'm sure you probably already know what a slash chord is, but just in case you're unclear, here's a definition.

TRIADIC SLASH CHORD DEFINED

A triadic "slash" chord is a chord whose symbol consists of two upper-case letters separated by a forward slash. The first letter is the root of a triad and may have other information before the slash, such as a lower-case m, making it a minor triad, for example. The letter after the slash is a bass note played under the triad.

I'm sure you noticed that all the examples in the previous chapter used many slash-chord symbols above the fingerboard diagrams to analyze what was literally being played. So, aren't we already masters of triadic slash chords? Well, no, because all the slash chords we've been using are actually just inversions of the triads since the bass notes were always the 3rds or 5ths of the triads. However, there are other kinds of slash chords.

TYPES OF TRIADIC SLASH CHORDS

As we have seen, one type of triadic slash chord is the triad inversion, where the bass note is the 3rd or 5th of the triad. All other types will have a bass note that is not a member of the triad.

Some of these other types turn out to be 7th chords in either root position or third inversion (with the 7th in the bass).

Ex. 5-2 is C/A, which turns out to be the same as Am7 in root position. The C/Ab in Ex. 5-1 could be called Abmaj7#5 (also in root position).

Ex. 5-2

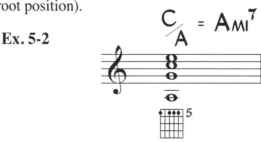

Ex. 5-3 is C/Bb, which is the same as C7 in the third inversion. Ex. 5-4 is C/B, which is a third inversion Cmaj7.

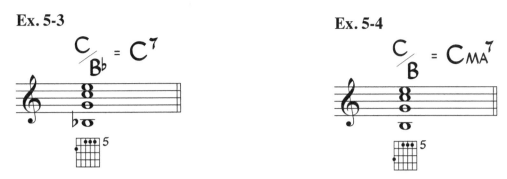

Notice that the root position 7th chords have the 6th or b6th of the triad in the bass, while the third inversion 7th chords have the b7th or maj7th in the bass. The other remaining types of triadic slash chords have either some kind of 2nd of the triad in the bass or some kind of 4th of the triad in the bass.

Ex. 5-5 is C/D, a major triad with the major 2nd in the bass. Ex. 5-6 is C/Db, a major triad with the minor 2nd in the bass. Triadic slash chords with 2nds in the bass are sometimes called "hybrid 11th" chords because the triad spells out the 7th, 9th, and 11th of the bass note. Occasionally a major triad will have an augmented 2nd in the bass, which isn't used as a hybrid 11th. We'll check it out when we run through all the triadic slash chord possibilities.

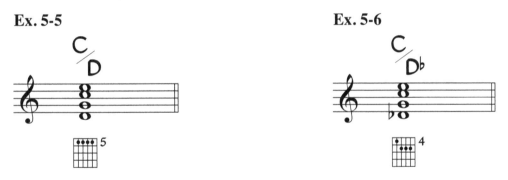

Ex. 5-7 is C/F, a major triad with the perfect 4th in the bass. Ex. 5-8 is C/F#, a major triad with the augmented 4th in the bass. Triadic slash chords with 4ths in the bass are sometimes called "hybrid 9th" chords because the triad spells out the 5th, 7th, and 9th of the bass note.

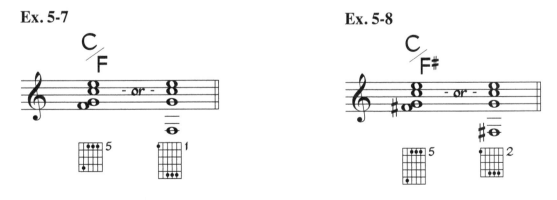

WHY "SLASH" CHORD SYMBOLS?

Since some types of triadic slash chords are really just 7th chords (or 9ths or 11ths), why should we ever bother with the more mysterious slash chord names at all? Sometimes it may be a matter of context.

Ex. 5-9 shows a passage where even the "never" used C/C chord symbol seems to make sense. It starts on E/C, which could be called Cmaj7#5, followed by Eb/C, which could be called Cm7. Next is D/C, which is a third inversion D7, followed by Db/C, which is a third inversion Dbmaj7. Now comes the C/C, then B/C, which could be called Cdim-maj7, followed by Bb/C, or C9sus, and finally A/C before resolving to Fmaj7.

Ex. 5-9

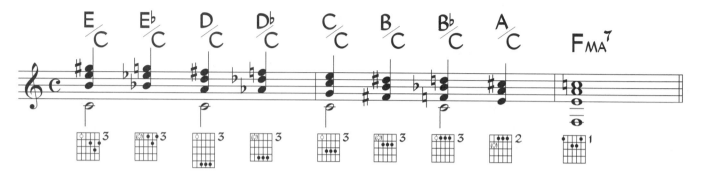

After playing the example, does it make more or less sense to use the slash chord symbols, or would you rather see something like Cmaj7#5-Cm7-D7/C-Dbmaj7/C-C-Cdim-maj7-C9sus-C13b9-Fmaj7? Which set of chord symbols gets the point across more effectively? For me, the slash-chord symbols indicate exactly what's actually going on while the conventional chord names might take several minutes to "solve the puzzle" (certainly not very good for sight reading).

Did you notice that all the slash chords in Ex.5-9 had the same bass note (a C)? This is an example of pedal point, which is one voice remaining motionless while the others move. A pedal could happen in any voice, but is commonly used in the bass voice. A bass pedal is frequently a great place, although certainly not the only place, to use slash chords. One famous example of slash chords over a pedal bass note occurs in "Aguas de Marco (Waters of March)" by Antonio Carlos Jobim, which happens to use the C pedal. The chords are named C-Cm7-D/C-Db/C-C, but could also be called C/C-Eb/C-D/C-Db/C-C/C, just to clarify what's going on. The melody uses a sequence that shifts from major (Ionian) to minor (aeolian), and finally to phrygian on the Db/C. For a complete discussion of chord-scale relationships on slash chords see *The Jazz Theory Book* by Mark Levine, published by Sher Music Co..

Did you notice that all the examples from 5-2 through 5-7 used a C major triad over various bass notes to create a variety of different sounding chords? The C triad seems to become different things when placed over different bass notes. Barry Finnerty's great book, *The Serious Jazz Book II - The Harmonic Approach,* has a very interesting section called "What a C can be" that explores all the possible contexts for the note C. Perhaps this would be a good time to explore the vertical harmonic contexts for triads in order to fully comprehend the use of triads in slash chords and in upper struture voicings.

WHAT TRIADS CAN BE

Ex. 5-10 shows many harmonic structures that contain a C major triad. The whole-notes are the triad while the additional notes use quarter-note heads. Notice there are no guitar chord diagrams. These are for analysis only and should be played on a keyboard since most are impractical or impossible on guitar in this configuration. The first three are C chords with extensions (the Cmaj7 and the C7) or added notes (the C6). Any of these chords could also have further extensions such as 9ths, etc., so I'm not going to list them as separate chords. All the others have notes under the C triad and have roots that are not C. Many of these might also have extensions added above the C triad without changing the underlying chord. Again, I am not going to show them all. What I am showing should be enough to keep you thinking for years (it has been for me).

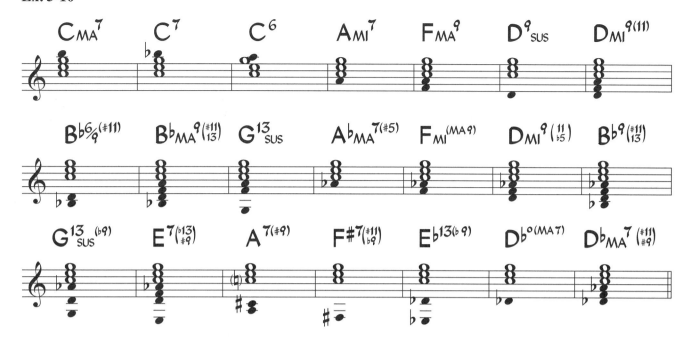

Ex. 5-11 shows the same concept exactly using a C minor triad this time. All the same instructions still apply.

Ex. 5-11

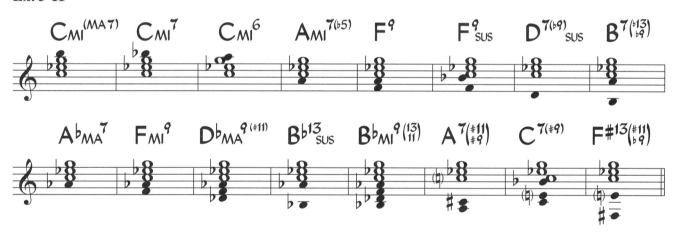

Ex. 5-12 shows the same thing using a C diminished triad.

Ex. 5-12

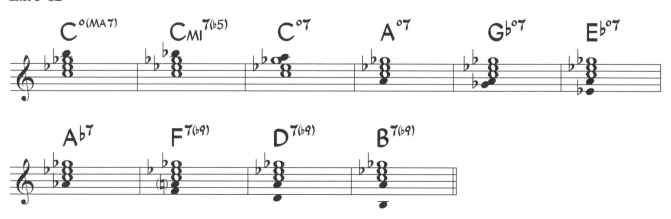

Ex. 5-13 is the same thing using the C augmented triad.

Ex. 5-13

I think that's enough of that for now. Let's get back to playing slash chords on our guitars.

MAJOR TRIAD SLASH CHORDS

All the slash chord examples we've seen so far used major triads, which are the most common. As you can see from the "What triads can be" section, we should also do slash chords using minor, diminished, and augmented triads as well. But first, major triads.

Ex. 5-14 shows all twelve major triads in root position (close voicing) on the upper-middle set of three consecutive strings over the bass note G. Notice that when the triad makes the low G hard to reach we move it up an octave, placing it on the fifth string. The last chord, E/G, can have the G on either the fifth or the sixth string. Learn and practice both versions.

Ex. 5-14

Ex. 5-15 shows all twelve close-voiced first-inversion major triads on the upper-middle set over the G bass notes.

Ex. 5-15

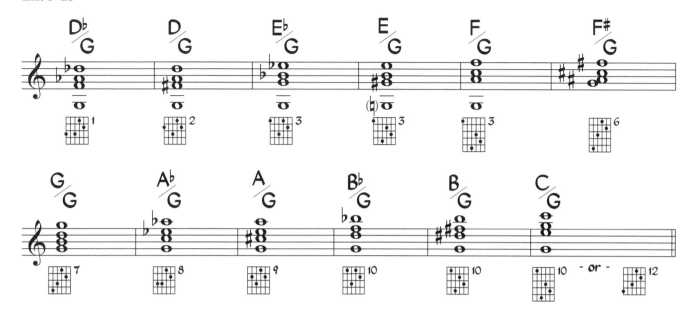

Ex. 5-16 shows all twelve second inversion close-voiced major triads on the upper-middle set over the G bass notes. Notice that the Db/G and the D/G are practical with both the lower octave G bass and the higher octave G bass, so do both. In fact, wherever it says "or" in the examples, think "and". Of course in real playing you'll use one "or" the other according to context—you'll need to know both so you'll be ready.

Ex. 5-16

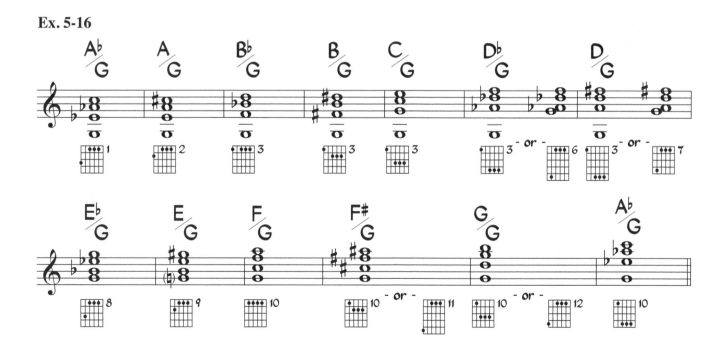

Ex. 5-17 shows all twelve close-voiced root position major triads on the top three strings over the higher octave G bass note. As the reach becomes difficult we move the G from the fourth string to the fifth string, keeping it in the same octave.

Ex. 5-17

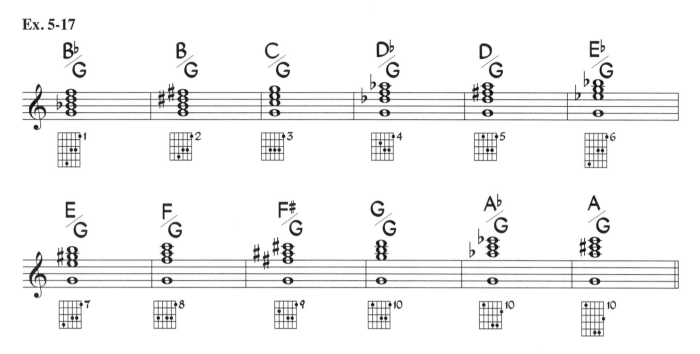

Ex. 5-18 shows all twelve first inversion close-voiced major triads on the top strings over the G bass note.

Ex. 5-18

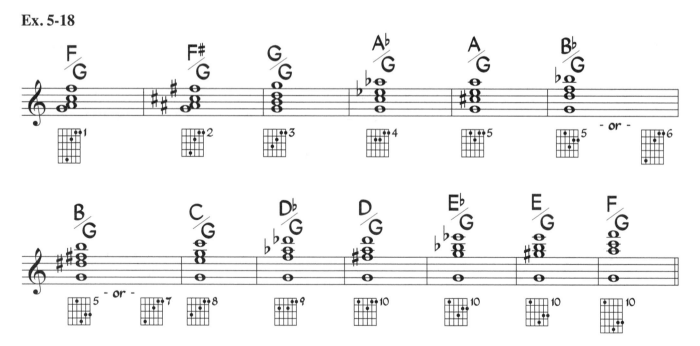

Ex. 5-19 shows all twelve second inversion close-voiced major triads on the top strings over the G bass.

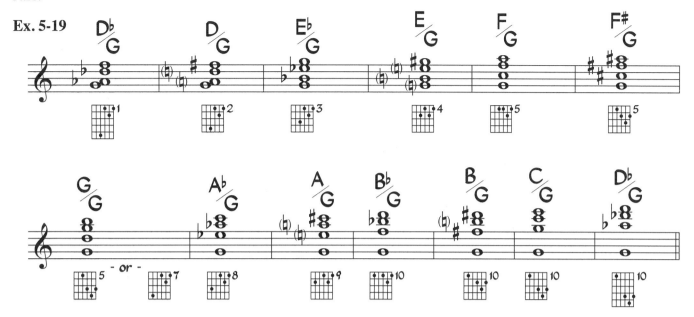

Ex. 5-19

MAJOR TRIAD SLASH CHORDS ANALYZED

G/G needs no analysis. Ab/G has a b9, sus4, and b13 of G, so is a phrygian chord. A/G has a 9, #11, and 13 of G, which indicates maj7#11 (lydian) or 7#11 (lydian-dominant). Bb/G is Gm7. B/G is Gmaj7#5 (lydian-augmented). C/G is a triad inversion. Db/G has a b7, b9, and b5(#11) of G, which could be Galt (superlocrian) or a diminished scale (half-whole). D/G has a maj7, 9, and 5th of G, probably Gmaj9 (there's no 3rd). Eb/G is a triad inversion, but might make a nice aeolian chord with its b3 and b6. E/G has a b9, maj3, and a 6th of G. The b9 combined with the maj3 makes it a dominant chord, so the 6 is a 13 making the chord a G13b9 (half-whole diminished). F/G has a b7, 9, and a 4th of G, so it's G9sus (probably mixolydian). F#/G has a maj7, min3 (or #9), and a b5 (or #11) of G, so it may be Gdim-maj7 (whole-half diminished), or it may represent part of Gmaj7#9#11 (sixth mode of B harmonic minor).

MINOR TRIAD SLASH CHORDS

Ex. 5-20 shows all twelve close-voiced root position minor triads on the upper-middle set of strings over the G bass notes.

Ex. 5-20

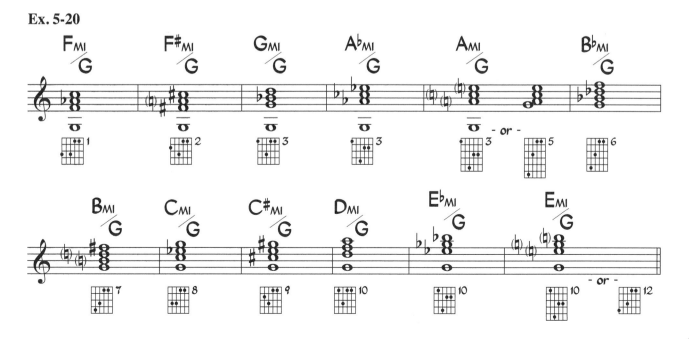

Ex. 5-21 shows all twelve first inversion close-voiced minor triads on the upper-middle strings over the G notes.

Ex. 5-21

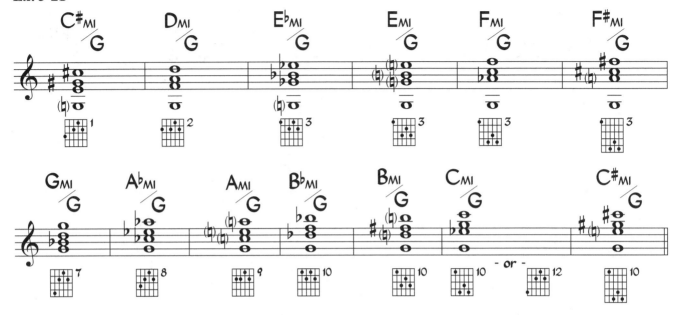

Ex. 5-22 shows all twelve second inversion close-voiced minor triads on the upper middle set over the G notes.

Ex. 5-22

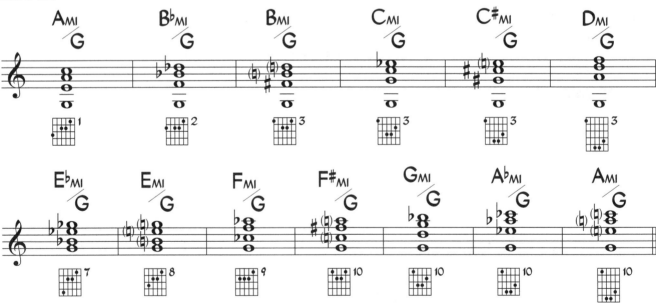

Ex. 5-23 shows all twelve root position close-voiced minor triads on the top set of strings over the G bass.

Ex. 5-23

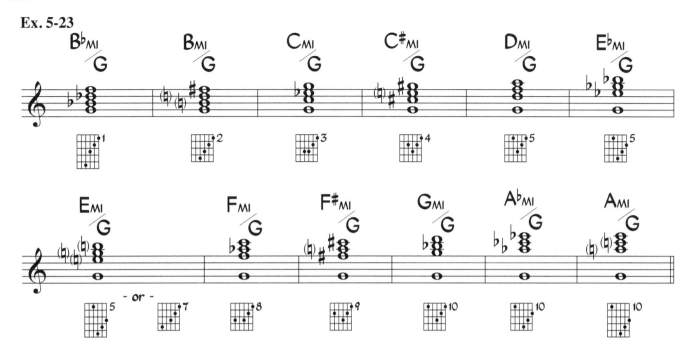

Ex. 5-24 shows all twelve first inversion close-voiced minor triads on the top strings over the G bass.

Ex. 5-24

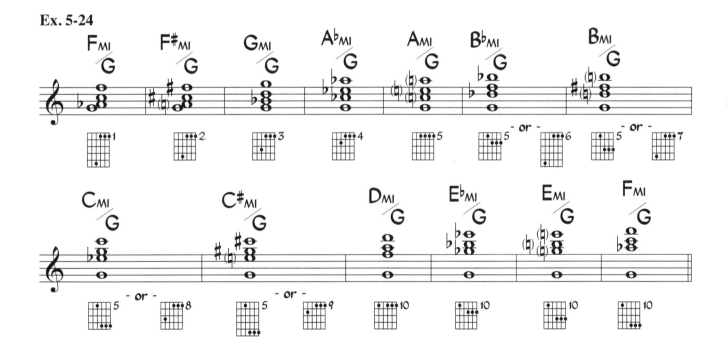

Ex. 5-25 shows all twelve second inversion close-voiced minor triads on the top set over the G bass.

Ex. 5-25

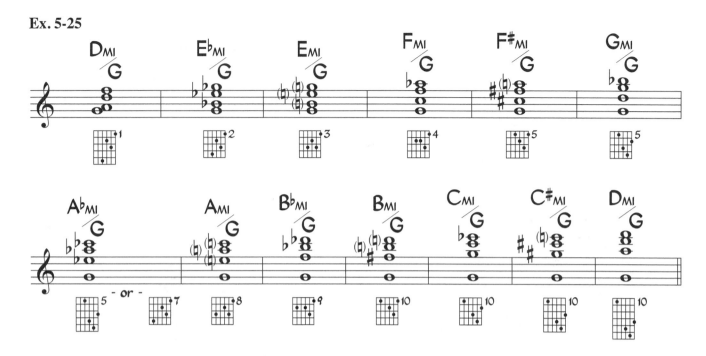

I'll leave it to you to do the analysis for the minor-triad slash chords.

OTHER TRIADIC SLASH CHORDS

Most slash chords use major triads, but many also use minor. Diminished and augmented triadic slash chords are much less common, but they do occur so you need to know them. Now I'm going to give you an assignment. Using the various close-voiced dim. and aug. triad forms from the triad review chapter that are located on the top three strings and the upper-middle set of strings, create the dim. and aug. triadic slash chords using the ones we just did (the maj. and the min.) as a model. If this seems too difficult, you need to review the triad chapter again, and this chapter as well.

By the way, the G bass note was arbitrarily chosen. All the fingerings are moveable so it's easy to transpose any voicing to a different pitch without changing fingering or form. Feel free to invent "key-specific" voicings using open strings if you like. The string groupings were chosen because their register allows the triads to be clearly heard as separate entities from the bass notes. Also, the close-voiced triads are easiest to hear this way too. Again, feel free to experiment with alternate ideas, such as open-voiced triads in slash chords, or even placing the "bass" note inside an open-voiced triad (see Ex.s 3-26 and 3-27).

UPPER STRUCTURE VOICINGS

Play Ex. 5-26, the last four bars of "There Will Never Be Another You" reharmonized using some triadic slash chords. The Bb/Eb functions as Ebmaj9. The Bb/Gb is a Gbmaj7#5 functioning as Ab13#11. The Eb/B is a Bmaj7#5 functioning as a G7#9b13 and the Ab/E is Emaj7#5 functioning as a C7#9b13. The remaining voicings are some basic three-note structures. (See next page.)

Ex. 5-26

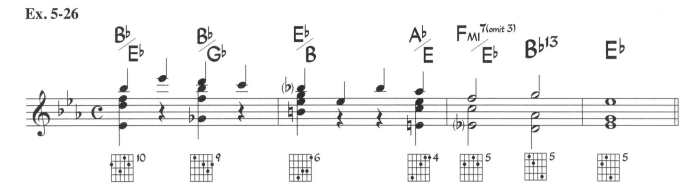

UPPER STRUCTURE VOICINGS DEFINED

This example is actually a simplified version of upper structure voicings, which are similar to triadic slash chords in the fact that they have a triad on top of the voicing, but the upper structure voicings generally have more notes under the triad than just the bass note, and are played over another bass note played by someone else (or imagined if playing solo).

SOME UPPER STRUCTURES DEMONSTRATED

Ex. 5-27 is the actual upper structure version of the last four bars of "There Will Never Be Another You." I changed the Bb/Eb to a fourth chord, which is a "stack" of 4th intervals used here because it voice-leads perfectly to the Ab13#11 voicing.

Ex. 5-27

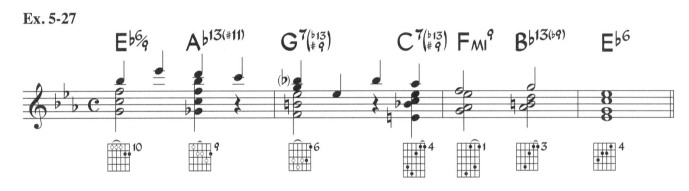

To play the Ab13#11 voicing, try this trick: start with the fingering for the Bb/Gb slash chord we used in Ex. 5-26, then pick up the second finger and place it on the fourth string (playing the C note), then roll the fingertip to flatten the finger to cover the F note with a partial barre while keeping the fourth finger arched so as not to mute the high D note.

To play the G7#9b13 voicing let's try the same kind of trick. Start with the Eb/B slash chord, pick up the second finger and place it on the fifth string (the F) and flatten into a partial barre covering three strings to play the note Eb.

For the C7#9b13, start with the Ab/E. Now replace the fourth finger with the third finger so the fourth finger can now play the Bb on the fourth string. This creates a stretch between the second and third fingers, which may take a little getting used to, but it is practical. What were three-note voicings in Ex. 5-26 are now four-note chords (for better compatibility) and the Bb13b9 is also an upper structure voicing (notice the G triad on top).

UPPER STRUCTURES ANALYZED

All the upper structure voicings in the last example are extended and/or altered dominant chords. Did you notice that the first three upper structures used all three major triad inversions? Let's start with those.

The Ab13#11 has a second inversion Bb major triad on top. From the top down it spells out the #11, 9, and 13 of the Ab. Under that we find the tritone C-Gb, the 3rd and 7th of the Ab. The Bb triad root is the major 2nd of Ab, so we call this voicing US II (for "upper structure II").

The G7#9b13 has a root position Eb major triad on top spelling (from the top down) the #9, root, and b13 of the G. Under that we find the tritone B-F, the 3rd and 7th of G7. The Eb triad root is the b6th of G, so we call this voicing US bVI.

The C7#9b13 has a first inversion Ab major triad on top, spelling the b13, #9, and root of the C. Under that we find the tritone Bb-E, the 7th and 3rd of C7. The Ab triad root is the b6th of C, so again we have a US bVI.

THE SAME UPPER STRUCTURES ANALYZED AS TRITONE SUBSTITUTIONS

Now let's re-analyze the voicings using tritone substitution. The symmetry of the tritone allows it to represent two dominant chords whose roots are also a tritone apart, so let's leave the voicings alone but replace the "imaginary" bass notes with new bass notes a tritone away.

The Ab13 #11 will now be some kind of D7. The Bb triad spells, from the top down, the root, b13, and #9 of the D, while the tritone swaps from being 3rd-7th of Ab to being 7th-3rd of D7. The Bb triad root is the b6th of D, so it's another US bVI now instead of being a US II (notice that II and bVI are also a tritone apart from each other).

The G7#9b13 will become Db13#11. The Eb triad now spells 13, #11, and 9 of the Db and it has become a US II.

The C7#9b13 becomes Gb13#11, the last US II.

We now have all three practical voicings for US II and for US bVI on the guitar by using just those three forms. Since we're not playing the roots as bass notes on the guitar, we have to practice thinking how to find them in various keys quickly on the instrument.

Now let's check out the remaining US voicing from the example, the Bb13b9. The first inversion G major triad spells, from the top down, the 13, the maj3, and the b9 of Bb. Notice that this is a four-note voicing rather than five. This is because one member of the tritone, the 3rd, is already present in the triad, so rather than having a cumbersome doubling, we just place the b7th (the Ab) under the triad. The G triad root is the 6th of Bb, so we have a US VI voicing.

Applying the tritone substitution to the Bb13b9 we get E7#9 with a natural 5th. The G triad root is the min3rd of E, so we have a US bIII (notice that VI and bIII are also a tritone apart from each other).

Ex. 5-28 shows Bb13b9 (US VI) and E7#9 (US bIII) using a second inversion G major triad.

Ex. 5-28

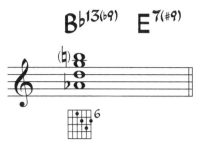

Ex. 5-29 shows them using the root position G triad.

Ex. 5-29

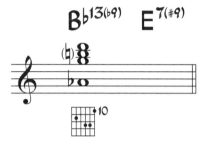

Ex.s 5-30, 5-31 and 5-32 show the same voicings transposed to F13b9 and B7#9 and moved over to the next set of strings.

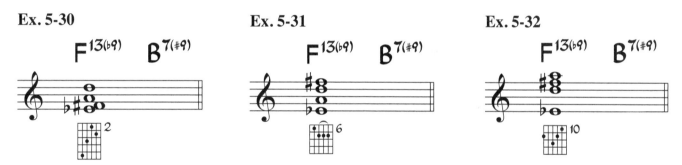

Ex. 5-30

Ex. 5-31

Ex. 5-32

SOME MORE DOMINANT US VOICINGS

We might as well finish the dominant US voicings first since we've done so many already. All the US triads used so far have been major triads. We still have one more major to look at, the US bV.

On a C7 the US bV triad is Gb major, which already contains the 7th of C (the note Bb), so we'll have four-note voicings again. When we place the 3rd of C under the triad, we get a plain unaltered Gb7 chord. This will only be usable when we have another actual instrument playing the C root as a bass note. When the bass is imaginary, it's much better to omit the 3rd in favor of a low C root (making it the already familiar Gb/C slash chord). For this reason all the US bV examples will have two versions. Version A has the 3rd of C7 under the Gb triad while version B has the root of C7 under the Gb triad.

Ex. 5-33 shows US bV using a first inversion Gb triad over C7. The Gb triad spells, from the top down, the b5 (#11), b9, and 7 of C7. Hence the name, C7b9#11. In addition to showing both version A and version B, each voicing is also shown in two different positions on different groupings of strings. The next two examples will do the same.

Ex. 5-33

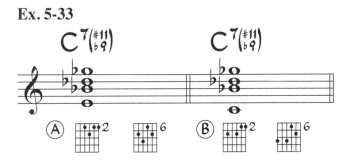

Ex. 5-34 shows C7b9#11 using a second inversion Gb triad.

Ex. 5-34

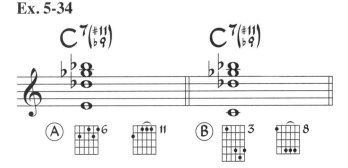

Ex. 5-35 shows C7b9#11 using a root position Gb triad.

Ex. 5-35

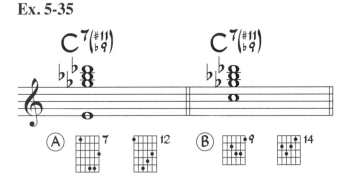

The tritone substitution technique doesn't apply to US bV because the triad is already a tritone away from the root of the C7 chord, so if we move the root by a tritone the triad becomes root, 3rd, and 5th (not exactly an upper structure).

DOMINANT US VOICINGS USING MINOR TRIADS

A I minor triad has the #9 of the I dom7 chord, so it can be used as an upper structure, as well as its tritone substitute, the #IV minor. Play Ex. 5-36. This could be played over E7 as a US I minor, creating E7#9 (with a natural 5th), or over Bb7 as a US #IV minor, creating Bb13b9#11. You might be complaining that the form requires five fingers (not counting the thumb) to play. You can actually find the "fifth-finger" on the side of the second joint of the first finger by rolling the fingertip so the second joint collapses away fom the rest of the hand to play the G while the tip still plays the B. In fact George Van Eps called this "the fifth-finger technique".

Ex. 5-36

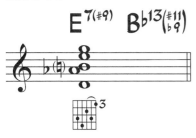

Ex. 5-37 is a variation that replaces the D with a low Bb, making it Bb13b9#11 only. You may find this better for Bb7 when no other actual instrument is there to supply the root bass note. This form also uses the "fifth-finger".

Ex. 5-37

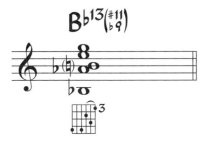

The last two examples used the second inversion Em triad. Let's try the root position. On the guitar it is almost impossible, and certainly impractical, to add both the 3rd and 7th, so if we're thinking E7 we must choose the 3rd or we'll end up with a simple m7 chord. The result is shown in Ex. 5-38, US I minor for E7#9 and US #IV minor for Bb13b9#11.

Ex. 5-38

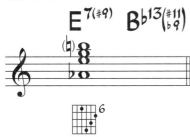

Ex. 5-39 shows the first inversion Em used as US I minor for E7 and as US #IV minor for Bb7. If, like me, you find the four-string barre difficult, try barring the upper-middle three strings with the second finger and catch the high E with the tip of the third finger.

Ex. 5-39

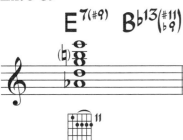

Ex. 5-40 uses a root position Fm triad on the upper-middle three strings as a US bII minor for E7 and as a US V minor for its tritone sub, Bb7. The Ab in the Fm functions as the 3rd of E7 and the 7th of Bb7, so we only need to place D under the triad to create E7#5b9 and Bb9.

Ex. 5-40

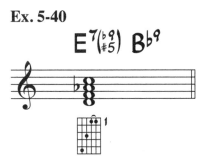

Ex. 5-41 uses the first inversion Fm triad.

Ex. 5-41

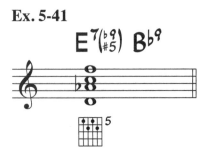

Ex. 5-42 uses the second inversion Fm triad.

Ex. 5-42

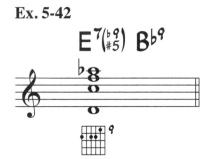

Ex. 5-43 moves the second inversion Fm triad to the top three strings.

Ex. 5-43

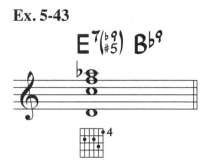

Ex. 5-44 uses the root position Fm on the top strings.

Ex. 5-44

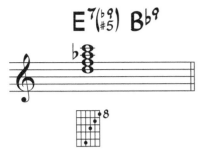

Ex. 5-45 uses the first inversion Fm on the top strings.

Ex. 5-45

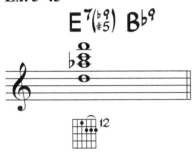

There's one last set of US minor voicings with tritone subs for dominant chords. Ex. 5-46 shows F13 or B7#9#11 using a second inversion Dm triad, forming US VI minor for the F7 and US bIII minor for the B7. Two forms are shown on different strings.

Ex. 5-46

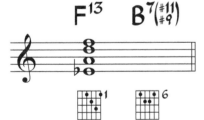

Ex. 5-47 uses the root position Dm triad for the same chords, again showing two forms.

Ex. 5-47

Ex. 5-48 uses the first inversion Dm triad for the same chords. This time it's only practical on the top strings, so only the one form is shown (the guitar can be really weird at times - please let me know if you ever figure it out!).

Ex. 5-48

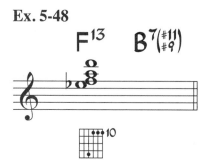

US VOICINGS USING DIMINISHED AND AUGMENTED TRIADS

Major and minor triads are the most used for upper structure voicings, but diminished and augmented triads are also useful. If I show them to you it will deprive you of the satisfaction of finding them yourself. You can use Ex. 5-12 and Ex. 5-13 to help you figure them out. Many may already be familiar to you, but it will give you a fresh perspective to see them as US voicings.

UPPER STRUCTURE TRIADS ON NON-DOMINANT CHORDS

Play Ex. 5-49. This is the top five notes of a six-note voicing that Mark Levine might call "the Herbie Hancock minor 11th" (the full six-note version isn't practical on guitar except on Em11). This Fm11 clearly has a second inversion Eb major triad on top, so it could be thought of as US bVII over Fm7. Like most voicings, this one has plural applications. In addition to Fm11, it can be used for Abmaj9 (US V), Bb13sus (US IV), and Dbmaj9#11 (US II).

Ex. 5-49

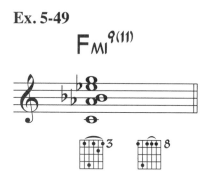

Ex. 5-50 uses the root position Eb to create the same harmonies as Ex. 5-49.

Ex. 5-50

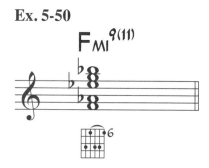

Ex. 5-51 uses the first inversion Eb triad.

Ex. 5-51

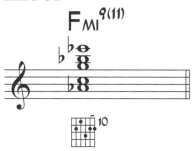

Play Ex. 5-52. This is the top four notes of a six-note voicing that Mark Levine might call "the Kenny Barron minor 11th" (the full six-note version is only playable as Em11 on guitar). This time the Fm11 has a first inversion open-voiced Eb major triad with the Ab inside the voicing rather than on the bottom under the triad. Again, it can be used for Abmaj9, Bb13sus, and Dbmaj9#11. Two forms are shown on different groups of strings.

Ex. 5-52

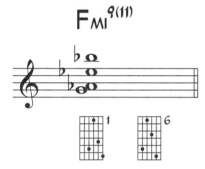

Ex. 5-53 uses the second inversion open-voiced Eb triad with the Ab added inside.

Ex. 5-53

Ex. 5-54 uses the root position open-voiced Eb triad with the inside Ab.

Ex. 5-54

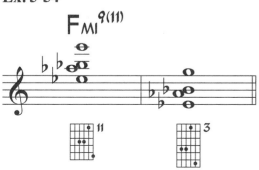

Ex. 5-55 is an example of what is called a "So What" voicing. It has the second inversion Eb major triad on top. Here I'm calling it an F9sus (US bVII), but it can be used as Cm11 (US bIII), Eb6/9, Abmaj13 (US V), and Dbmaj13#11 (US II).

Ex. 5-55

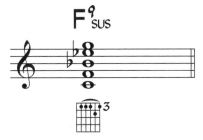

Ex. 5-56 uses the root position Eb triad for F9sus, but again can be the same chords as Ex. 5-55.

Ex. 5-56

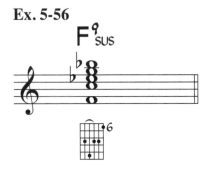

Ex. 5-57 uses the first inversion Eb triad.

Ex. 5-57

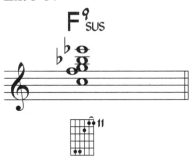

Ex. 5-58 is the top four notes of the "So What" voicing, which is also the slash chord Eb/F, shown on the top-four strings and on the middle-four strings. It's not only F9sus (US bVII), but also Ebadd9, Abmaj13 (US V), Db6/9#11 (US II), and Cm11 (US bIII).

Ex. 5-58

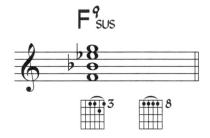

Ex. 5-59 uses an open-voiced first inversion Eb triad with the F added inside for all the same chords as in Ex. 5-58, shown on the top and middle string groups. This is literally an inversion of the previous voicing.

Ex. 5-59

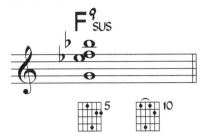

Ex. 5-60 uses the second inversion open Eb with the F added inside, again shown on the two string groups. This is the next inversion of the previous voicing.

Ex. 5-60

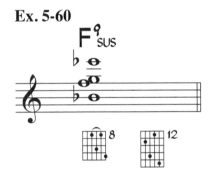

Ex. 5-61 uses a close-voiced root position Eb triad with the F added above, shown two different registers to make it easier to show on both the top and middle strings. Again, it's the last inversion of the previous voicing and works for all the chords named in Ex. 5-58.

Ex. 5-61

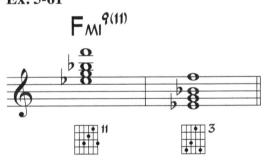

All the voicings in the last four examples are what we call "drop 2", and some of the other four-note voicings shown earlier are as well. For a complete explanation see my *Jazz Guitar Voicings Vol.1 - The Drop 2 Book*.

Ex. 5-62 is a Bbmaj9 voicing using a second inversion F major triad on the upper-middle strings.

Ex. 5-62

Ex. 5-63 is a Bb6/9#11 voicing using a second inversion C major triad on the upper-middle strings.

Ex. 5-63

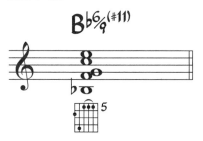

Changing one note transforms the previous chord into a beautiful Dm9/11 chord shown in Ex. 5-64.

Ex. 5-64

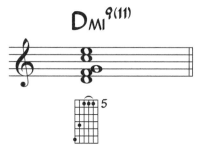

NON-DOMINANT MELODIC MINOR US VOICINGS

Since the melodic minor chordscale modes have no avoid notes, all the voicings are somewhat interchangable. Try the dom7#9b13 (US bVI) and dom13#11 (US II) voicings from Ex. 5-27 for all the melodic minor chords. For instance, the Ab13#11 voicing can be used for Gbmaj7#5, Ebm-maj7, Cm9b5, F13susb9, and D7alt. Your assignment is to work out these applications in all keys and forms.

A BILL EVANS TRICK

I will show one example, though. It's based on a neat trick I heard Bill Evans do on piano on his recording of Earl Zindars' "Elsa" from Explorations. Bill played it over a dominant chord (F7#11), but being from the C melodic minor scale it has vast potential applications. Play Ex. 5-65. It has two distinct parts. The bottom line is a wholetone melody while the top three voices are two second inversion major triads a whole-step apart from each other (G and F), alternating back and forth. All the notes are diatonic members of C melodic minor. The two alternating triads on top are a good example of what's called a triad pair, so let's check them out next.

Ex. 5-65

Chapter 6 - Triad Pairs

MAJOR TRIAD PAIRS

Play Ex. 6-1, the first three bars of Duke Pearson's "Jeannine."

Ex. 6-1

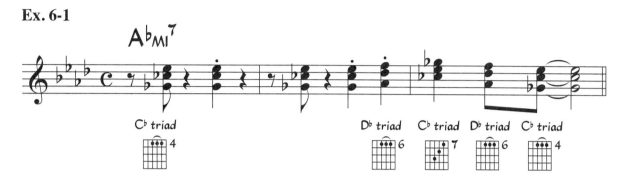

Now play Ex. 6-2, the seventh and eighth bars of Oliver Nelson's "Stolen Moments."

Ex. 6-2

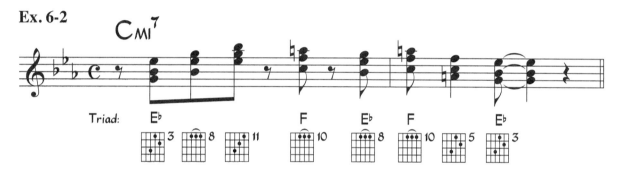

These are both examples of using triad pairs to harmonize the melodies on guitar.

DEFINITION OF TRIAD PAIR

A triad pair could be any two triads, but what we mean when we use the term is two triads that have no notes in common, resulting in a six-note (hexatonic) collection. A more accurate name would be "mutually-exclusive triad pair", but that's too long so we'll just use "triad pair" for short. Triad pairs that have both triads belonging to the same seven-note scale are always adjacent triads, that is, their roots are next to each other in the scale, such as I and II or IV and V. Major and minor triad pairs a tritone apart can be found in the eight-note diminished scale. Most of the popular triad pairs use two major triads or two minor triads, but mixed versions and versions using diminished and augmented triads also exist and are used. Let's look at major triad pairs first.

TYPES OF MAJOR TRIAD PAIRS

If we start with a C major triad and add a triad down a half-step (B major), we have a hexatonic collection. If we instead add a triad down a whole-step (Bb major) we still get a hexatonic collection. If we try down a minor 3rd instead (an A major triad) we have a common tone, the E note, so that won't be a triad pair according to our definition. Down a major 3rd, Ab, has a C common tone. Down a 4th, G, has a G common tone, so no cigar. Down a tritone, Gb, yields a hexatonic collection.

Everything past the tritone is just an inversion of the relationships we just did, so we've discovered that there are only three types of major triad pairs. They are: 1) a half-step apart, 2) a whole-step apart, and 3) a tritone apart.

The triad pair of B and C can be found in the E harmonic minor scale.

The Bb-C triad pair can be found in the F major scale and all the modes it generates, as well as in the F melodic minor scale and all the modes it generates, so the whole-step pair will be very useful. Notice that Ex. 6-1 and Ex. 6-2 both used major whole-step pairs to harmonize dorian mode melodies.

The Gb-C pair can be found in the half-whole diminished scale from Gb, A, C, and Eb, as well as the whole-half diminished scale from G, Bb, Db, and E.

PRACTICING THE BASIC MAJOR WHOLE-STEP PAIR

Ex. 6-3 is similar to the close-voiced triad inversion review, but connecting each inversion with an up-a-whole-step move in between. It starts with the lowest Bb triad on the guitar, then moves up to the lowest C triad before inverting and continuing on the same strings. It switches up to the lower-middle set on the next inversion, etc. until the whole range of the guitar is covered. It's only shown ascending, but when you get to the top, reverse direction and descend using the same forms. This could represent Bb lydian, C mixolydian, or G dorian, among others (including E7alt, surprisingly enough).

Ex. 6-3

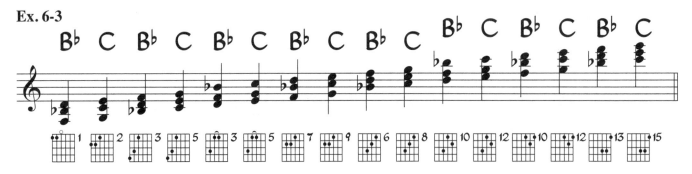

Ex. 6-4 uses open-voiced triads and changes the forms on the parallel whole-step moves for variety and extra fun.

Ex. 6-4

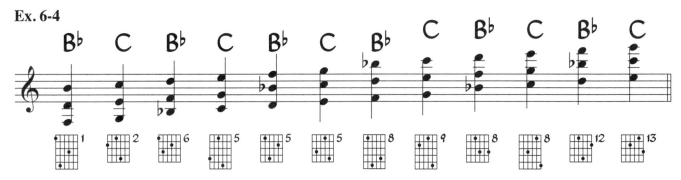

Of course, practice them in all keys, ascending and descending.

PRACTICING THE MAJOR TRITONE PAIR

Ex. 6-5 is the close-voiced tritone pair using Gb and C.

Ex. 6-5

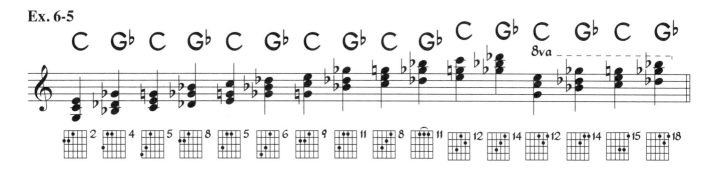

Ex. 6-6 is the open-voiced tritone pair.

Ex. 6-6

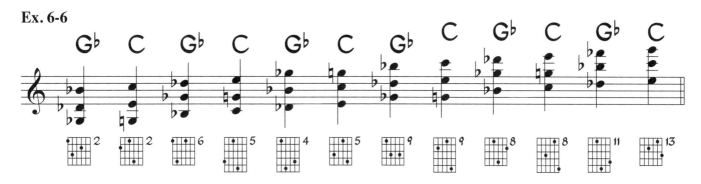

PRACTICING THE MAJOR HALF-STEP PAIR

Your homework assignment is to work out the half-step pair.

MINOR TRIAD PAIRS

TYPES OF MINOR TRIAD PAIRS

Since the minor triad is actually an upside-down major triad (same intervals in reverse order) the same relationships will occur at the same distances, so we'll have the same three types of pairs: 1) a half-step apart, 2) a whole-step apart, and 3) a tritone apart.

The half-step pair Bm-Cm can be found in the G harmonic major scale (a G major scale with Eb replacing E natural).

The whole-step pair Bbm-Cm can be found in the Ab major scale and its modes, as well as in Bb melodic minor and its modes.

The tritone pair F#m-Cm can be found in the same diminished scales as the major tritone pair shown above.

PRACTICING THE BASIC MINOR WHOLE-STEP PAIR

Ex. 6-7 is the close-voiced minor whole-step pair, full range, using Bbm and Cm. This works great for Bb dorian, Eb mixolydian, and G locrian#2 (for Gm7b5) among many others. Practice descending as well as ascending.

Ex. 6-7

Now more homework for you. Work out the open-voiced version.

PRACTICING THE MINOR TRITONE PAIR

Ex. 6-8 is the close-voiced minor tritone pair using F#m and Cm.

Ex. 6-8

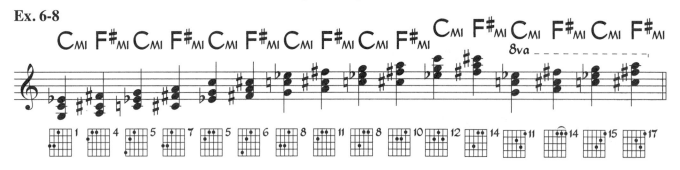

Ex. 6-9 is the open-voiced minor tritone pair.

Ex. 6-9

PRACTICING THE MINOR HALF-STEP PAIR

Ex. 6-10 is one possible set of forms for the open-voiced (I'm sure it will be easy for you to do the close-voiced version) minor half-step pair using Bm-Cm. (See next page.)

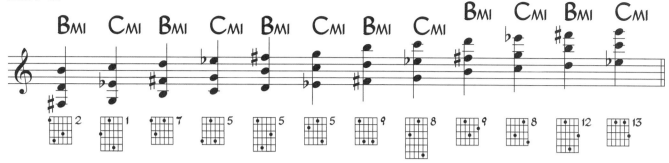

Practice all the pairs ascending and descending, eventually in all keys.

COMBINING MAJOR AND MINOR WHOLE-STEP PAIRS TO HARMONIZE MAJOR MODES

Play Ex. 6-11, the major whole-step pair using F and G on the upper-middle strings. This can represent the modes of the C major scale (C Ionian, D dorian, E phrygian, F Lydian, G Mixolydian, A aeolian, and B locrian), but the E note is missing.

Ex. 6-11

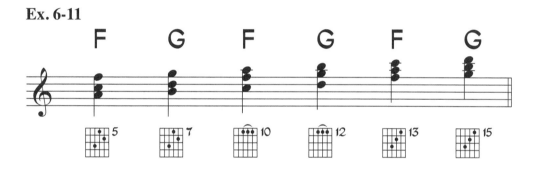

Play Ex. 6-12, the minor whole-step pair using Dm and Em on the upper-middle strings. This can also represent the same modes of the C major scale we looked at above. This time it's the C note that's missing, but the E is present so various combinations of the two triad pairs should be able to harmonize the entire scale containing all the modes mentioned.

Ex. 6-12

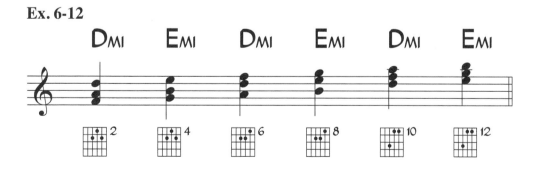

THE COMBINATIONS

Ex. 6-13 is one possible combination. It starts with the first two chords from the minor version, harmonizing the D and E melody notes, so the the E is already done. The rest of the scale uses the major pair. (See next page.)

Ex. 6-13

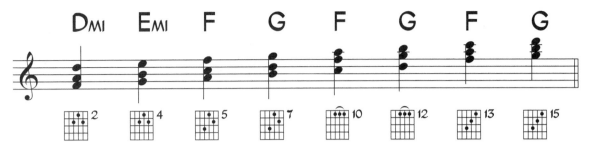

Ex. 6-14 is another combination, alternating between two chords from the minor pair, then two from the major pair, two from the minor pair again, and finishing with two from the major pair.

Ex. 6-14

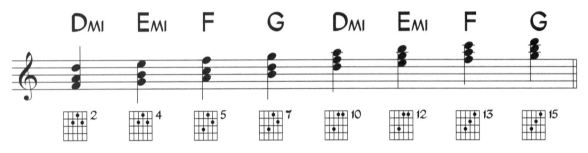

Ex. 6-15 starts with the first four chords from the minor pair and finishes with the last four chords from the major pair.

Ex. 6-15

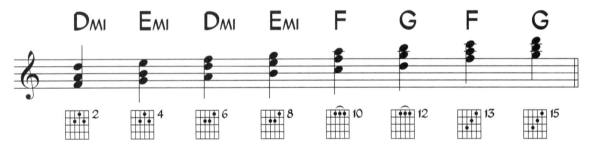

Ex. 6-16 uses the entire minor pair and ends with the last two chords from the major pair.

Ex. 6-16

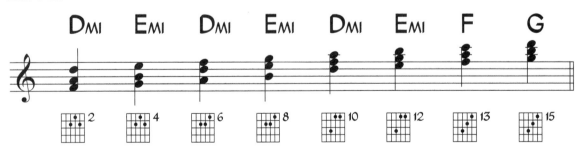

These combinations spell out the D dorian mode, but can be used for the other modes of C major as well.

"STOLEN MOMENTS" REVISITED

All the combinations sound good so what combinations you use will be a matter of personal preference. Play Ex. 6-17. It's the seventh and eighth bars of "Stolen Moments" again, but this time uses a combination of major whole-step triad pair (Eb and F) and relative minor whole-step triad pair (Cm and Dm).

Ex. 6-17

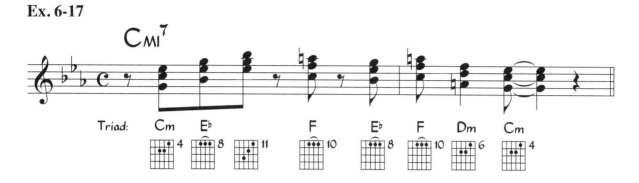

COMBINING MINOR AND DIMINISHED WHOLE-STEP PAIRS TO HARMONIZE MELODIC MINOR MODES

Play Ex. 6-18, the minor whole-step pair using Fm and Gm on the upper-middle strings. This can represent F melodic minor and all of its modes, but the E note is missing.

Ex. 6-18

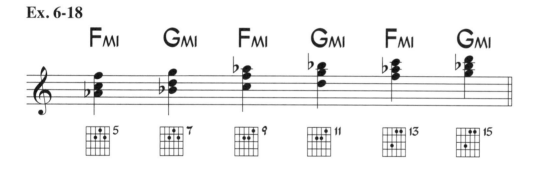

Play Ex. 6-19, the diminished whole-step triad pair using Ddim and Edim on the upper-middle strings. The E is present but now the C is missing, so again we'll use combinations to harmonize the entire scale.

Ex. 6-19

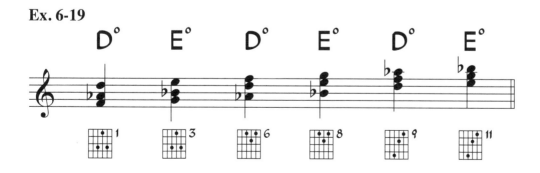

THE MELODIC MINOR COMBINATIONS

Ex.6-20 starts with the first two chords from the diminished pair followed by the entire minor pair.

Ex. 6-20

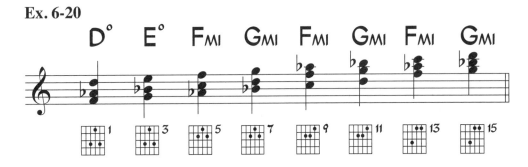

Ex. 6-21 alternates two chords from the diminished pair with two chords fom the minor pair, etc.

Ex. 6-21

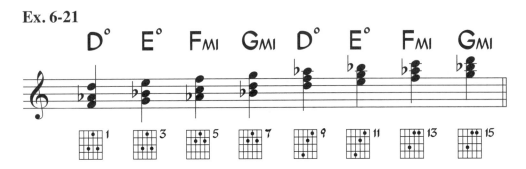

Ex. 6-22 starts with the first four chords from the diminished pair and ends with the last four chords from the minor pair.

Ex. 6-22

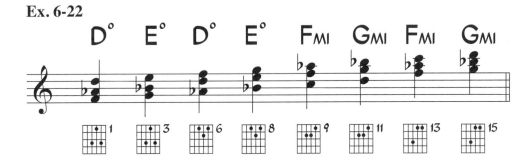

Ex. 6-23 starts with the entire diminished pair and ends with the last two chords from the minor pair.

Ex. 6-23

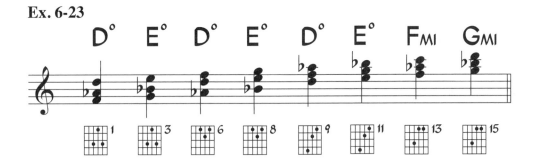

These combinations spell out the D locrian#2 mode (the sixth mode of melodic minor), but can be used for the other modes of F melodic minor as well. They sound great for Abmaj7#5, Fm-maj7, Dm9b5, Bb13#11, G13susb9, and E7alt.

MORE TRICKS WITH TRIAD PAIRS

TWO FAVORITE HEXATONIC SCALES

By definition mutually-exclusive triad pairs form hexatonic (six-note) scales. Therefore hexatonic scales can also be divided into triad pairs. Two of my personal favorite hexatonic scales are what I might call the maj13-relative m11 hexatonic and the melodic minor hexatonic.

The Cmaj13-Am11 hexatonic is basically a C major scale with the 4th, the note F, omitted (see Ex. 6-24). As you probably already know, the 4th is the "avoid" note on a C major chord, so omitting it eliminates the problems it can create. F is also an avoid note on the A minor chord, so ditto. To find the triad pair start on the first note above the omitted note and build the triads in 3rds from adjacent roots. G is the first note above F so we'll find a G major triad and an A minor triad. This scale and triad pair can be used for Cmaj7, Am7, Fmaj7#11, and D13sus for starters.

Ex. 6-24

C Major Hexatonic Scale

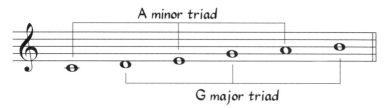

The C melodic minor hexatonic is basically a C melodic minor scale with the 4th, again the note F, omitted (see Ex. 6-25). As you probably already know, there really is no avoid note in the melodic minor scale, so for now let's just use this hexatonic scale as an excuse to find another cool triad pair. The pair is a G major triad and an A diminished triad. This scale and triad pair can be used for Ebmaj7#5, Cm-maj7, Am7b5, F13#11, D13susb9, and B7alt.

Ex. 6-25

C Melodic Minor Hexatonic Scale

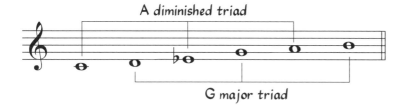

THE CLOSE-VOICED MAJOR HEXATONIC TRIAD PAIR

Ex. 6-26 shows the C major hexatonic scale harmonized with a close-voiced triad pair on the top three strings.

Ex. 6-26

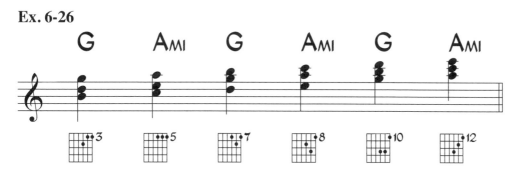

Ex. 6-27 shows the C major hexatonic scale harmonized with a close-voiced triad pair on the upper-middle three strings.

Ex. 6-27

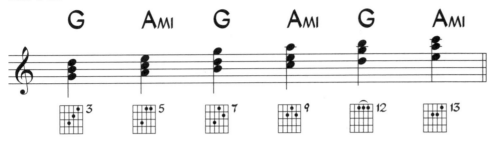

THE CLOSE-VOICED MELODIC MINOR HEXATONIC TRIAD PAIR

Ex. 6-28 shows the C melodic minor hexatonic scale harmonized with a close-voiced triad pair on the top three strings.

Ex. 6-28

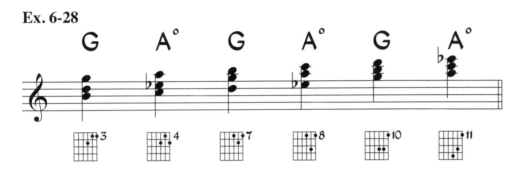

Ex. 6-29 shows the C melodic minor hexatonic scale harmonized with a close-voiced triad pair on the upper-middle three strings.

Ex. 6-29

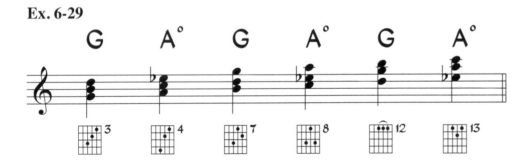

REPLACING THE MIDDLE NOTES WITH OPPOSITE-TRIAD NOTES

Now we're ready to try a new trick. Let's replace the middle note of each triad with a note from the opposite triad, making each chord a hybrid of C major and A minor triads. There are two different notes from each opposite triad that are practical to use, so we'll end up with two complete sets of voicings.

Ex. 6-30 shows one set of middle-note replacements for the C major hexatonic scale on the top three strings, while Ex. 6-31 (see next page) shows the other.

Ex. 6-30

Ex. 6-31

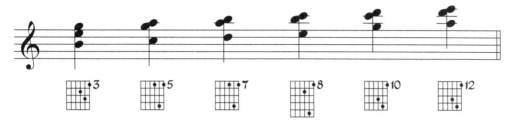

Ex. 6-32 shows one set of middle-note replacements for the C major hexatonic scale on the upper-middle three strings, while Ex. 6-33 shows the other.

Ex. 6-32

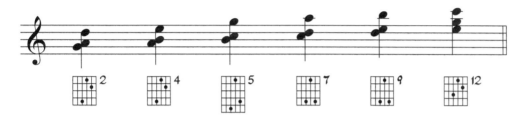

Ex. 6-33

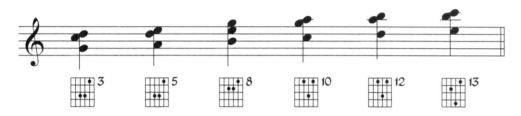

Ex. 6-34 shows one set of middle-note replacements for the C melodic minor hexatonic scale on the top three strings, while Ex. 6-35 shows the other.

Ex. 6-34

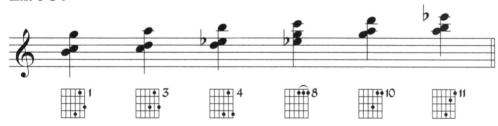

Ex. 6-35

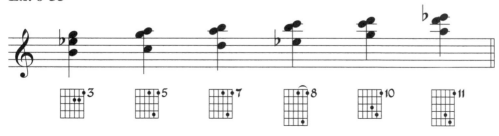

Ex. 6-36 shows one set of middle-note replacements for the C melodic minor hexatonic scale on the upper-middle three strings, while Ex. 6-37 shows the other. These voicings can be useful on the lower-middle set of three strings as well, so more homework for you.

Ex. 6-36

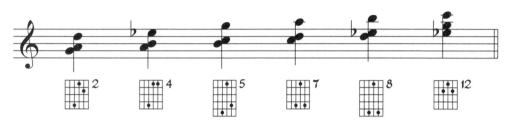

Ex. 6-37

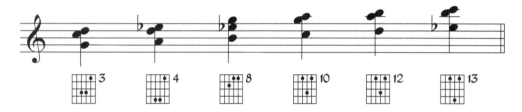

REPLACING THE BOTTOM NOTES WITH OPPOSITE-TRIAD NOTES

The next trick is a variation of the last trick. This time we'll keep the top two notes of each triad while replacing the bottom note with a note from the opposite triad. Again there are two practical note choices so we'll get two complete sets of voicings.

Ex. 6-38 shows one set of bottom-note replacements for the C major hexatonic scale on the top three strings, while Ex. 6-39 shows the other.

Ex. 6-38

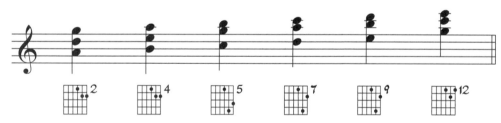

Ex. 6-39

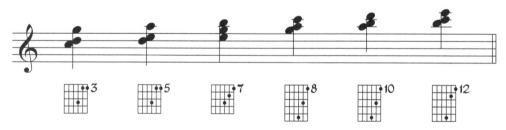

Ex. 6-40 shows one set of bottom-note replacements for the C major hexatonic scale on the upper-middle three strings, while Ex. 6-41 shows the other. (See next page.)

Ex. 6-40

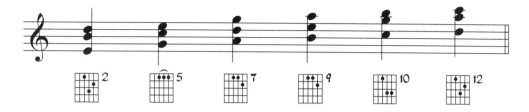

Ex. 6-41

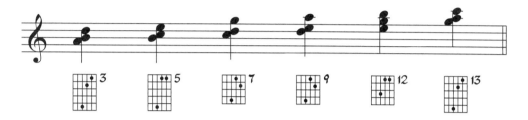

Ex. 6-42 shows one set of bottom-note replacements for the C melodic minor hexatonic scale on the top three strings, while Ex. 6-43 shows the other.

Ex. 6-42

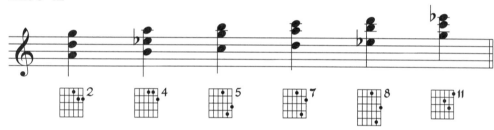

Ex. 6-43

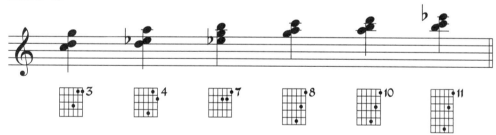

Ex. 6-44 shows one set of bottom-note replacements for the C melodic minor hexatonic scale on the upper-middle three strings, while Ex. 6-45 (see next page) shows the other.

Ex. 6-44

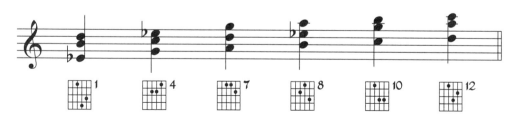

Ex. 6-45

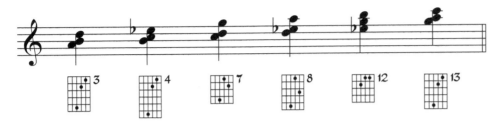

REPLACING THE TOP NOTES WITH OPPOSITE-TRIAD NOTES

Now we'll keep the bottom two notes of each triad while replacing the top note with a note from the opposite triad. Once again there will be two complete sets of voicings.

Ex. 6-46 shows one set of top-note replacements for the C major hexatonic scale on the top three strings, while Ex. 6-47 shows the other.

Ex. 6-46

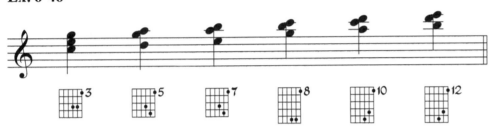

Ex. 6-47

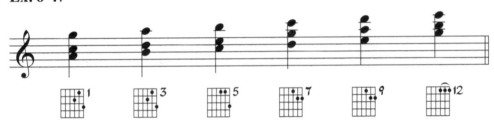

Ex. 6-48 shows one set of top-note replacements for the C major hexatonic scale on the upper-middle three strings, while Ex. 6-49 shows the other.

Ex. 6-48

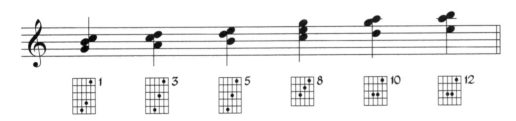

Ex. 6-49

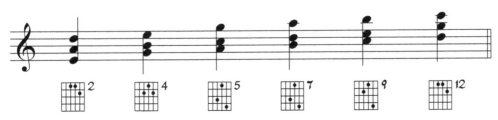

Ex. 6-50 shows one set of top-note replacements for the C melodic minor hexatonic scale on the top three strings, while Ex. 6-51 shows the other.

Ex. 6-50

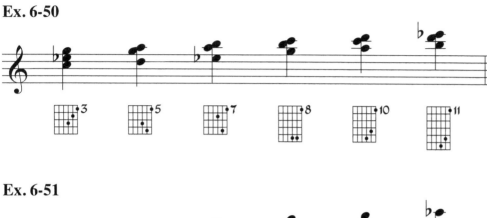

Ex. 6-51

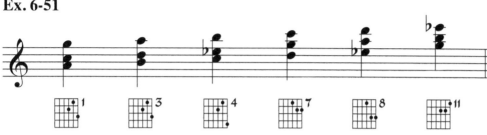

Ex. 6-52 shows one set of top-note replacements for the C melodic minor hexatonic scale on the upper-middle three strings, while Ex. 6-53 shows the other.

Ex. 6-52

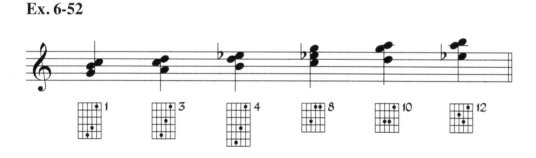

Ex. 6-53

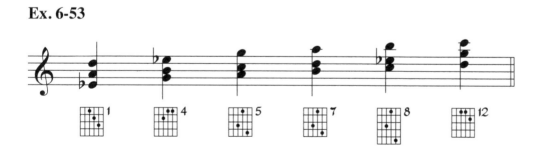

Most of the voicings we've looked at for these favorite hexatonic scales can be used on the lower middle set of three strings, so, you guessed it, more homework for you.

THE OPEN-VOICED MAJOR HEXATONIC TRIAD PAIR

Ex. 6-54 shows the C major hexatonic scale harmonized with the open-voiced triad pair on the first, third, and fourth strings.

Ex. 6-54

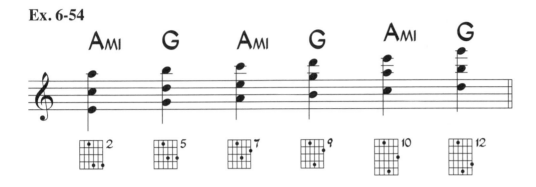

Ex. 6-55 shows the C major hexatonic scale harmonized with the open-voiced triad pair on the first, second, and fourth strings.

Ex. 6-55

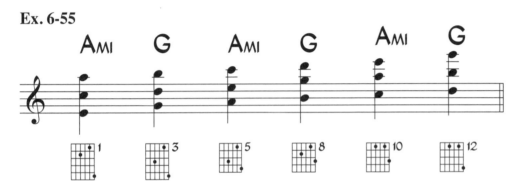

THE OPEN-VOICED MELODIC MINOR HEXATONIC TRIAD PAIR

Ex. 6-56 shows the C melodic minor hexatonic scale harmonized with the open-voiced triad pair on the first, third, and fourth strings.

Ex. 6-56

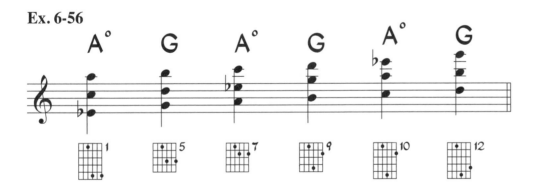

Ex. 6-57 shows the C melodic minor hexatonic scale harmonized with the open-voiced triad pair on the first, second, and fourth strings.

Ex. 6-57

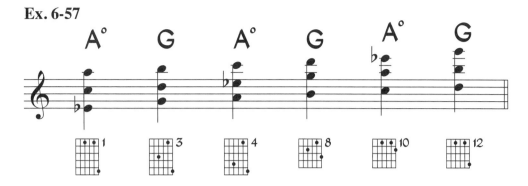

ADDING OPPOSITE-TRIAD NOTES TO THE OPEN VOICINGS

Ex. 6-58 shows a set of four-note voicings derived from the C major hexatonic scale open-voiced triad pair on the first, third, and fourth strings by adding opposite-triad notes on the second string.

Ex. 6-58

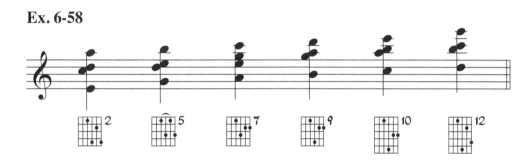

Ex. 6-59 shows a set of four-note voicings derived from the C major hexatonic scale open-voiced triad pair on the first, second, and fourth strings by adding opposite-triad notes on the third string.

Ex. 6-59

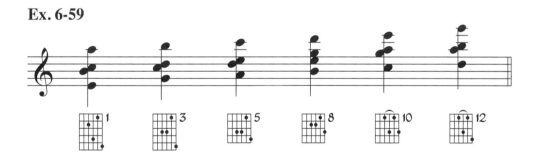

Ex. 6-60 shows a set of four-note voicings derived from the C melodic minor hexatonic scale open-voiced triad pair on the first, third, and fourth strings by adding opposite-triad notes on the second string.

Ex. 6-60

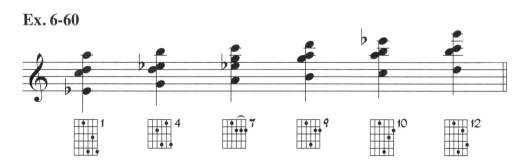

Ex. 6-61 shows a set of four-note voicings derived from the C melodic minor hexatonic scale open-voiced triad pair on the first, second, and fourth strings by adding opposite-triad notes on the third string.

Ex. 6-61

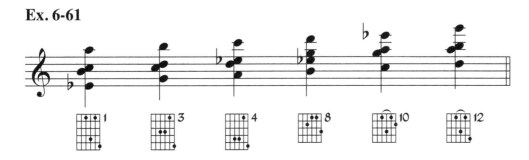

All the four-note chords in the last four examples are actually drop 2 voicings (see my *Jazz Guitar Voicings, Vol. 1 - The Drop 2 Book*).

ONE LAST BIG TRICK WITH TRIAD PAIRS

Play Ex. 6-62. This is an example of an improvised chord-melody over Dm7b5 going to G7alt going to Cmaj7 (a minor-key II-V going to a major-key I chord).

Ex. 6-62

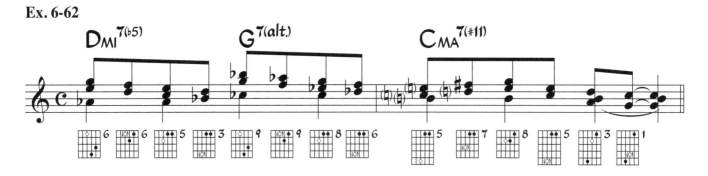

On the Dm7b5 the descending 3rds are two-note reductions from the whole-step major triad pair C and Bb representing D locrian#2 from F melodic minor. The note Ab is missing from the triad pair, so that note is added as a pedal tone.

Similarly, the descending 3rds on the G7alt are two-note reductions from the whole-step triad pair Eb and Db representing the G altered scale from Ab melodic minor. The note Cb is missing from the triad pair, so this time Cb is the added pedal tone.

The Cmaj7 uses two-note reductions from the whole-step pair C and D representing C lydian. The note B is missing from the triad pair so it becomes the pedal tone. Notice that on the last note the reduction is the root, D, and 5th, A, of the D triad, surrounding the pedal B, which had to be moved from the fourth string to the third string to make it playable.

MAJOR SCALE REDUCTIONS WITH "MISSING NOTE" PEDAL

Ex. 6-63 (on next page) shows two-note reductions from the triad pair G and F with the pair's "missing-note," E, used as a pedal tone throughout. The example is shown descending, but should be practiced both ascending and descending. Notice that as the reductions surround the pedal, the pedal is moved up a string, and as the reductions drop under the pedal it is, again, moved up a string. These harmonies are diatonic from the key of C major, but don't work well on a C major chord because of the F "avoid" note. They work great for Fmaj7 (lydian with the #11), Dm7 (dorian with the 13), G13sus (mixolydian), and Esusb9 (phrygian).

Ex. 6-63

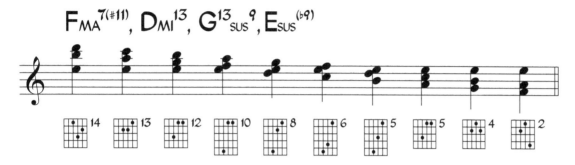

MELODIC MINOR SCALE REDUCTIONS WITH "MISSING NOTE" PEDAL

Ex. 6-64 shows two-note reductions from the triad pair G and F with the pair's "missing-note," Eb, used as a pedal tone throughout. Practice descending, as shown, and ascending. These harmonies work great for Ebmaj7#5, Cm-maj7, Am7b5, F7#11, D13susb9, and B7alt.

Ex. 6-64

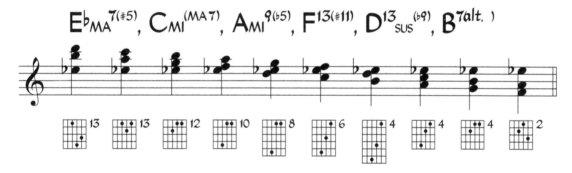

OPEN-VOICED REDUCTIONS WITH "MISSING NOTE" PEDALS

In Ex. 6-65, the two-note triad reductions from the whole-step pair have been opened from 3rds and 4ths to 6ths and 5ths, using the missing major scale note E as the added pedal. Try holding down the third finger on the E note (fourth string) for the first four voicings. These work for the same chords as found in Ex. 6-63.

Ex. 6-65

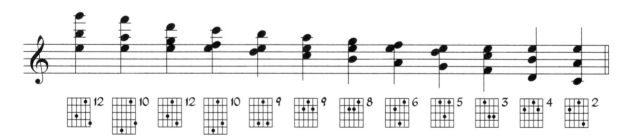

Ex. 6-66 uses the same open-voiced reductions with the missing melodic minor scale note Eb added as the pedal. Try holding down the second finger on the Eb note (fourth string) for the first four voicings. These work for the same chords as found in Ex. 6-64.

Ex. 6-66

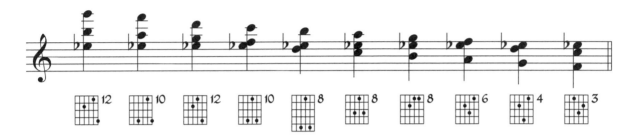

Keep in mind you might never (or rarely) use an example in its entirety in actual playing. The triad pairs and their tricks supply us with a vast arsenal of voicings to use for a variety of purposes, including melody harmonization, background patterns for comping, improvised chord solos, etc. Frequently four or even just two of the consecutive voicings in a row can be surprisingly effective at creating the perception of full, complex harmony enhanced by the dynamic motion in the voices.

Chapter 7 - Dominant Cycles Revisited plus Diminished and Wholetone Scales

A FRESH LOOK AT DOMINANT CYCLES

Play Ex. 7-1, the first four bars of the A section of George Gershwin's "Nice Work If You Can Get It."

Ex. 7-1

The melody starts in quarter notes against a half-note harmonic rhythm of dominant7 chords moving counter-clockwise around the circle of fifths. Make sure you select fingerings that enable the chord tones to sustain while the melody notes move. For example, the tritone on the middle two strings in the first chord can be played with the first and third fingers, leaving the second and fourth fingers free to play the melody, while the second chord can have the tritone fingered with the first two fingers, leaving the third and fourth fingers free to play the melody. The A13 should be grabbed with fingers two, three, and four to make the chromatic counter-melody playable.

Now let's look at some exercises based on this idea that will develop a more sophisticated finger control as well as developing ideas for intros, interludes, fills, cadenzas and endings.

INTRODUCTION TO THE BASIC EXERCISES

For the basic exercises we'll take the 3rd-7th tritone and add a simple two-note melody above, either the root and 9th or the 5th and 13th. The two-note melodies may ascend or descend in any order, so each exercise will have permutations.

Since the voicings have no bass notes, they work over tritone substitute roots as well. This would convert the root-9th voicings into b5-#5 voicings, and would convert the 5th-13th voicings into b9-#9 voicings. This remains true throughout this chapter.

When the dominant chord goes around the cycle the tritone descends chromatically. When the first chord has a root-9th melody the second chord will have a 5th-13th melody, which will be the same two notes. Then it will happen again on the next two chords in the cycle, but a whole-step lower, etc.

The examples will show the first four chords of each cycle, but you should continue each one down the fingerboard as far as possible. The first four examples will show four permutations on the first exercise: 1) two-note melodies all going up, 2) melodies all going down, 3) going up-down-up-down and 4) going down-up-down-up. They can go in any random mixed order but these four permutations "contain" all the others so they are the essential ones to practice.

THE FIRST EXERCISE

Ex. 7-2 shows the first permutation on the lower-middle set of three strings. To make it work we must select the best fingering. The tritone in the first chord (G9) should be played with the second and fourth fingers, leaving the third finger free to play the 9th (the A note) while the tritone sustains. When the chord changes to C13 we must exchange fingers so the tritone is now the second and third fingers.

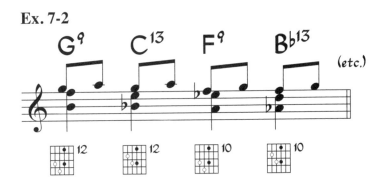

Ex. 7-3 shows the second permutation on the lower-middle set of three strings. The initial form must be grabbed using fingers two and four on the tritone and the third finger on the A (the 9th). The first finger is ready to play the root, G. Now the third finger is lifted while continuing to hold down the second and fourth fingers, making this a great finger-control study. Then the fingers exchange for the C13, with the fourth finger playing the A (the 13th) and the middle two fingers doing the tritone.

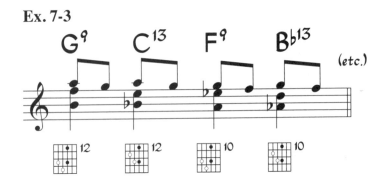

Ex. 7-4 shows the third permutation (up-down-up-down, etc.) on the lower-middle set of three strings. It combines the fingering solutions from the last two examples.

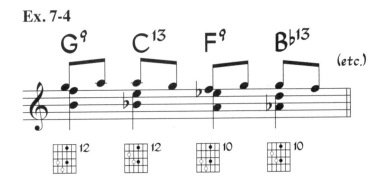

Ex. 7-5 shows the fourth permutation (down-up-down-up, etc.) on the lower-middle set of three strings. Continue to use the good fingerings.

Ex. 7-5

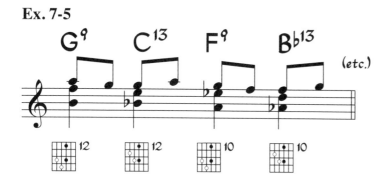

The next four examples will show the four permutations of the second exercise.

THE SECOND EXERCISE

Ex. 7-6 shows the first permutation on the upper-middle set of three strings. These strings, as you know, have a different tuning so we'll use a different fingering. The first tritone will be played by the middle two fingers, with the melody played by the first and fourth fingers. When the chord changes we finger the tritone with the first and third fingers while playing the melody with the second and fourth. Notice the 8va. The examples in the second exercise are written down an octave to avoid excessive ledger lines.

Ex. 7-6

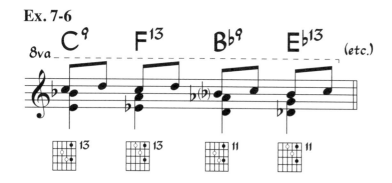

Ex. 7-7 shows the second permutation on the upper-middle set of three strings. The melodic directions are reversed but we use the same fingers for the same notes as we did in the last example.

Ex. 7-7

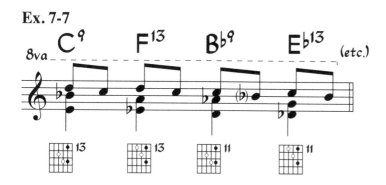

Ex. 7-8 shows the third permutation on the upper-middle set of three strings.

Ex. 7-8

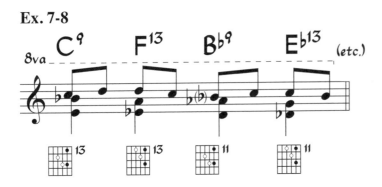

Ex. 7-9 shows the fourth permutation on the upper-middle set of three strings.

Ex. 7-9

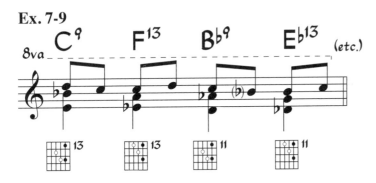

I'm not going to show all the permutations on the following exercises because by now you know how it's done. Even though they're not shown you should still practice each exercise in all four permutations (where they apply) and all the way down the guitar.

THE THIRD EXERCISE

Ex. 7-10 shows the first permutation of the third exercise, which is similar to the first two but with the tritones inverted to open the space between the tritones and the melody notes. This results in forms that skip a string between the tritone and the melody. The third exercise uses the forms on the second, fourth and fifth strings. The first tritone uses fingers one and three with the melody using fingers two and four. The second tritone uses fingers one and two with the melody using fingers three and four. Remember to do the other three permutations.

Ex. 7-10

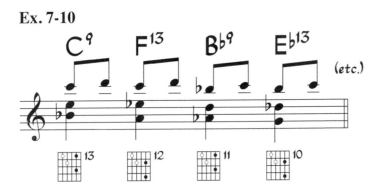

THE FOURTH EXERCISE

Ex. 7-11 shows the first permutation of the fourth exercise, which is the same as the third exercise except this time the forms are located on the first, third and fourth strings. Since both the third and fourth exercises skip the second-to-third string major 3rd tuning, their forms and fingerings are identical. Don't forget the other three permutations.

Ex. 7-11

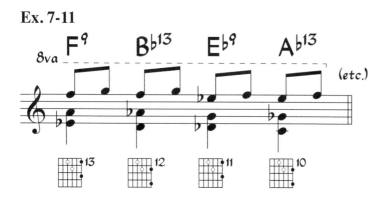

THE FIFTH EXERCISE

The fifth exercise combines the 9th chord forms from the first exercise with the 9th chord forms from the third exercise. Ex. 7-12 shows the first permutation, but do all four.

Ex. 7-12

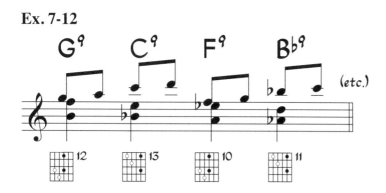

THE SIXTH EXERCISE

The sixth exercise combines the 9th chord forms from the second exercise with the 9th chord forms from the fourth exercise. Ex. 7-13 shows the first permutation, but do all four.

Ex. 7-13

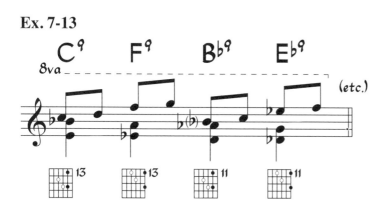

THE SEVENTH EXERCISE

The seventh exercise combines the 13th chord forms from the first exercise with the 13th chord forms from the third exercise. Ex. 7-14 shows the first permutation, but do all four.

Ex. 7-14

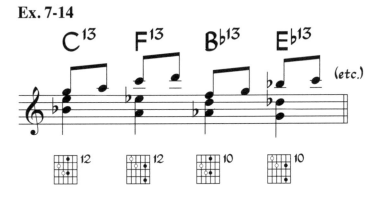

THE EIGHTH EXERCISE

The eighth exercise combines the 13th chord forms from the second exercise with the 13th chord forms from the fourth exercise. Ex. 7-15 shows the first permutation, but do all four.

Ex. 7-15

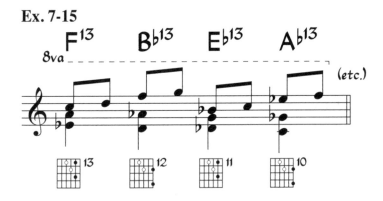

The following exercises do not have permutations.

THE NINTH EXERCISE

The ninth exercise uses a new melody. After starting on the root it ascends chromatically to the 13th of the second chord before skipping up a 3rd. Ex. 7-16 shows the first four chords of the ninth exercise, beginning on the lower-middle string group. This new melody calls for a change in fingering. All the examples starting on the G9 up to this point have fingered the tritone with fingers two and four, but here it's fingered with three and four, and the C13 starts with fingers one, three and four so the second finger is free to play the last melody note (the C).

Ex. 7-16

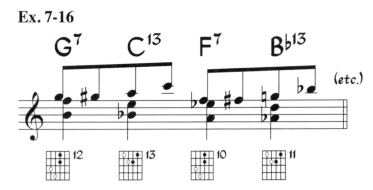

THE TENTH EXERCISE

The tenth exercise uses the same melody as the ninth, but starts on the upper-middle string group. Ex. 7-17 shows the first four chords. Again the new melody requires a change of fingering. It's kind-of the reverse of the last example, with the first tritone fingered with two and four rather than the previously used two and three. This leaves the third finger free to play the chromatic passing note (the C#).

Ex. 7-17

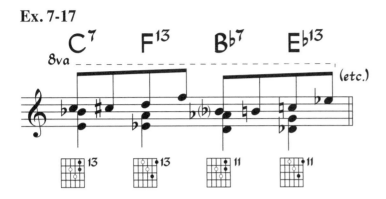

THE ELEVENTH EXERCISE

Ex. 7-18 shows the first four chords of the eleventh exercise. This is another new melody, a slight variation of the last one, going back down a step at the end instead of the up-a-3rd skip. This set of voicings is located on the spread string group of two, four, and five. The fingerings should be no problem if you've done all the previous examples.

Ex. 7-18

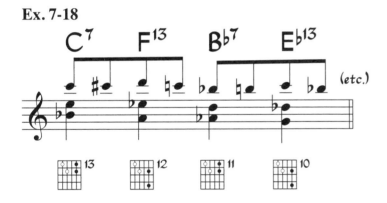

THE TWELFTH EXERCISE

Ex. 7-19 shows the first four chords of the twelfth exercise. It uses the same melody, forms, and fingerings as the eleventh but is located on the sting group of one, three, and four.

Ex. 7-19

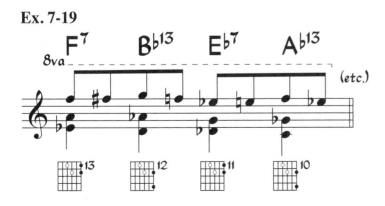

THE THIRTEENTH EXERCISE

Now we encounter another new melody. It starts on the 9th of the first chord and descends chromatically to the #11 of the second chord. Ex. 7-20 shows the first four chords, located on the lower-middle string group. The G9 starts with its original fingering while the C7 should be played with fingers two, three, and four so the first finger can play the #11 (the F#).

Ex. 7-20

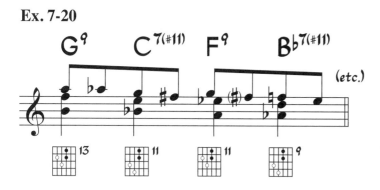

THE FOURTEENTH EXERCISE

Ex. 7-21 is the first four chords of the fourteenth exercise. It has the same melody as the thirteenth, but is found on the upper-middle string group. The first tritone is played by fingers one and three, with the first two melody notes played by four and two. The second tritone must be played with fingers two and four, with the next two melody notes played by three and one.

Ex. 7-21

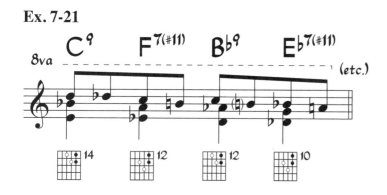

THE FIFTEENTH EXERCISE

Play Ex. 7-22 using exactly the same forms and fingerings as Ex. 7-21, except moved over to the lower- middle string group. Because of the tuning difference we now have a melody starting on the 13th of the first chord and descending chromatically to the chromatic lower neighbor of the 13th of the third chord, where the pattern begins again.

Ex. 7-22

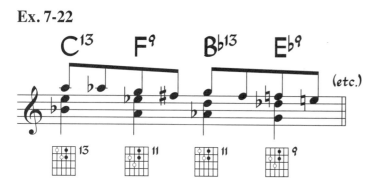

131

THE SIXTEENTH EXERCISE

Ex. 7-23 shows the first four chords of the fifteenth exercise, which uses the same melody as the fourteenth, but moved up to the upper- middle string group. I'm showing the forms but I'll have you work out your own fingering.

Ex. 7-23

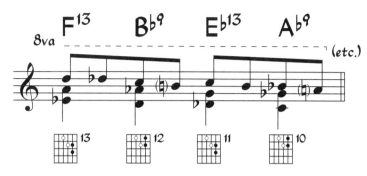

THE SEVENTEENTH EXERCISE

This study (Ex. 7-24) introduces something new, a melody in quarter-note triplets moving independently over the chords in straight quarter-notes. To achieve this the fingers have to really know what they're doing. Start with the first finger playing the first melody note while the third and fourth fingers play the tritone. The tritone sustains while the second finger plays the second melody note. Now the melody sustains while the first and third fingers grab the second tritone. Finally the fourth finger easily plays the third melody note. All this takes place on the lower-middle strings.

Ex. 7-24

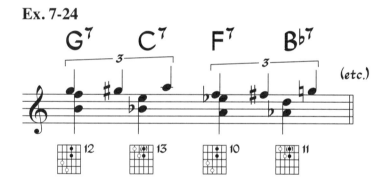

THE EIGHTEENTH EXERCISE

Ex. 7-25 moves the quarter-note triplet study up to the upper-middle strings, requiring a new set of fingerings. Begin with the first finger playing the first melody note and fingers two and four playing the first tritone. The tritone sustains as the third finger plays the second melody note. Sustain the melody note while grabbing the second tritone with fingers one and two. Then play the third melody note with the fourth finger.

Ex. 7-25

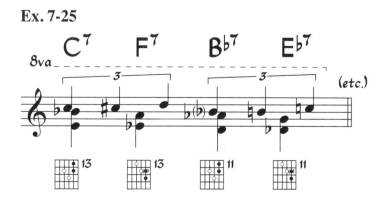

These first eighteen exercises show us that applying the dynamic concept of harmony to the guitar requires great flexibility in choices for fingerings, even within the same forms. In the dynamic concept the melodies are changing and the fingerings are changing according to where the melodies are going; so we keep the notes moving, we have to keep the fingers moving, and we have to keep the mind moving.

THE NINETEENTH EXERCISE

Now let's go back to half-note durations for the dominant chords, with eighth-note melodies, so we'll have the tritones sustaining for two beats each with a very common eighth-note melody above, using the 13th and #11th surrounding the 5th. Ex. 7-26 shows the first four chords with the tritones voice-leading on the fourth and fifth strings while the melody is on the third string for the first chord but jumps to the second string for the second chord. On the first chord the first melody note is played by finger four, with the next three notes played by the first finger and the tritone played by the middle two. The second chord begins with its standard fingering with the first finger playing the lowest note on its tip while damping the unused strings. For the third melody note press the side of the first finger down, forming a barre, to keep the half-notes sustaining as the melody moves.

Ex. 7-26

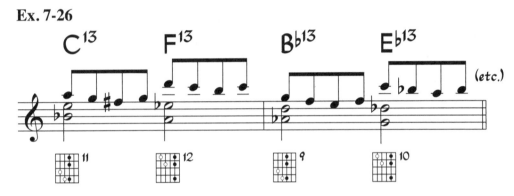

THE TWENTIETH EXERCISE

Ex. 7-27 is the same as Ex. 7-26, but with the tritones voice-leading on the middle-two strings and the melodies bouncing back and forth between the top-two strings. Even though some of the shapes look different, this time the fingerings are the same.

Ex. 7-27

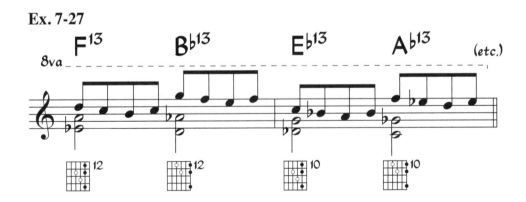

A FRESH LOOK AT DIMINISHED SCALES

A curious thing happens if I take the four-eighth-note melody over a half-note tritone we've just done and move it up by minor 3rds. All the notes in the tritones and in the eighth-note melody are members of one diminished scale, and spell out the entire scale as well. Ex. 7-28 shows this starting on E13 to give us room to go up in minor 3rds. All the forms and fingerings can be found in the nineteenth and twentieth exercises above. (See next page.)

Ex. 7-28

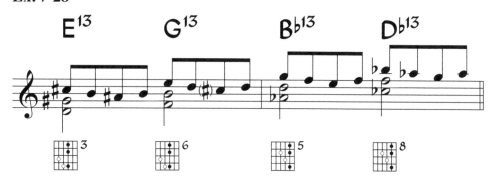

Ex. 7-29 skips a string between the tritone and the melody and starts on G13. Again, all the forms and fingerings can be found in the nineteenth and twentieth exercises above.

Ex. 7-29

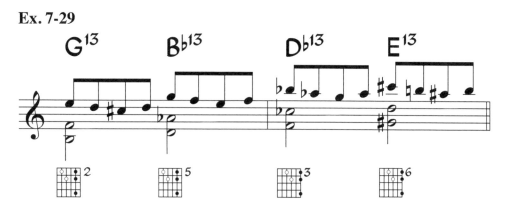

I'm sure you probably already know about the application of diminished scales not only to diminished chords, but to dominant chords as well. Looking at the last example, the chord names follow the forms as they move up by minor 3rds, but, being a diminished scale, it can all happen over one chord. Let's call the entire example G7 and see what's happening. The first chord is still G13#11. The second chord is G13b9. The third chord is G7#9b9. The fourth chord is G7#9b9#11. Of course the entire example could also be Bb7, Db7, E7, Bdim7, Ddim7, Fdim7, or Abdim7! You can see how important these diminished scale harmonies are, so let's see what else we can find.

Ex. 7-30 uses the dom13 forms first introduced in Ex. 7-2 and in Ex. 7-6 to play a melody going straight up the diminished scale. Since it's two notes per voicing, all the permutations (up-up, down-down, up-down, and down-up) can and should be applied. The chord names refer to the original forms, but the entire study can be used for all the chords mentioned in the previous paragraph. The forms are only shown ascending in minor 3rds, but should also be practiced descending as well.

Ex. 7-30

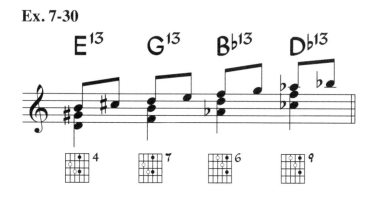

Ex. 7-31 uses the dom13 forms first introduced in Ex. 7-10 and in Ex. 7-11 to play up the diminished scale. Also do the melodic permutations and the descending version.

Ex. 7-31

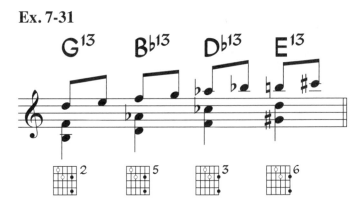

Ex. 7-32 is an extended version of Ex. 7-30 introducing some new forms on the top-three strings. Use a partial barre with the first finger on the new forms. Also play it descending and do all the melodic permutations.

Ex. 7-32

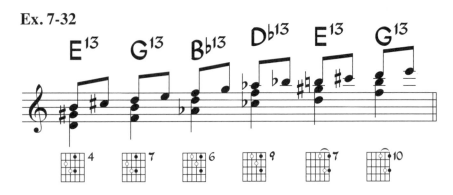

Ex. 7-33 starts with the same voicing as Ex. 7-32, but this time the middle voice teams-up with the top voice, harmonizing it in parallel minor 3rds, with the bottom voice simply outlining a dim7 arpeggio in quarter notes. Start with the first three fingers, then hold down the second while playing the second melody and harmony notes with the third and fourth fingers. On the upper-middle strings and on the top strings use a partial barre with the first finger. Practice it both ascending and descending, and try all the melodic permutations.

Ex. 7-33

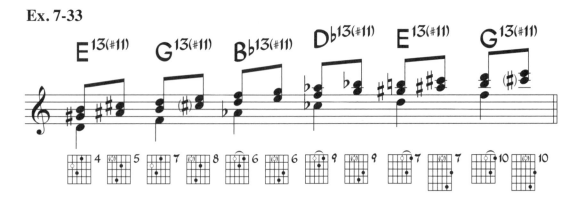

Ex. 7-34 gives the bottom voice a new melody while the 3rds on top are the same. The new melody for the bottom voice still outlines the dim7 arpeggio but is an eighth-note pattern going down-a-minor 3rd, up-a-tritone, down-a-minor 3rd, up-a-tritone, etc. Play the first voicing with the first three fingers and the second with fingers two, three, and four. On the upper-middle and top strings, use the partial barres and the second voicings are always done with fingers two, three, and four. (This is not "etched in stone," just a suggestion. Feel free to experiment.) Practice ascending and descending and do all the permutations.

Ex. 7-34

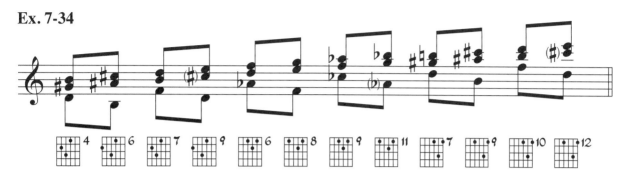

Ex. 7-35 shows a neat two-voice trick. The major 3rd G-B moves in contrary motion (the top note goes up a whole-step while the bottom note goes down a whole-step) to the augmented 5th F-C#. This group of four notes spells a G7b5 (it's literally a G7#11, but since the 5th isn't present I'm calling it G7b5 for convenience), which can be found in the diminished scale we've been playing. If we move it up by a minor 3rd (to Bb7b5) we're ascending the diminished scale again.

Ex. 7-35

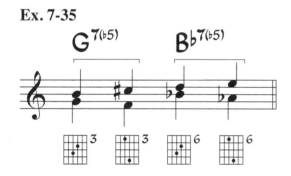

Ex. 7-36 shows a third voice that we're going to add to the two-voice trick. It's a dim7 arpeggio pattern again, this time going up-a-tritone, down-a-minor 3rd, up-a-tritone, down-a-minor 3rd, etc.

Ex. 7-36

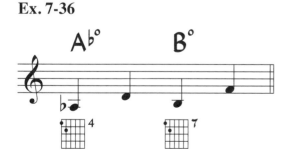

Ex. 7-37 shows the full-range combination of the two-voice trick with the dim7 arpeggio pattern. Choose a fingering that works and practice ascending and descending, and do all the permutations.

Ex. 7-37

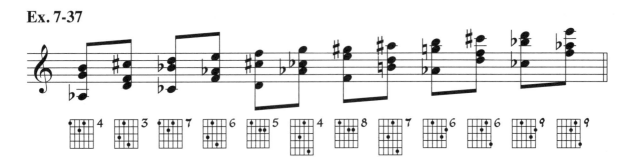

The next two examples are derived from Ex. 7-37. In addition to being useful as they are, they are preparing us for some amazing elaborations of Ex. 7-37.

Ex. 7-38 should present no fingering problems if you've been practicing the material up to now. Do it ascending and descending, and also all the permutations.

Ex. 7-38

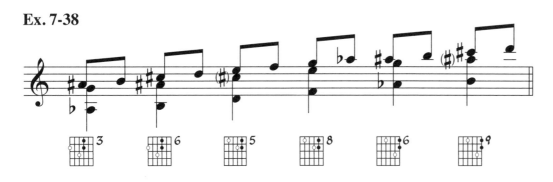

The same goes for Ex. 7-39.

Ex. 7-39

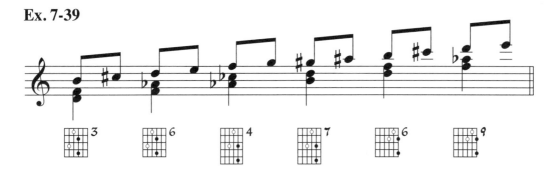

Ex. 7-40 puts the last two examples together to create a four-note melodic pattern in eighth-notes riding on top of the interesting quarter-note voicings. Practice ascending and descending and try to find as many usable permutations as you can. Be creative. For example, you could even play the second voicing first and the first voicing second, etc. (See next page.)

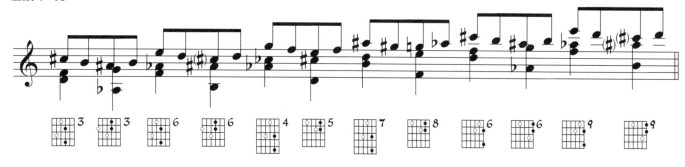

All the diminished scale examples were in the same diminished scale, but there are actually three so start all the examples a half-step lower and a half-step higher to cover all the "keys".

I think these examples have demonstrated the superiority of the dynamic concept of harmony over the static concept. These amazing forms and fingerings emerge from the process of treating harmony as a collection of good melodies rather than as isolated blocks of sound.

Ex. 7-41 uses all diminished scale harmonies, but applied to a dominant cycle. The bass line is in quarter-note triplets under the straight quarter-notes above. Play the first chord with fingers one, two, and four. Continue holding down two and four while playing the second bass note with finger three. Now continue holding down three while playing the second quarter-note pair with fingers two and four. The next chord begins with fingers one, two, and four. The first finger moves to play the next bass note while holding down two and four. Finger one stays put as fingers three and four grab the next quarter-note pair. The last bass note in the pattern is played by finger two.

Ex. 7-41

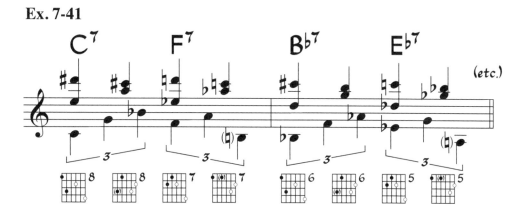

A FRESH LOOK AT WHOLETONE SCALES

A curious thing happens if I take the dom9 chord forms with melodies from Ex. 7-2 and from Ex. 7-6 and move them up by major 3rds. All the melody notes and all the chord tones are members of one wholetone scale, and spell out the entire scale as well. Ex. 7-42 shows this starting with a low A9 form to make room to go up by major 3rds. (See next page.)

Ex. 7-42

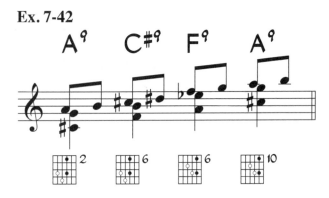

The chord names come from how we named the forms originally, but the entire example can be played over any harmony from the same wholetone scale (such as G9b5, B7#5 etc.). When you get to the top, reverse direction and descend all the way back down. Also experiment with melodic permutations.

Ex. 7-43 is a variation using the same forms. This melodic pattern can be continued up the neck as far as practical, then reversed back down.

Ex. 7-43

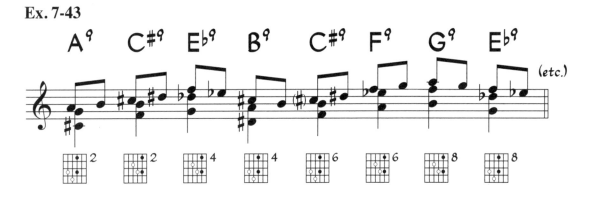

Ex. 7-44 uses the same melodic pattern as the last example, but has been moved up to higher strings resulting in the introduction of new forms on the top strings. Continue all the way up and all the way back down.

Ex. 7-44

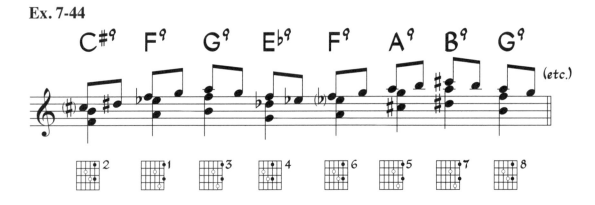

Ex. 7-45 again uses the same melodic pattern but moves the tritones in contrary motion to the melody. All the forms and fingerings should be familiar by now. Continue on up and back down.

Ex. 7-45

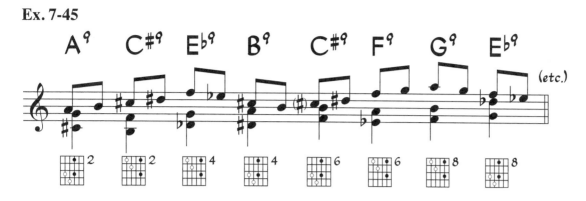

Ex. 7-46 is the same as 7-45 but moved up onto the higher strings, still using familiar forms and fingerings. Continue up and down.

Ex. 7-46

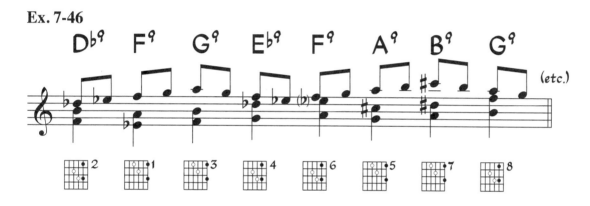

Now let's get away from familiar forms. We'll create new forms "out of thin air" by combining some simple melodies.

Ex. 7-47 harmonizes the top melody in parallel major 3rds, while the bottom line is a mirror image of the top melody, creating continuous contrary motion. Continue up the fingerboard and back down.

Ex. 7-47

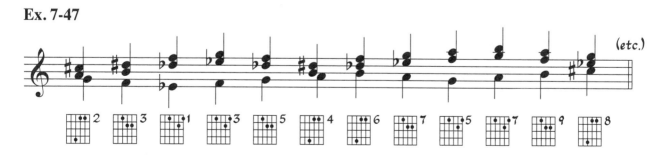

Ex. 7-48 is the same thing moved down onto lower strings.

Ex. 7-48

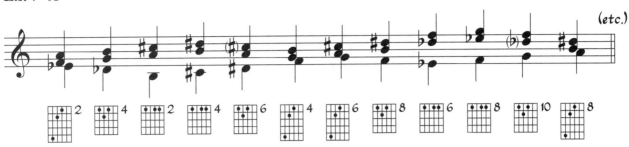

Ex. 7-49 uses a melodic pattern harmonized in parallel major 3rds played in quarter-note triplets against a straight quarter-note bottom melodic pattern. This example is only practical on the strings shown (the upper-middle set). The bottom line is played by fingers two and four, while the parallel 3rds use partial barres by the first and third fingers.Continue up and back.

Ex. 7-49

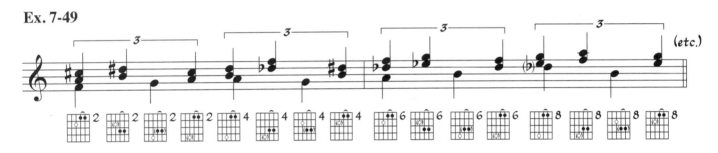

Things start to get interesting in Ex. 7-50. It uses the same melodic pattern found in the last example, but instead of parallel 3rds we find an inversion of the melody (the mirror image again). It's still in quarter-note triplets over a stright quarter-note line. This time the bottom melody is a permutation of the bottom line from the last example. It's only practical on the upper-middle strings. The top two voices use the first and third fingers. The bottom voice is done by fingers two and four. Continue up the fingerboard and back down.

Ex. 7-50

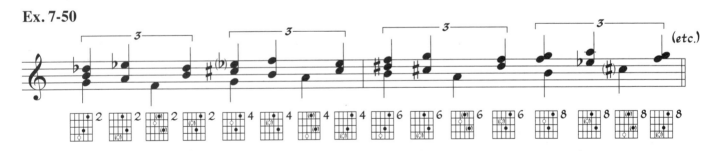

All the wholetone examples here used one wholetone scale. Be sure to practice all the examples in the other wholetone scale by moving them up or down a half-step.

Chapter 8 - Quartal Harmony and Secundal Harmony

QUARTAL HARMONY DEMONSTRATED

Play Ex. 8-1, the first three measures of Bronislau Kaper's "Invitation." This is the sound of quartal harmony (harmony built from 4th intervals). The melody is harmonized with three-note modal fourth chords. This portion of the melody is pure dorian mode, which lends itself to diatonic parallel quartal voicings.

Ex. 8-1

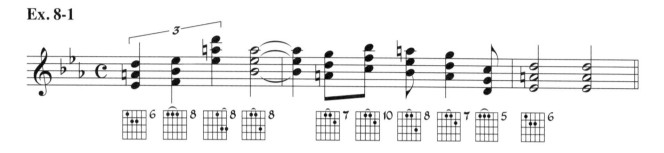

Ex. 8-2 is an alternate harmonization of the first three of "Invitation." It's still quartal harmony because it's derived from 4ths, but uses a mixture of the other two inversions of three-note fourth chords.

Ex. 8-2

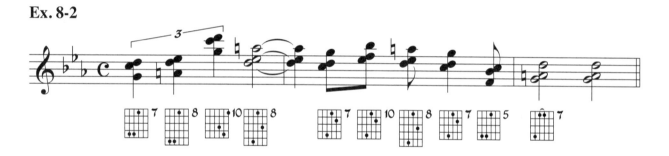

SECUNDAL HARMONY DEMONSTRATED

Ex. 8-3 shows another alternate harmonization of the same phrase. This is the sound of secundal harmony (harmony derived from 2nd intervals). Root-position secundal triads are frequently impractical on guitar, so this example uses a mixture of the two inversions.

Ex. 8-3

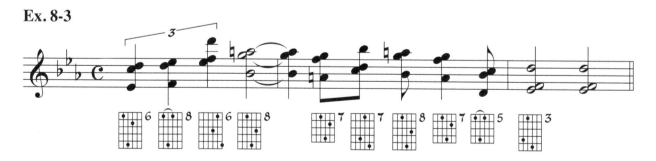

If either or both of these last two examples seem too difficult for you right now, please come back and try them again after you've worked through this chapter.

QUARTAL HARMONY

DIATONIC QUARTAL TRIADS - ROOT POSITION

Play Ex. 8-4. This is a quartal triad, a three-note stack of perfect 4ths.

Ex. 8-4

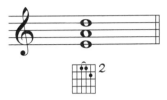

What is the name of this chord? Our way of naming chords is derived from the tertian harmonic system (harmony derived from 3rd intervals), so some possible tertian-related names are shown in Ex. 8-5. These names are usually unnecessary, but might occasionally prove useful for naming quartal slash chords, such as the one shown in Ex. 8-6. It is named Asus4/F#, but could also be called Dadd9/F#, or even F#m7#5.

Ex. 8-5

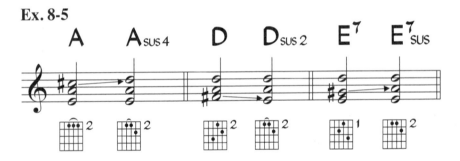

Ex. 8-6

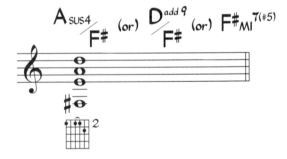

The notes in Ex. 8-4, E, A, and D, located on the upper-middle strings, are all diatonic members of the key of C major, so let's move the voicing up the C scale on the same strings to derive all the diatonic quartal triads for the modes of C major. These will be especially useful for Fmaj7(lydian), Dm7(dorian), G7sus(mixolydian), and Esusb9(phrygian). Ex. 8-7 shows the result. As usual, practice both ascending and descending. (See next page.)

Ex. 8-7

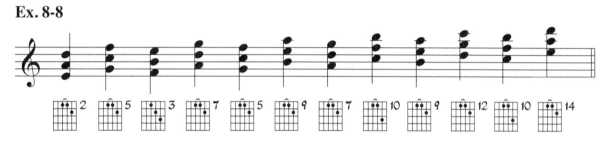

Notice that all the voicings and forms are identical except for two. All the 4ths in the major scale are perfect except for one, which is an augmented 4th (tritone). Since the chords all have three notes, there are two places in their voicings where the tritone could be located. The second chord has the tritone between the bottom two notes, and the sixth chord has the tritone between the top two notes. All the other chords are all perfect 4ths. It's a good idea to locate the voicings with the tritones first when learning a new key or string group.

Ex. 8-8 shows the voicings harmonizing a melodic pattern in 3rds. This type of study is great for internalizing the forms and fingerings. When you get to the top, reverse the pattern back down to the starting point.

Ex. 8-8

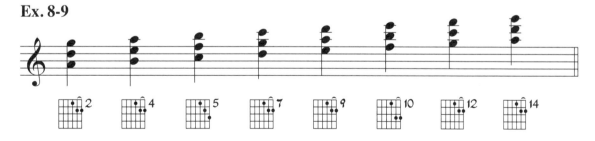

To transpose to other keys, leave the notation unchanged and add whatever key signature you want. You should (ultimately) be able to do this on the guitar without writing them out. This will apply to the forms we're about to show on other string groups as well.

Ex. 8-9 shows the diatonic quartal triads in root position for the key of C on the top three strings. Practice ascending and descending. Also do them in the pattern of 3rds, up and down the fingerboard.

Ex. 8-9

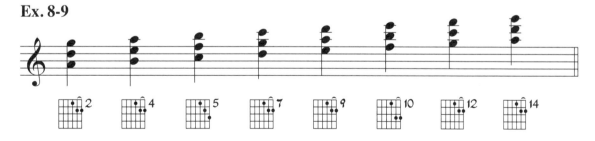

Ex. 8-10 shows the diatonic quartal triads in root position for the key of C on the lower-middle strings. Practice ascending and descending. Also do them in the pattern of 3rds, up and down the fingerboard.

Ex. 8-10

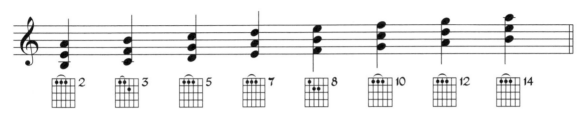

FIRST INVERSION DIATONIC QUARTAL TRIADS

Ex. 8-11 shows an easy way to create a first inversion quartal triad from a root position. Take the second chord from Ex. 8-7 and move the bottom note up an octave, placing it on the top string while leaving the other two notes where they are. This results in a first inversion fourth chord on the top three strings. You will probably want to exchange some fingers to make this practical.

Ex. 8-11

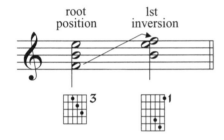

Ex. 8-12 shows the diatonic quartal triads in the first inversion in the key of C on the top three strings. Practice ascending and descending. Also do them in the pattern of 3rds, up and down the fingerboard.

Ex. 8-12

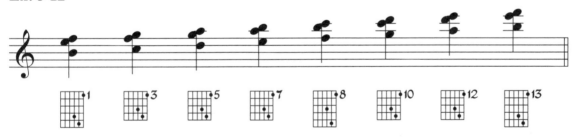

Ex. 8-13 shows the diatonic quartal triads in the first inversion in the key of C on the upper-middle three strings. Practice ascending and descending. Also do them in the pattern of 3rds, up and down the fingerboard.

Ex. 8-13

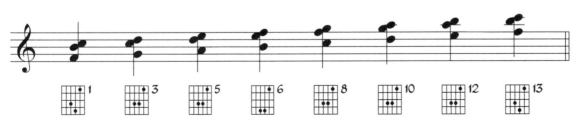

Ex. 8-14 shows the diatonic quartal triads in the first inversion in the key of C on the lower-middle three strings. Practice ascending and descending. Also do them in the pattern of 3rds, up and down the fingerboard.

Ex. 8-14

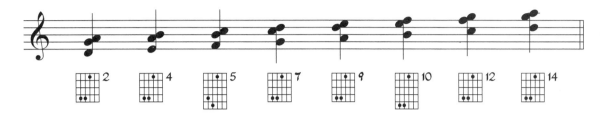

SECOND INVERSION DIATONIC QUARTAL TRIADS

Ex. 8-15 shows the easy way to derive a second inversion quartal triad from a first inversion. Take the first chord from Ex. 8-13 and move the bottom note up an octave, placing it on the top string while leaving the other two notes where they are. This results in a second inversion fourth chord on the top three strings.

Ex. 8-15

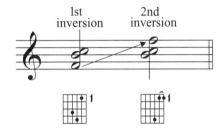

Ex. 8-16 shows the diatonic quartal triads in the second inversion in the key of C on the top three strings. Practice ascending and descending. Also do them in the pattern of 3rds, up and down the fingerboard.

Ex. 8-16

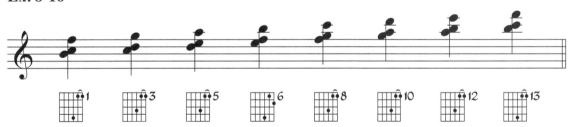

Ex. 8-17 shows the diatonic quartal triads in the second inversion in the key of C on the upper-middle three strings. Practice ascending and descending. Also do them in the pattern of 3rds, up and down the fingerboard.

Ex. 8-17

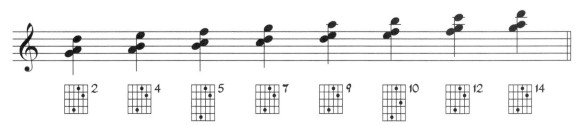

Ex. 8-18 shows the diatonic quartal triads in the second inversion in the key of C on the lower-middle three strings. Practice ascending and descending. Also do them in the pattern of 3rds, up and down the fingerboard.

Ex. 8-18

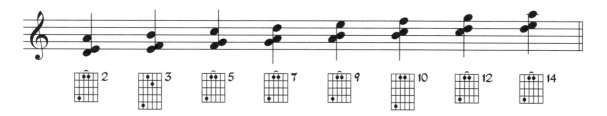

APPLYING THE QUARTAL TRIADS

Now we have a good arsenal of quartal triads. Try voicing the melody from Ex. 6-2, the seventh and eighth bars of "Stolen Moments," with root position quartal triads, then first inversion quartal triads, and finally with second inversion quartal triads. You can also mix the inversions. Ex. 8-19 shows one possible mixture applied to the melody fragment from "Stolen Moments."

Ex. 8-19

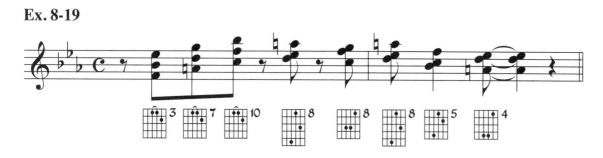

Another good tune to try is the A-section from Freddie Hubbard's "Little Sunflower." I'm not going to show examples, but you can work out many great variations using the "Stolen Moments" fragments as a model.

Quartal triads derived from the melodic minor scale are generally not very effective because of the presence of a diminished 4th, sounding like a major 3rd and creating false tertian-sounding chords. Four-note and especially five-note quartal voicings from melodic minor can be effective since the diminished 4th gets hidden inside the larger 4th chords, so be sure to check them out.

OPENING THE QUARTAL VOICINGS

All the quartal triads we've done so far have been close-voiced, spanning less than the range of an octave. The voicings can be opened by inverting the 4ths into 5ths. Two 5ths span the interval of a 9th, which, being larger than an octave, opens the voicing. An easy way to do this on the guitar is to keep the middle voice of a close-voiced root position 4th chord where it is, while exchanging the registers of the outer two voices. Ex. 8-20 shows this procedure applied to the voicing from Ex. 8-4. The A in the middle remains unchanged, while the low E below and the high D above swap places, creating a stack of 5ths, the open inversion of 4ths. (See next page.)

147

Ex. 8-20

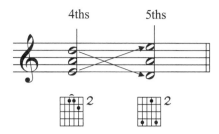

Opening the quartal voicings that contain an augmented 4th results in chords containing the difficult-to-use minor 9th interval, so we'll skip them for now. Ex. 8-21 shows all the close-voiced quartal triads made up of all perfect 4ths diatonic to the key of F major. These are great for using over Bbmaj7 (lydian), Gm7 (dorian), and C13sus (mixolydian) among others.

Ex. 8-21

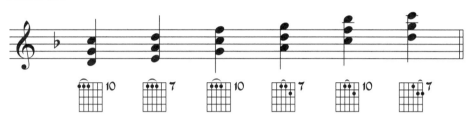

Ex. 8-22 opens all the perfect 4th voicings in F major shown in Ex. 8-21, making them perfect 5th voicings. They work for all the same chords as Ex. 8-21. Notice that the top voice follows the C major pentatonic scale, starting on D. Practice both ascending and descending.

Ex. 8-22

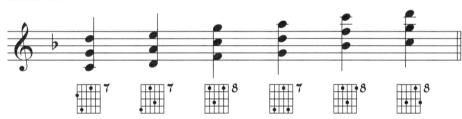

Ex. 8-23 shows an alternate harmonization of the same pentatonic line using three of the close-voiced 4th chords changing into their open 5th counterparts. Practice both ascending and descending.

Ex. 8-23

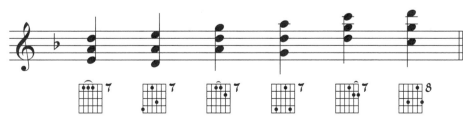

148

Ex. 8-24 uses the other three close-voiced 4th chords and their open 5th counterparts to create a harmonized Bb major pentatonic melody starting on C. As usual, practice both ascending and descending.

Ex. 8-24

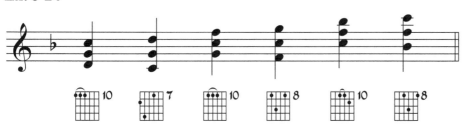

These 4th-5th combinations were originally inspired by some single-note intervallic studies from Joe Diorio's influencial book Intervallic Designs. By the way, all the voicings we've done and will do can be broken-up into single-note lines (arpeggios) and I advise that you do so.

So far all the open 5th voicings have been in root position, but they can be inverted. Ex. 8-25 shows a root position open 5th voicing built from C on the sixth string (containing C, G, and D), followed by its first inversion, then its second inversion, then back to root position an octave higher, and finally another first inversion up an octave. The forms are worked out going across the strings. Practice both ascending and descending.

Ex. 8-25

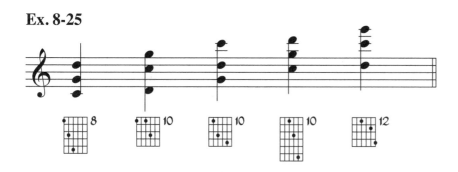

Ex. 8-26 shows the open inversions starting with a lower-register second inversion and working across the fingerboard. As usual, practice both ascending and descending.

Ex. 8-26

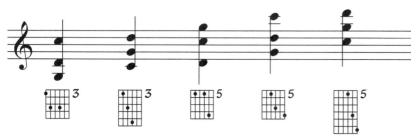

SECUNDAL HARMONY

Now let's take a look at a basic secundal triad, the notes A, B, and C. In the root position it is not practical to create a movable form without any open strings, so let's try the first inversion, created by moving the A up an octave. The result is shown in Ex. 8-27, voiced on the top three strings. There's a bit of a stretch, but it is practical for most players.

Ex. 8-27

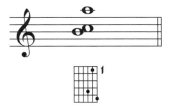

FIRST INVERSION DIATONIC SECUNDAL TRIADS

All three notes in the voicing shown in 8-27 are diatonic to the key of C major, so let's move the voicing up the C scale on the same strings to derive all the diatonic secundal triads for the modes of C major. These will be especially useful for Fmaj7(lydian), Dm7(dorian), G7sus(mixolydian), and Esusb9 (phrygian). Ex. 8-28 shows the result. Practice both ascending and descending.

Ex. 8-28

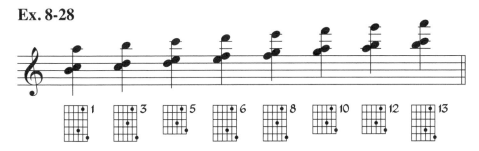

Ex. 8-29 shows the first inversion diatonic secundal triads in C major voiced on the upper-middle strings.

Ex. 8-29

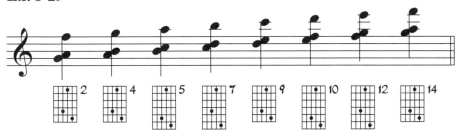

Ex. 8-30 shows them on the lower-middle strings.

Ex. 8-30

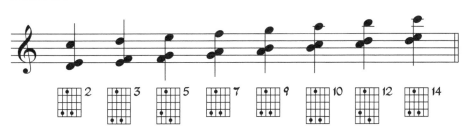

SECOND INVERSION DIATONIC SECUNDAL TRIADS

Ex. 8-31 shows the second inversion diatonic secundal triads in the key of C major on the lower-middle strings. Practice both ascending and descending.

Ex. 8-31

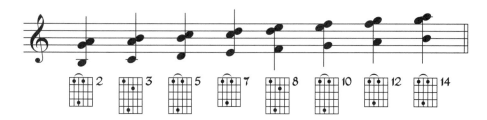

Ex. 8-32 shows them on the upper-middle strings.

Ex. 8-32

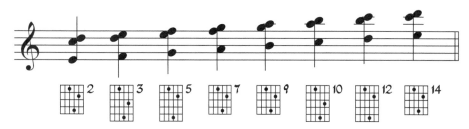

The second inversion secundal triads are quite difficult on the top three strings, so we need a new set of forms to voice the top melody on the high E string. These are shown in Ex. 8-33.

Ex. 8-33

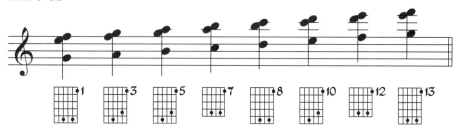

Ex. 8-34 shows similar forms used for melodies on the B string, giving an alternate choice. As usual, practice both ascending and descending.

Ex. 8-34

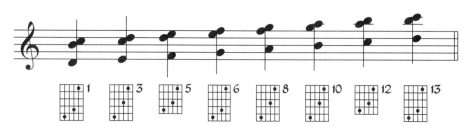

OPENING THE SECUNDAL VOICINGS

The inversion of a 2nd is a 7th, so the open secundal voicings consist of consecutive 7ths. Using the voicing from 8-27, we can lower the C by one octave to give us a stack of 7ths, shown in Ex. 8-35.

Ex. 8-35

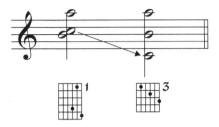

Ex. 8-36 moves the open voicings up the scale. Practice both ascending and descending.

Ex. 8-36

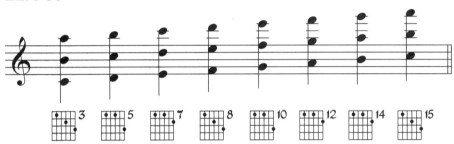

USING HEXATONIC SECONDS TO HARMONIZE MELODIES

Now let's check out one of my very favorite things to do with three-note voicings. If you recall, one of my favorite hexatonic scales is the maj13- relative m11. The avoid note 4 on the maj7 (b6 on the relative m7) is omitted, eliminating certain problems and making all the derived voicings very user-friendly. We'll use Fmaj13-Dm11 hexatonic for now. Ex. 8-37 shows a series of two-note structures, hexatonic 2nds, on the second and third strings, leaving the first string free to add a melodic line. We omit Bb (or B), so the lowest note is C and the highest is A. Since they are two-note structures using six notes, we get five voicings.

Ex. 8-37

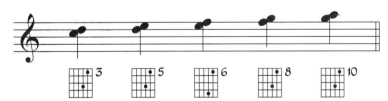

Ex. 8-38 adds an Fmaj7 arpeggio on the first string, resulting in five interesting three-note voicings. You probably recognize some or most of the voicings as ones we've already looked at, but here they are the result of our current process, creating a unique combination. The arpeggio going up in thirds is harmonized by the series of 2nds walking up step-wise underneath. The Fmaj7 may also be used to represent Dm9. Practice both ascending and descending.

Ex. 8-38

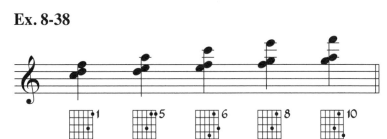

Ex. 8-39 shows a solution to the problem that arises if the Fmaj7 arpeggio is changed to an Fmaj9 arpeggio. The problem is that the last two-note structure, G and A, doubles the 9th of the Fmaj9, the G. If we skip up to the next hexatonic 2nd, the high C and D, we've jumped more than a tritone, ruining the melodic effect. Instead we back down to the next lower 2nd, and everything sounds great. Notice that in order to make the high G melody note reachable, the E-F second is placed on the middle two strings. This time the example is shown both ascending and descending.

Ex. 8-39

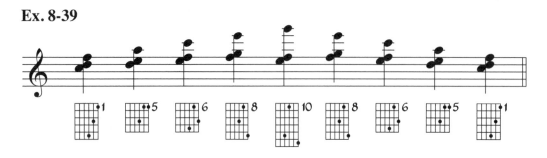

Ex. 8-40 replaces the first F melody note with G, making the arpeggio literally Am7, but representing Fmaj9 or Dm11.

Ex. 8-40

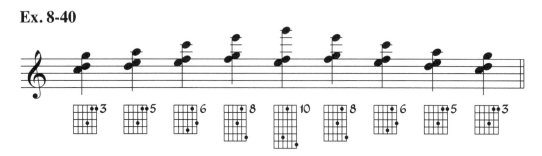

These apeggio harmonizations should be transposed to other keys. Work out forms starting with a Cmaj7 arpeggio on the second string, then forms starting with an Abmaj7 arpeggio on the third string.

Ex. 8-41 shows a melodic line that I wanted to harmonize using this system, but notice how low it goes. How do we solve the problem this time? If we skip down from the lowest 2nd, the C-D, to a lower octave of the highest 2nd, the G-A, we stay under the melody and have only dropped by a 4th, less than a tritone, keeping the melodic effect intact.

Ex. 8-41

Ex. 8-42 shows the solution. Notice how the 2nds continue down at the end rather than paralleling the melody, giving a touch of contrary motion as the phrase resolves. The harmony underlying the phrase could be Fmaj7, Dm7, Bbmaj7#11, G13sus, or E7susb9.

Ex. 8-42

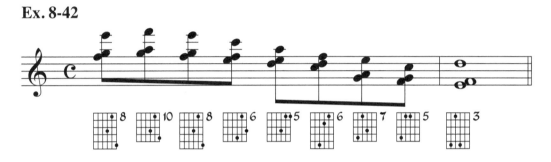

Ex. 8-43 shows the same phrase and harmonization converted to F melodic minor hexatonic. The harmony underlying the phrase could be Abmaj7#5, Fm-maj7, Dm7b5, Bb13#11, G13susb9, or E7alt.

Ex. 8-43

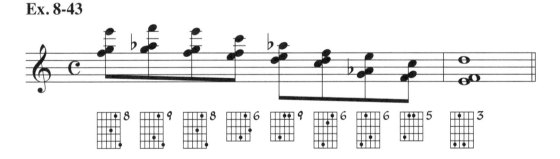

Chapter 9 - Drop 2 Reductions

Play Ex. 9-1, the first two measures of Jimmy Van Heusen's "Polkadots And Moonbeams," demonstrating the sound of what I'll call drop 2 reductions. Drop 2 voicings are four-note chords derived from four-note close voicings by lowering the second note from the top by an octave. For a complete explanation, see my *Jazz Guitar Voicings Vol.1 - The Drop 2 Book*. Notice the voicings here are only three notes each. They are reductions of the four-note drop 2 created by omitting the bottom note, in this case, leaving the top three notes.

Ex. 9-1

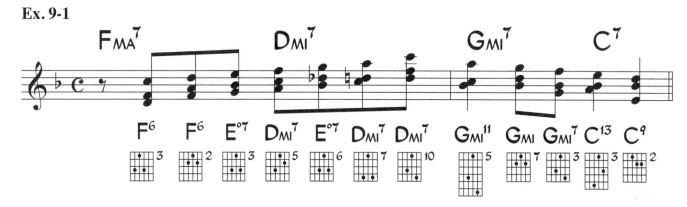

Ex. 9-2 demonstrates modal drop 2 reductions created the same way. This time they are applied to the by now familiar melodic fragment from the seventh and eighth bars of "Stolen Moments."

Ex. 9-2

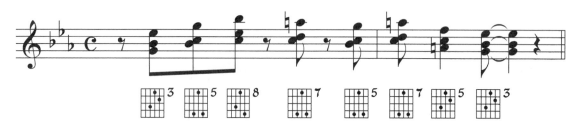

Ex. 9-3 shows the same fragment, but in this example the drop 2 reductions are created by omitting the top note of the standard drop 2, leaving the bottom three notes, and using the new highest note for the melody. This example is almost identical to Ex. 6-17, but derived through an entirely different method.

Ex. 9-3

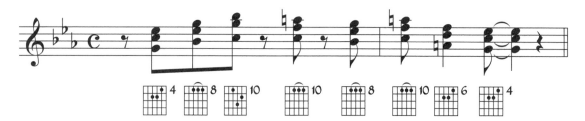

TOP-THREE-NOTE DROP 2 REDUCTIONS

BEBOP MAJOR SCALE

Ex. 9-4 shows the top-three-note drop 2 reductions harmonizing the C bebop major scale on the first three strings. These are reduced from standard drop 2 voicings, so it's also the A bebop natural minor scale. Practice both ascending and descending.

Ex. 9-4

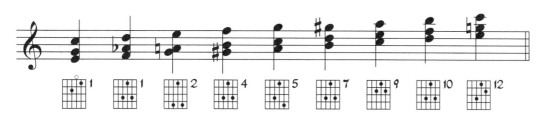

Ex. 9-5 shows the top-three-note drop 2 reductions harmonizing the C bebop major scale on the upper-middle three strings.

Ex. 9-5

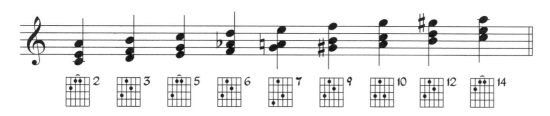

Ex. 9-6 shows the top-three-note drop 2 reductions harmonizing the C bebop major scale on the lower-middle three strings. Practice both ascending and descending.

Ex. 9-6

BEBOP MELODIC MINOR SCALE

Ex. 9-7 shows the top-three-note drop 2 reductions harmonizing the C bebop melodic minor scale on the first three strings. Practice both ascending and descending.

Ex. 9-7

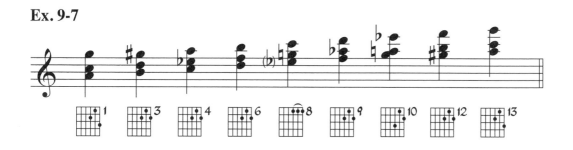

Ex. 9-8 shows the top-three-note drop 2 reductions harmonizing the C bebop melodic minor scale on the upper-middle three three strings. Practice both ascending and descending.

Ex. 9-8

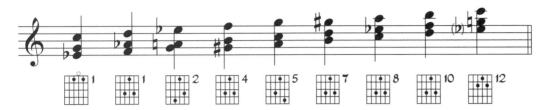

Ex. 9-9 shows the top-three-note drop 2 reductions harmonizing the C bebop melodic minor scale on the lower-middle three three strings. Practice both ascending and descending.

Ex. 9-9

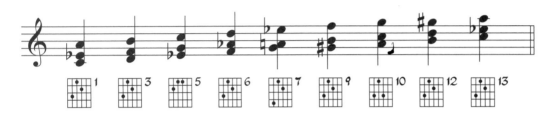

Notice that the voicings for the G melody notes, a chord tone, have no Eb and don't sound like C minor chords (at least not by themselves). They are still useful in scale passages as they are. However, if we try top-three-note drop 2 reductions on bebop dominant scales, we get some pretty vague "dominant" chords with no tritone, so we need to check out some bottom-three-note drop 2 reductions before we can continue.

BOTTOM-THREE-NOTE DROP 2 REDUCTIONS

Ex. 9-10 shows the bottom-three-note drop 2 reductions on the upper-middle three strings (derived from standard drop 2 on the top four strings) harmonizing the C bebop major scale. Practice ascending and descending.

Ex. 9-10

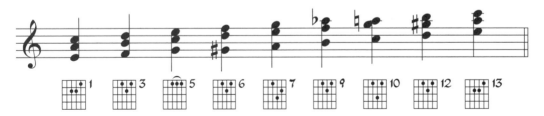

Ex. 9-11 shows the bottom-three-note drop 2 reductions on the upper-middle three strings harmonizing the C bebop melodic minor scale. Practice ascending and descending.

Ex. 9-11

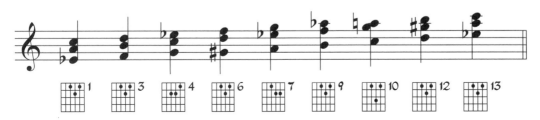

Now, more homework for you. Work out the forms and fingerings for bottom-three-note drop 2 reductions for both C bebop major and C bebop melodic minor scales on both the top three strings and the lower-middle three strings.

If you try bottom-three-note reductions on the bebop dominant scale, you'll discover that it's not too bad, but still has at least one voicing that doesn't quite cut it as a dominant chord, so let's try some combinations.

MIXING THE TOP AND BOTTOM DROP 2 REDUCTIONS

BEBOP DOMINANT SCALE
Ex. 9-12 shows one possible solution to the dominant problem. It's a mixture of bottom-three-note and top-three-note reductions, shown on the upper-middle strings, resulting in the tritone being present in every chord-tone voicing. Many other satisfactory combinations may be possible as well, but this is the one I liked today (Dec.9, 2009). Notice that the A melody note uses a chromatic approach chord. The voice leading makes it work both ascending and descending.

Ex. 9-12

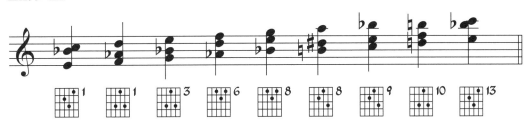

Ex. 9-13 shows the same voicings as Ex. 9-12 but placed on the top three strings. As usual, practice both ascending and descending.

Ex. 9-13

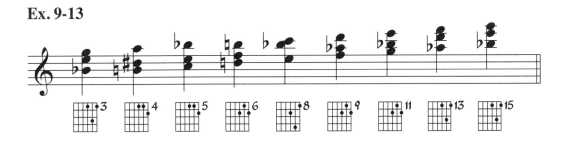

Ex. 9-14 shows them on the lower-middle three strings.

Ex. 9-14

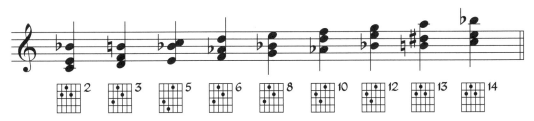

158

COMBINATIONS FOR BEBOP MELODIC MINOR AND BEBOP MAJOR

Ex. 9-15 shows a mixture for C bebop melodic minor on the upper-middle three strings that results in Eb being present in every chord-tone voicing, addressing the problem mentioned earlier. Practice ascending and descending.

Ex. 9-15

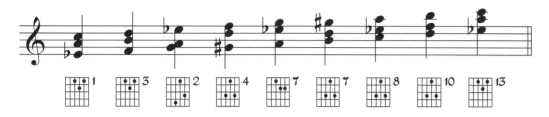

Ex. 9-16   shows a mixture for C bebop major on the upper-middle three strings that results in E natural being present in every chord-tone voicing. As usual, practice both ascending and descending.

Ex. 9-16

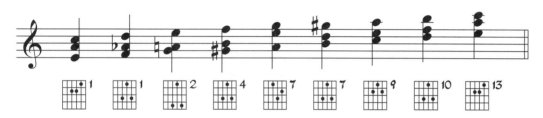

Once again, more homework for you. Work out the forms and fingerings to place the last two examples on the top three strings and on the lower-middle three strings.

MODAL DROP 2 REDUCTIONS

DORIAN TOP-THREE-NOTE DROP 2 REDUCTIONS

As you might recall from my first book, a dorian mode can be harmonized by two m7 chords built from the 1st and 2nd degrees of the mode. The m7 chords alternate and go through their inversions as you go up and down the scale. They are perfect for reductions, so let's check them out.

Ex. 9-17 is the top-three-note drop 2 reduction for the A dorian mode on the lower-middle three strings. As usual, practice both ascending and descending. These forms are ideal for Ab dorian and up chromatically through at least C# dorian. The A dorian forms also work great for C lydian, D mixolydian, and B phrygian. Did you notice that Ex. 9-17 starts out with a triad-pair combination? First there's a minor pair followed by its relative major pair bfore morphing into something different.

Ex. 9-17

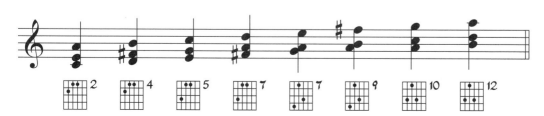

159

Ex. 9-18 is the top-three-note drop 2 reduction for the D dorian mode on the upper-middle three strings. Practice ascending and descending. These forms are ideal for Db dorian and up chromatically through at least F dorian.

Ex. 9-18

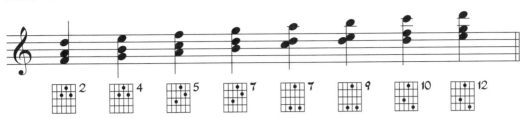

Ex. 9-19 is the top-three-note drop 2 reduction for the G dorian mode on the top three strings. Practice ascending and descending. These forms are ideal for F dorian and up chromatically through at least A dorian.

Ex. 9-19

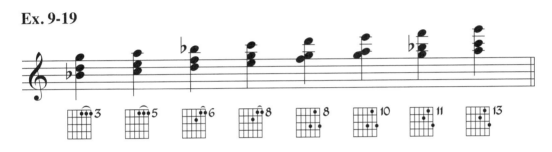

DORIAN BOTTOM-THREE-NOTE REDUCTIONS

Ex. 9-20 is the bottom-three-note drop 2 reduction for the A dorian mode on the lower-middle three strings. As usual, practice both ascending and descending. These forms are ideal for Ab dorian and up chromatically through at least C# dorian.

Ex. 9-20

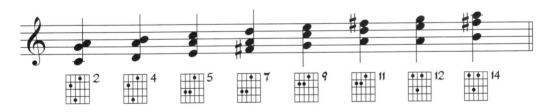

Ex. 9-21 is the bottom-three-note drop 2 reduction for the D dorian mode on the upper-middle three strings. Practice ascending and descending. These forms are ideal for Db dorian and up chromatically through at least F dorian.

Ex. 9-21

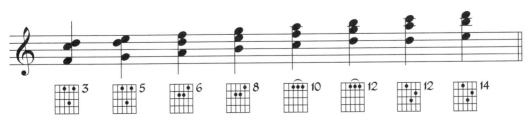

Ex. 9-22 is the bottom-three-note drop 2 reduction for the G dorian mode on the top three strings. Practice ascending and descending. These forms are ideal for F dorian and up chromatically through at least A dorian.

Ex. 9-22

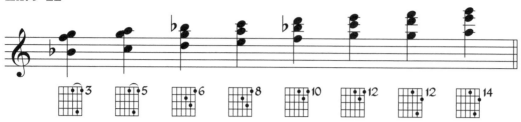

LOCRIAN#2 TOP-THREE-NOTE DROP 2 REDUCTIONS

The locrian#2 mode (the sixth mode of melodic minor) can be harmonized by two m7b5 chords built from the 1st and 2nd degrees of the mode. The m7b5 chords alternate and go through their inversions as you go up and down the scale.

Ex. 9-23 is the top-three-note drop 2 reduction for the A locrian#2 mode on the lower-middle three strings. As usual, practice both ascending and descending. These forms are ideal for A locrian#2 and up chromatically through at least C# locrian#2. The A locrian#2 forms also work great for C melodic minor, Eb lydian augmented, F lydian dominant, D13susb9, and B7alt.

Ex. 9-23

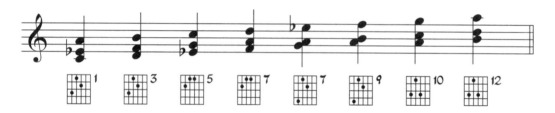

Ex. 9-24 is the top-three-note drop 2 reduction for the D locrian#2 mode on the upper-middle three strings. Practice ascending and descending. These forms are ideal for D locrian#2 and up chromatically through at least F# locrian#2.

Ex. 9-24

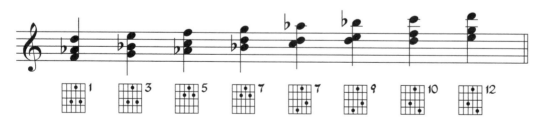

161

Ex. 9-25 is the top-three-note drop 2 reduction for the G locrian#2 mode on the top three strings. Practice ascending and descending. These forms are ideal for F# locrian#2 and up chromatically through at least A locrian#2.

Ex. 9-25

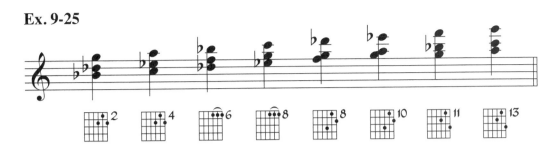

LOCRIAN#2 BOTTOM-THREE-NOTE DROP 2 REDUCTIONS

Ex. 9-26 is the bottom-three-note drop 2 reduction for the A locrian#2 mode on the lower-middle three strings. As usual, practice both ascending and descending. These forms are ideal for G# locrian#2 and up chromatically through at least C# locrian#2.

Ex. 9-26

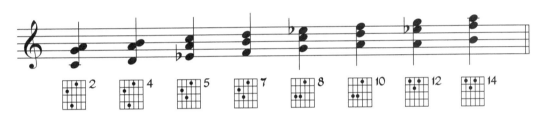

Ex. 9-27 is the bottom-three-note drop 2 reduction for the D locrian#2 mode on the upper-middle three strings. Practice ascending and descending. These forms are ideal for D locrian#2 and up chromatically through at least F locrian #2.

Ex. 9-27

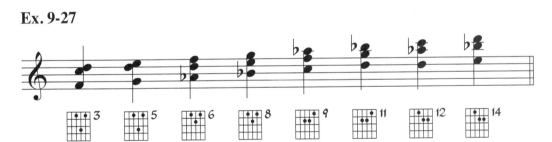

Ex. 9-28 is the bottom-three-note drop 2 reduction for the G locrian#2 mode on the top three strings. Practice ascending and descending. These forms are ideal for F# locrian#2 and up chromatically through at least A locrian#2.

Ex. 9-28

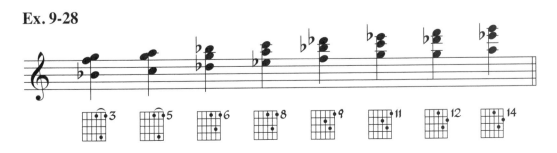

SOME TOP-BOTTOM MIXTURES FOR MODAL DROP 2 REDUCTIONS

The modal reductions generally don't require combinations, but they are possible and useful, so let's check out a few.

Ex. 9-29 shows one possible D locrian#2 mixture on the upper-middle three strings. It switches from "top" to "bottom" on the last two chords in order to keep the note Ab in the Dm7b5 voicing, which is the minor 3rd of the parent scale, F melodic minor. Practice ascending and descending. Work it out for A locrian#2 on the lower-middle strings and for G locrian#2 on the top strings.

Ex. 9-29

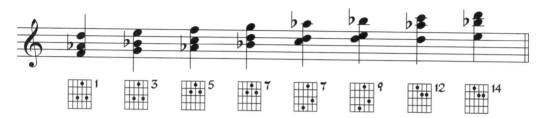

Ex. 9-30 shows one possible D dorian mixture on the upper-middle three strings. It switches from "top" to "bottom" on the last two chords in order to keep the note A in the Dm7 voicing, which is the major 3rd of F lydian. Practice ascending and descending. Work it out for A dorian on the lower-middle strings and for G dorian on the top strings.

Ex. 9-30

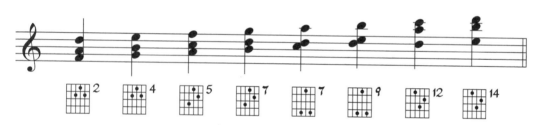

Ex. 9-31 shows another possible D dorian mixture on the upper-middle three strings. This time the switch is on the fifth and sixth chords, keeping the note F in the Dm7 voicing, which is the minor 3rd of D dorian. Practice ascending and descending. Work it out for A dorian on the lower-middle strings and for G dorian on the top strings.

Ex. 9-31

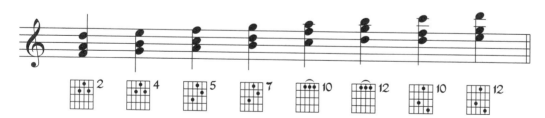

Feel free to experiment with more combinations on your own.

SOME MISCELLANEOUS DROP 2 REDUCTIONS

It is also possible to create interesting drop 2 reductions by omitting one of the inner voices from a drop 2 chord. This leaves both of the outer voices, which generally have a very pleasant voice-leading together.

I'm going to leave it up to you to discover all the reductions leaving out the second highest voice, then all the reductions leaving out the third highest voice. I am going to show you a few of my favorite combinations.

A BEBOP MAJOR SCALE MIXTURE

Ex. 9-32 shows a combination on the upper-middle strings harmonizing the C bebop major scale. Remember, it is also the A bebop natural minor scale. Practice both ascending and descending.

Ex. 9-32

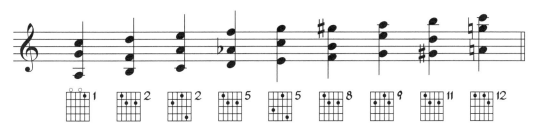

A BEBOP MELODIC MINOR SCALE MIXTURE

Ex. 9-33 shows a combination on the upper-middle strings harmonizing the C bebop melodic minor scale. Practice both ascending and descending.

Ex. 9-33

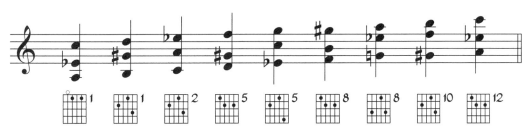

A BEBOP DOMINANT SCALE MIXTURE

Ex. 9-34 shows a combination on the upper-middle strings harmonizing the C bebop dominant scale. Practice both ascending and descending.

Ex. 9-34

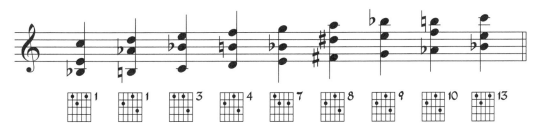

A HOMEWORK ASSIGNMENT

Your assignment is to work out the forms and fingerings for the last three examples across the top four strings.

THE ALTERED BEBOP MINOR REDUCTION

If you've been through my earlier book, you may be wondering about the altered bebop minor scale. Most of the reductions just don't yield useful results. The one exception may be the omitting of the second highest note. Ex. 9-35 shows it on the middle strings. The resulting triads give it a pleasant "quasi-classical" sound. As usual, practice both ascending and descending. Also work out the forms and fingerings across the top four strings.

Ex. 9-35

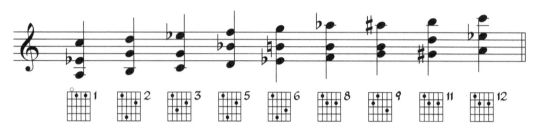

Now the real homework begins. Try working out the melodies of tunes using the various drop 2 reductions. Some suggested tunes include "Blue Bossa," "My One And Only Love," and "Little Sunflower." You should also refer to my *Jazz Guitar Voicings Vol.1* and try reductions on enclosures, chromatic approach chords, and elaborated enclosures.

Chapter 10 - Deriving Simulated Shearing-Style Block Chords from Drop 2 Reductions

SIMULATED SHEARING-STYLE BLOCK CHORDS DEMONSTRATED

Play Ex. 10-1, the first two measures of Jimmy Van Heusen's "Polkadots And Moonbeams."

Ex. 10-1

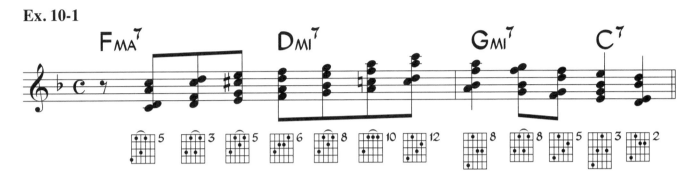

Now play Ex. 10-2, the ninth, tenth, and eleventh bars of Victor Young's "Stella By Starlight."

Ex. 10-2

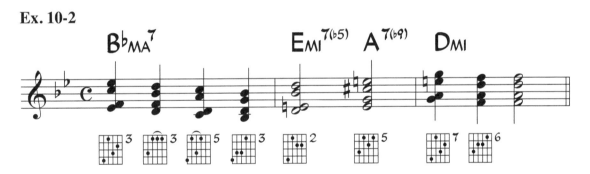

These demonstate the sound of simulated Shearing-style block chords. Why simulated? The actual piano voicings popularized by George Shearing are five-note close voicings, so they would require extra hands, strings, and probably brains to be playable on guitar. The closely packed notes surrounded by the melody in octaves is so appealing that the temptation to try simulating them on guitar is impossible to resist.

The voicings in the first measure of Ex. 10-1 are bottom-three-note drop 2 reductions with the melody doubled an octave below, going up the F bebop major scale voicings. The second measure uses some extension voicings (see my *Vol.1*) that have been reduced, with the added octaves.

The voicings in Ex. 10-2 are all derived from bottom-three-note reductions, and treats all the non-chord tones as if they were extensions, including the natural 11th on the Bbmaj7 chord. Why? Because it sounds so good to my ear.

In a way, these four-note structures are really just three-note chords with an octave double added.

BEBOP SCALE SHEARING-STYLE VOICINGS

In general, the bottom-three-note drop 2 reductions make easier simulated Shearing-style voicings, so let's get started by checking them out first.

SIMULATED SHEARING-STYLE VOICINGS DERIVED FROM BOTTOM-REDUCTIONS

Ex. 10-3 is a review of Ex. 9-10, the bottom-three-note drop 2 reductions harmonizing the C major bebop scale on the upper-middle strings.

Ex. 10-3

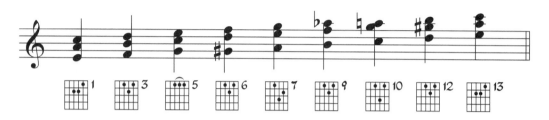

Ex. 10-4 shows the same thing converted into simulated Shearing-style by adding, on the fifth string, the lower octave doubling of the top voice. Play the scale both ascending and descending.

Ex. 10-4

Ex. 10-5 shows the bottom-reduction derived simulated Shearing-style C bebop major scale on the top four strings. Practice both ascending and descending.

Ex. 10-5

Ex. 10-6 shows the bottom-reduction derived simulated Shearing-style C bebop major scale on the bottom four strings. Practice both ascending and descending.

Ex. 10-6

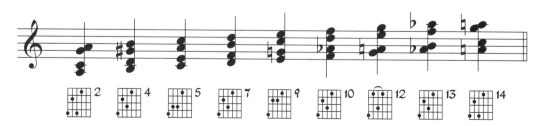

Many of the Shearing-style scales will work better using a few top-three-note reductions mixed in with the bottom-reductions to clarify the harmonies, so let's try some top-reduction simulated Shearing-style voicings.

SIMULATED SHEARING-STYLE VOICINGS DERIVED FROM TOP-REDUCTIONS

Ex. 10-7 is a review of Ex. 9-5, the top-three-note drop 2 reductions harmonizing the C major bebop scale on the upper-middle strings.

Ex. 10-7

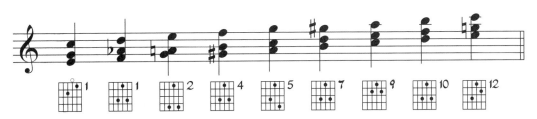

Ex. 10-8 shows the same thing converted into simulated Shearing-style by adding, on the fifth string, the lower octave doubling of the top voice. Play the scale both ascending and descending. Notice there's some fairly challenging finger stretches involved. (Don't hurt yourself!)

Ex. 10-8

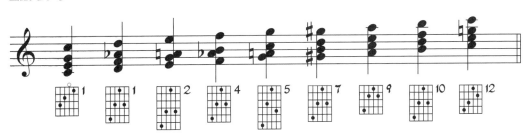

I'm leaving it up to you to try the top-reduction derivations on the top strings and on the bottom strings (generally impractical), and to convert them into bebop melodic minor scales and into bebop dominant scales. I am going to show what I think are some of the most useful combinations, so don't waste too much time checking out every concievable possibility.

SIMULATED SHEARING-STYLE VOICINGS DERIVED FROM USEFUL MIXED-REDUCTIONS

Ex. 10-9 shows the C bebop melodic minor scale in simulated Shearing-style voicings on the middle four strings. Practice both ascending and descending.

Ex. 10-9

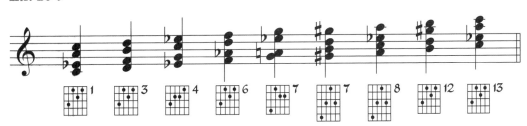

Ex. 10-10 shows the C bebop melodic minor scale in simulated Shearing-style voicings on the top four strings. Practice both ascending and descending.

Ex. 10-10

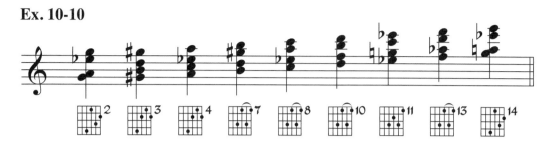

Ex. 10-11 shows it on the bottom four strings. Practice both ascending and descending.

Ex. 10-11

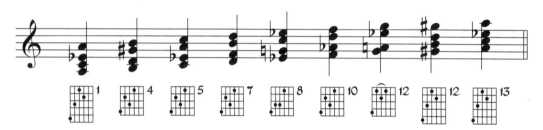

Ex. 10-12 shows the C bebop dominant scale in simulated Shearing-style voicings on the middle four strings. Practice both ascending and descending. The voicings for the E and Bb melody notes are not derived the same way as the other chords. They are bottom-reductions with the octave-doubled melody added above instead of below. This was done to create voicings that contain both notes of the tritone while remaining compatible with the surrounding chords and being practical to play on all the string groups.

Ex. 10-12

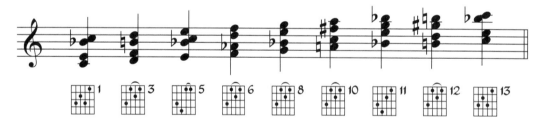

Ex. 10-13 shows the C bebop dominant scale in simulated Shearing-style voicings on the top four strings. Practice both ascending and descending.

Ex. 10-13

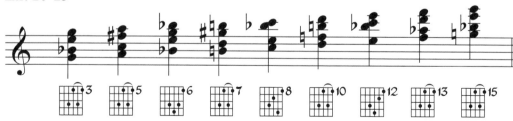

Ex. 10-14 shows the C bebop dominant scale in simulated Shearing-style voicings on the bottom four strings. Practice both ascending and descending.

Ex. 10-14

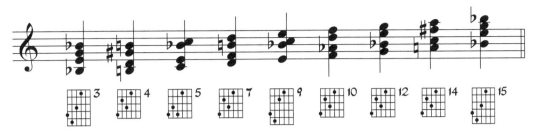

USING DROP 2 EXTENSION VOICING REDUCTIONS

Shearing-style block chords often sound better when the passing notes, the non-chord tones, are harmonized as extensions of the basic underlying chord, rather than with passing diminished chords. The extension may replace the basic chord tone beneath it (such as the 9th replacing the root) or may have the support of another extension (such as the 9th supported by the maj7th), but at least one basic chord tone from the original voicing should remain to keep the ear hearing the tension tone as an extension of the basic chord.

Since this device doesn't use the passing diminished chords, it won't harmonize the bebop scales, but harmonizes regular seven note modes instead.

SHEARING-STYLE EXTENSION VOICINGS

These extension voicings are generally not usable on the bottom four strings, but there are exceptions, as shown in Ex. 10-2. They are rare and I'm not going to show any. If you need one you can always work it out.

Ex. 10-15 shows the C lydian mode in simulated Shearing-style voicings, harmonizing the tension tones as extensions, on the middle four strings. This could also be used for the A dorian mode. As usual, practice both ascending and descending.

Ex. 10-15

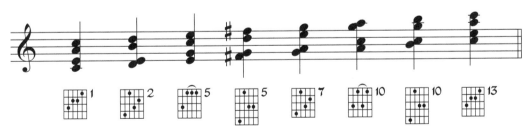

Ex. 10-16 shows the same voicings on the top four strings. Practice both ascending and descending.

Ex. 10-16

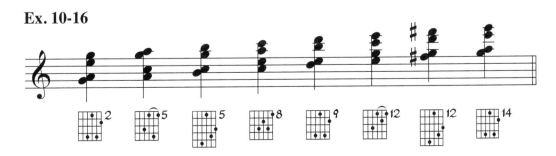

Ex. 10-17 shows the C lydian dominant scale in simulated Shearing-style voicings, harmonizing the tension tones as extensions, on the middle four strings. Practice ascending and descending.

Ex. 10-17

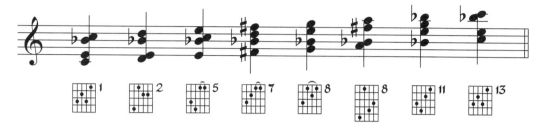

Ex. 10-18 shows the same voicings on the top four strings. Practice both ascending and descending.

Ex. 10-18

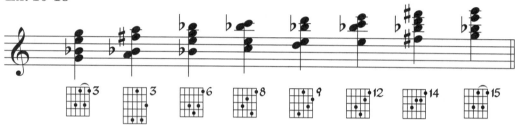

Ex. 10-19 shows the C melodic minor scale in simulated Shearing-style voicings, harmonizing the tension tones as extensions, on the middle four strings. These work for Ebmaj7#5 (lydian augmented), Cm-maj7, Am9b5 (locrian#2), D13susb9 and B7alt. Practice ascending and descending.

Ex. 10-19

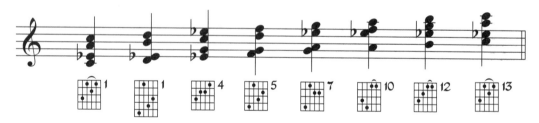

Ex. 10-20 shows the same voicings on the top four strings. Practice both ascending and descending.

Ex. 10-20

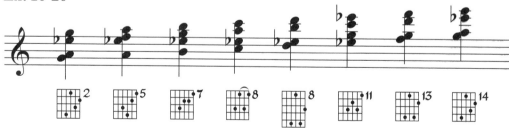

DIMINISHED SCALE IN SIMULATED SHEARING-STYLE

Ex. 10-21 shows the diminished scale in simulated Shearing-style block chords. It's based on some of the forms found in Ex. 7-33 with the lower octave doubling of the top voice added below. Because the scale is symetrical, the forms repeat as you go up, so this example crosses from the middle strings to the top strings to show all the practical forms.

Ex. 10-21

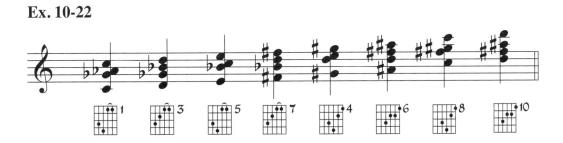

WHOLETONE SCALE IN SIMULATED SHEARING-STYLE

Ex. 10-22 is a wholetone scale in simulated Shearing-style block chords. Of course the wholetone scale is also symetrical, so again the forms repeat and cross from the middle to the top strings.

Ex. 10-22

SIMULATED SHEARING REDUCTIONS

Did you notice that, in the last four examples (Ex.s 10-19 through 10-22), the top two voices are parallel diatonic 3rds? If we omit the second voice from the bottom, we're left with 3rds and an octave doubling of the melody. Play Ex. 10-23. We return to the seventh and eighth bars of "Stolen Moments" to demonstrate the sound of these simulated Shearing reductions. Perhaps you recognize the sound as an important part of George Benson's style.

Ex. 10-23

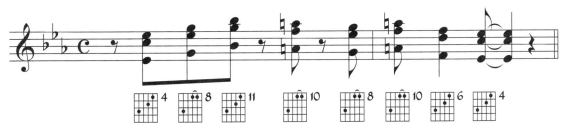

Since these voicings contain all the diatonic 3rds, they work best for modes without avoid notes, such as lydian, dorian, most modes of melodic minor, and diminished and wholetone scales. I'll demonstrate them using C dorian. It'll be up to you to work out the rest, and to transpose into all keys, etc.

Ex. 10-24 shows the simulated Shearing reductions for C dorian on the middle strings. Practice ascending and descending.

Ex. 10-24

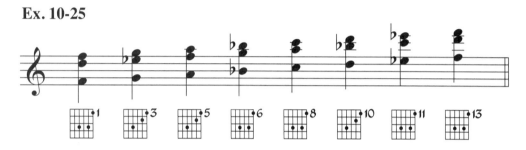

Ex. 10-25 shows them on the top strings. Practice ascending and descending.

Ex. 10-25

Chapter 11 - Comping Revisited

Play Ex. 11-1, a turnaround for blues in F. It's composed of the dominant chord tritones going up a minor 3rd and returning chromatically, with a simple blues scale melody played above.

Ex. 11-1

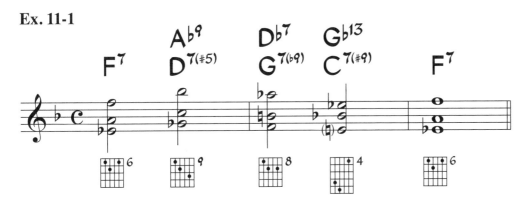

Now try Ex. 11-2. It's the same thing but has an extra voice added under the melody above the tritones to fill out the sound a bit.

Ex. 11-2

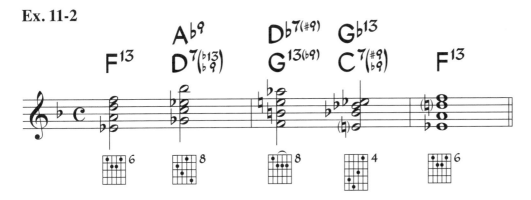

Let's check out some blues comping using these kind of sounds.

BLUES COMPING

THREE-NOTE BLUES IN F

We'll start with blues in F using the concept demonstrated in Ex. 11-1. Since it's a comp and not a solo, the melody should be simple enough not to distract from a soloist, but strong enough to sound good by itself. The blues is traditionally a very horizontal, tonic-oriented idiom, so let's try to emphasize the tonic note, and we'll limit our other melody note choices to a few simple blues scale notes.

Ex. 11-3 shows a possible solution with all the rhythms removed so you can concentrate on the movement of the voicings. Some of the chords have two names. These are chords in the turnarounds that the bassist may use tritone-substitutions on. The voicings work for both, so no need to worry. (See next page.)

Notice that each voice stays on the same string throughout the example. This is partly for sound, but also to leave the third string free to add another voice later. Once you get it down, try the next example.

Ex. 11-4 shows the same voicings, but with comp-rhythms added to make it sound more like music. Feel free to change the rhythms and create your own variations. This is just an example to use as a model.

Ex. 11-4

THREE-NOTE BLUES IN Bb

Ex. 11-5 is identical to Ex. 11-3, except it's in Bb and it's been relocated to the top strings. Once you get the forms down add comp rhythms.

Ex. 11-5

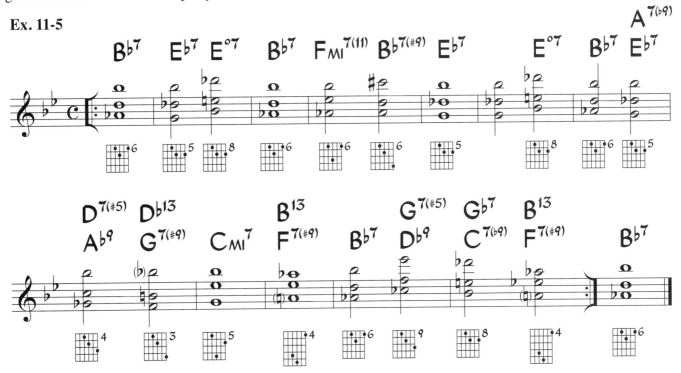

"SPLIT-TRITONE" VOICINGS IN Bb

Ex. 11-6 shows a new set of forms for blues in Bb on the top strings with a new melody, this time venturing outside the "minor" blues scale a bit by borrowing a note from the "major" blues scale (please see *The Blues Scales* by Dan Greenblatt, Sher Music Co., for a compete explanation). I call the new forms "split-tritone" voicings because the tritones are separated by a string, instead of being on consecutive strings. This leaves a different string free inside the voicing and inside the tritone for adding a different voice later on. Once you've mastered the forms add some comp rhythms.

Ex. 11-6

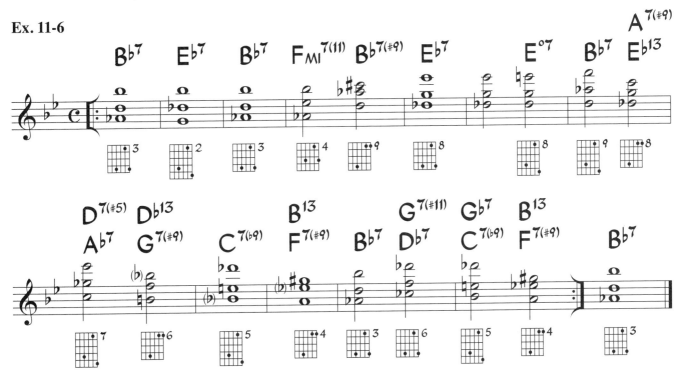

ADDING ANOTHER VOICE TO THE BLUES IN F

Ex. 11-7 shows our first blues in F with a fourth voice added inside. The three-note version sounds great as it is, but this four-note version gives another option in case you need a fuller sound.

Ex. 11-7

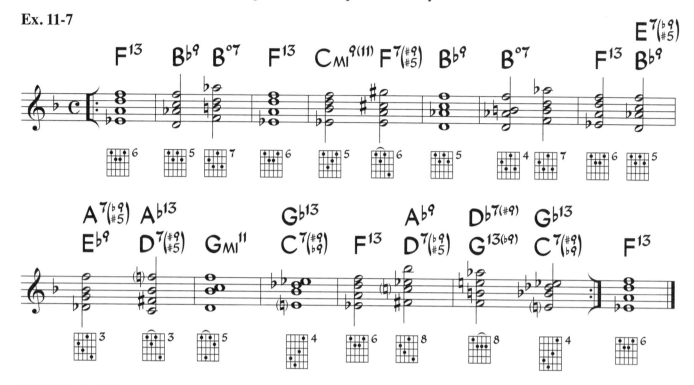

ADDING ANOTHER VOICE TO THE BLUES IN Bb

Ex. 11-8 shows the four-note version in Bb on the top strings.

Ex. 11-8

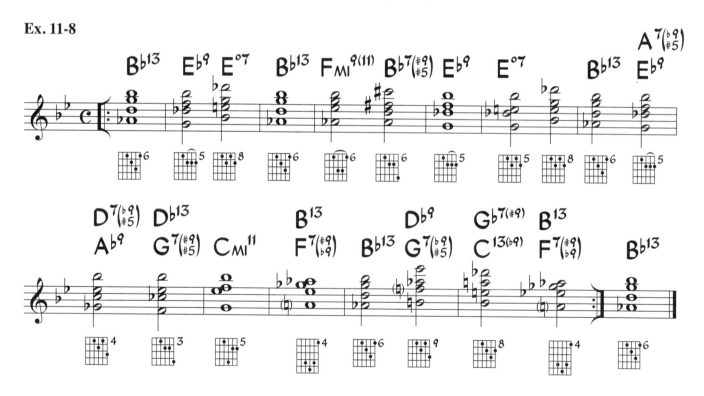

ADDING ANOTHER VOICE TO THE "SPLIT-TRITONE" VOICINGS IN Bb

Ex. 11-9 shows the split-tritone voicings in Bb with an added fourth-note. In the "standard" voicing at the beginning of Ex. 11-8 the added-note is the 13th on the second string, going to the 9th on the second chord (still on the second string). In the split-tritone voicing the added-note is the 9th on the first chord becoming the 13th on the second chord. This time the added notes are located on the third string.

Ex. 11-9

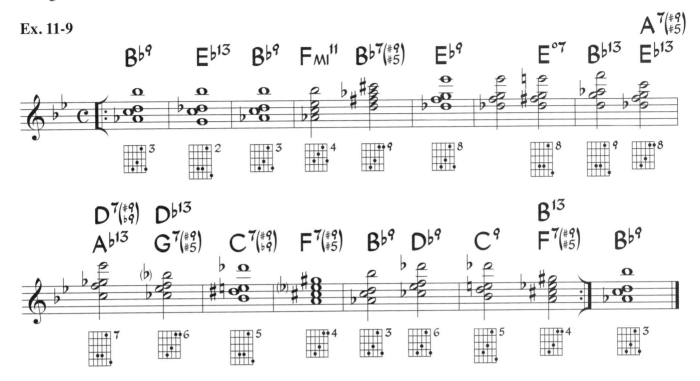

Incidently, if you always play the notes on the third and fourth strings in this example with the middle two fingers, it makes all the chord transitions easy to play, so give it a try.

Notice the interesting sequential motion that takes place in measures seven through ten. It even results in the II chord in the II-V progression being warped into an altered dominant chord, with the "blue" 3rd of the key on top.

Also notice the intriguing turnaround. The third chord of the turnaround might be called C9addb9, or its tritone substitute Gb7#5add natural5. Believe me, you'll probably never see either chord symbol. They technically don't exist, but the voice leading makes it work. In fact, in this context it's a more interesting sound than any "correct" voicing I might have used because I "knew" it was "right."

II-V-I COMP MELODIES

These next examples are half-note melodies used for comping on II-V-I progressions (see my *Vol.1*, page 33). The first six examples use the same melodies we used in the drop 2 versions, but this time it's all three-note voicings using many different things we've explored in this book, including (but not limited to) triads, quartal and secundal chords, voicings derived from mixing triad-pairs, and drop 2 reductions. The next six examples explore the same concept in the key of F major. Then I convert all the examples into the parallel minor keys (C minor and F minor). Please feel free to create your own variations.

The chord symbols generally reflect the basic IIm7-V7-Imaj7 (or IIm7b5-V7-Im6 in minor), without specifying the particulars of the voicings used, except alterations on the V chords are at least refered to if not specifically indicated.

II-V-I COMP MELODIES IN C MAJOR

Ex. 11-10 starts on the root of the II chord. Even though the melody is diatonic, I have altered the V chord to form more interesting counter melodies.

Ex. 11-10

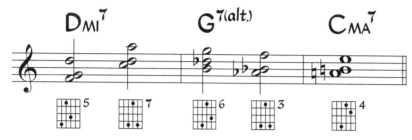

The same thing happens in Ex. 11-11, as it it frequently does in many of the examples. This time the melody starts on the 3rd of the II chord.

Ex. 11-11

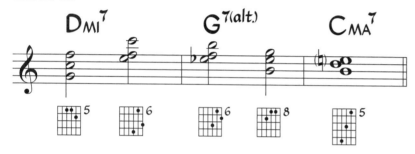

Ex. 11-12 starts on the 5th of the Dm7.

Ex. 11-12

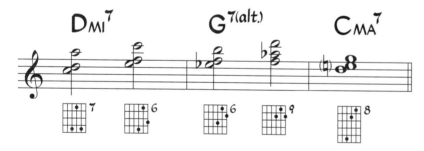

Ex. 11-13 starts on the 7th of the II chord.

Ex. 11-13

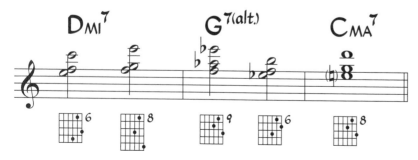

Ex. 11-14 starts on the 9th of the II chord.

Ex. 11-14

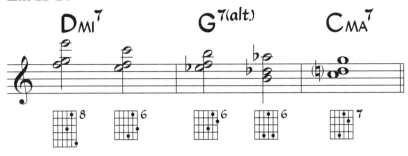

Ex. 11-15 starts on the 11th of the Dm7.

Ex. 11-15

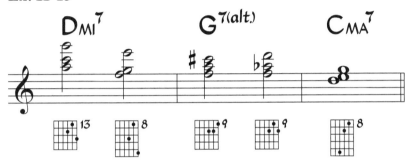

II-V-I COMP MELODIES IN F MAJOR

If we transpose the comp melodies we used in C major to the key of F major, many of the registers are either too high or too low to sound right, so we'll re-compose new lines for the key of F.

Ex. 11-16 starts on the root of Gm7.

Ex. 11-16

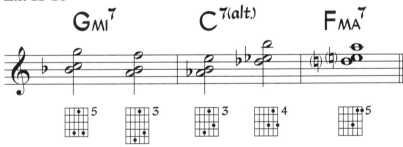

Ex. 11-17 starts on the 3rd of Gm7, and begins and ends with three-note stacks of 4ths.

Ex. 11-17

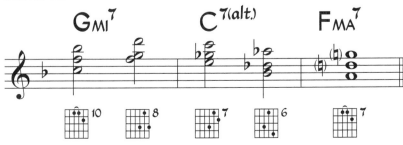

Ex. 11-18 starts on the 5th of Gm7.

Ex. 11-18

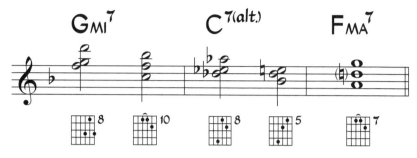

Ex. 11-19 starts on the 7th of Gm7.

Ex. 11-19

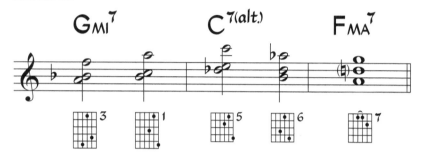

Ex. 11-20 starts on the 9th of Gm7. Notice that the bottom two voices are "walking" 2nds, with major 2nds climbing chromatically against the melody on the last three chords.

Ex. 11-20

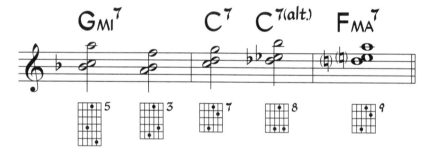

Ex. 11-21 starts on the 11th of Gm7.

Ex. 11-21

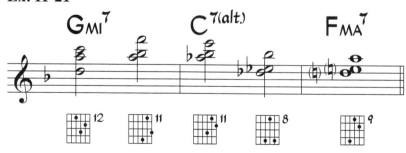

II-V-I COMP MELODIES IN C MINOR

Of course the melodies will be modified to fit the minor tonalities, but I'm still using the major key examples as models.

Ex. 11-22 starts on the root of Dm7b5.

Ex. 11-22

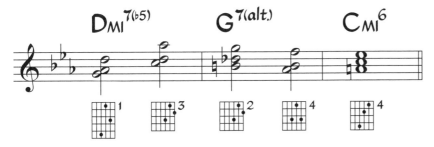

Ex. 11-23 starts on the 3rd of Dm7b5.

Ex. 11-23

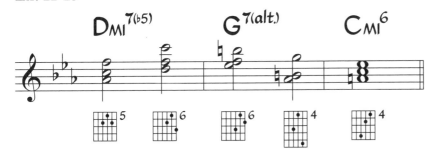

Ex. 11-24 starts on the 5th of Dm7b5.

Ex. 11-24

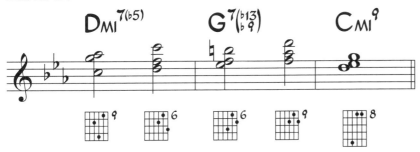

Ex. 11-25 starts on the 7th of Dm7b5.

Ex. 11-25

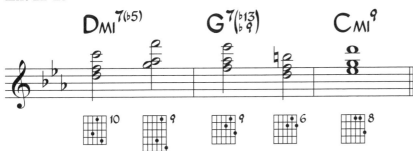

Ex. 11-26 starts on the 9th of Dm7b5. It's the natural 9th since the b9 is an avoid note, so it's outside of the C minor tonality. You can, if you wish, replace the first melody note, E, with an F, leaving the other notes where they are. This results in a much more inside sound.

Ex. 11-26

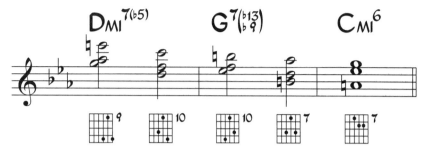

Ex. 11-27 starts on the 11th of Dm7b5.

Ex. 11-27

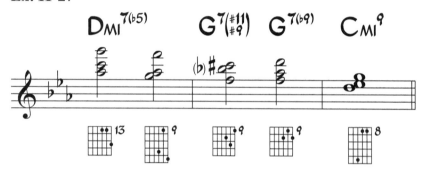

II-V-I COMP MELODIES IN F MINOR

Ex. 11-28 starts on the root of Gm7b5.

Ex. 11-28

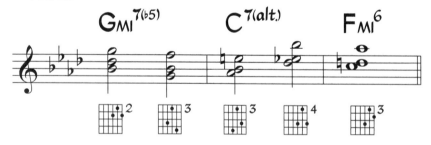

Ex. 11-29 starts on the 3rd of Gm7b5. The last chord is Fm-maj9, which is compatible with the Fm6 chord symbol.

Ex. 11-29

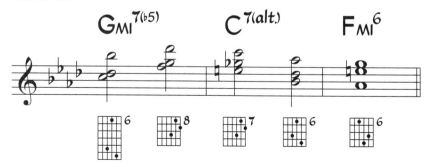

Ex. 11-30 starts on the 5th of Gm7b5.

Ex. 11-30

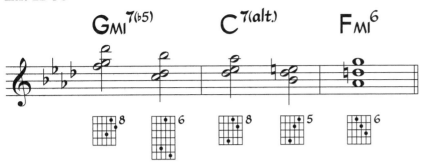

Ex. 11-31 starts on the 7th of Gm7b5. The second melody note is the natural 9th, so again you can replace it with the 3rd to make it more inside sounding.

Ex. 11-31

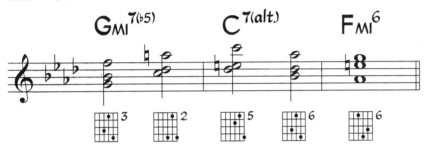

Ex. 11-32 starts on the 9th of Gm7b5. Being the natural 9th the same instructions still apply that applied to the previous examples wih natural 9ths.

Ex. 11-32

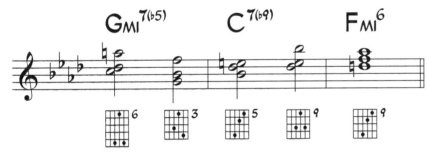

Ex. 11-33 starts on the 11th of Gm7b5.

Ex. 11-33

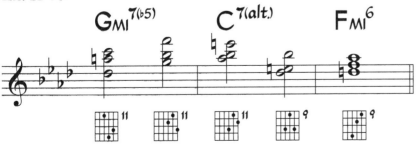

Hopefully these examples have shown how using melodies with skips can create more interesting harmonic combinations than you can achieve by following the standard textbook voice-leadings.

Chapter 12 - Melodies Revisited

HARMONIZING MELODIES WITH CHROMATIC PARALLEL VOICINGS

Play Ex. 12-1, the first four bars of Sonny Rollins' classic blues in Bb, "Sonnymoon For Two."

Ex. 12-1

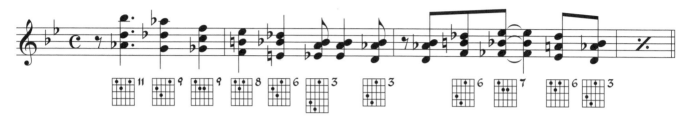

I'm not going to try to name the chords. They result from the chromatically descending tritones being forced in under the melody. A couple of the chords are technically "illegal" from a vertical, theory classroom viewpoint, but they work in context because of the logical melodies involved (although they may still be illegal in some states).

I'd like to try adding another note above the tritone, but the range doesn't permit. But if it's transposed to the key of F, I can give it a try.

Ex. 12-2 shows the same phrase as Ex. 12-1, but transposed into F with the tritones inverted so as to make more room to add another voice later.

Ex. 12-2

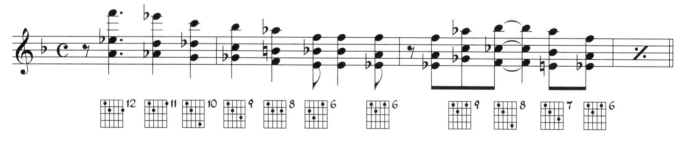

Ex. 12-3 shows the same phrase with the added notes. They are all a perfect 4th above the tritones, creating a chromatically descending three-note voicing under the melody.

Ex. 12-3

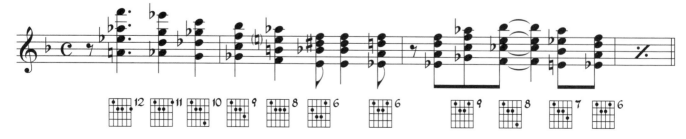

Next I'd like to try applying the chromatic parallel voices concept to a tune that's harmonically more complex.

Ex. 12-4 is the first four bars of Bernice Petkere's "Lullaby Of The Leaves."

Ex. 12-4

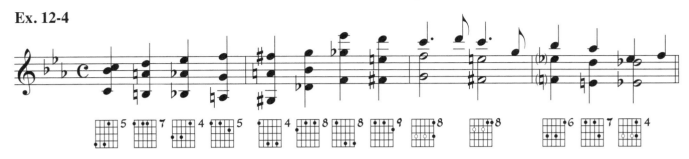

The ascending combined blues scale melody is, at first, harmonized by chromatically descending parallel minor 7th intervals. If we continued this motion when the melody reaches the F#, there would be an unwanted octave doubling of the melody by the middle voice, so here the middle voice leaps to the aid of the melody and begins following it in parallel major 6ths until the higher D melody note, at which time the middle voice resumes its role as a parallel minor 7th above the bottom voice.

Ex. 12-5 shows measures 28-31 of Victor Young's "Beautiful Love." It uses descending parallel tritones, mostly chromatic, to harmonize the melody. The first chord is a chromatic approach chord to the A7. It's played by the first, third, and fourth fingers. The A7 is played using the second and fourth fingers to play the tritone, while the F note is played by the third finger on the third string, followed by the G note played by the first finger on the second string. The Dm6 is followed by a chromatic approach chord to the B7.

Ex. 12-5

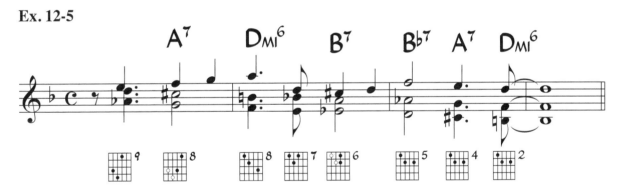

Ex. 12-6 shows measures 2-5 of Sigmund Romberg's "Softly, As In A Morning Sunrise" using parallel tritones descending and ascending to harmonize the melody.

Ex. 12-6

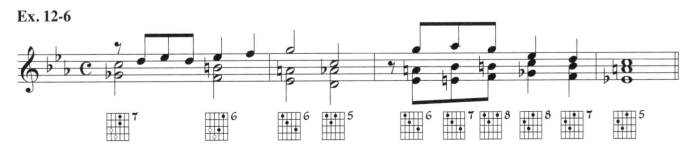

Ex. 12-7 revisits the first two bars of Jimmy Van Heusen's "Polkadots And Moonbeams." It starts with a single accompaniment voice in contrary motion, descending chromatically while the melody ascends the scale. It expands into three notes, a tritone moving under the melody, at the third note of the melody line. When the melody skips up to the high C, the expanded range requires something larger than a tritone, so the middle voice moves up to form parallel minor 7th intervals. All I can say is the rest is pure serendipity, especially since I intend to start the next bar with Am7.

Ex. 12-7

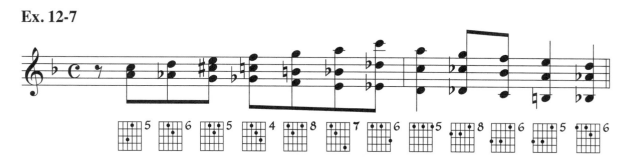

These chromatic parallel voicings frequently result in radical reharmonizations, making them potentially dangerous for use in a group setting. Some are relatively safe because they happen to fit the tunes changes well, as in the "Beautiful Love" excerpt above. Now let's try free combinations of all the types of three-note harmonizations we know to harmonize tunes without resorting to dangerous "reharms."

FREE THREE-NOTE COMBINATIONS

Ex. 12-8 is the last four measures of "Polkadots And Moonbeams."

Ex. 12-8

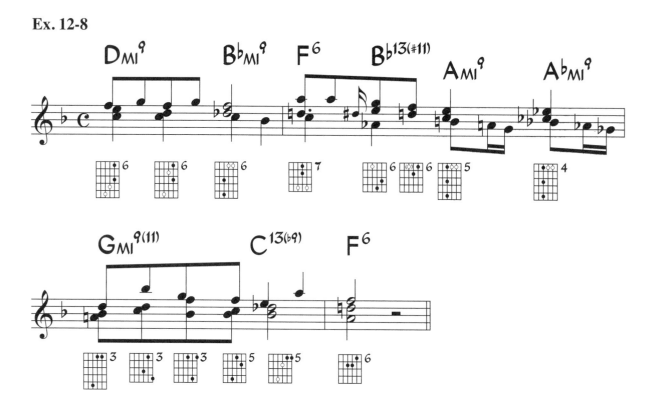

Ex. 12-9 is the first four bars of "Beautiful Love" without the pickup notes.

Ex. 12-9

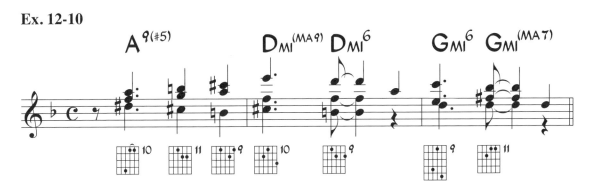

Ex. 12-10 shows bars 8-10 of "Beautiful Love." It starts with a wholetone scale invention similar to Ex. 7-47.

Ex. 12-10

Ex. 12-11 is the first four bars of Irving Berlin's "How Deep Is The Ocean?" The long notes in the original melody have been filled in with improvised melodies.

Ex. 12-11

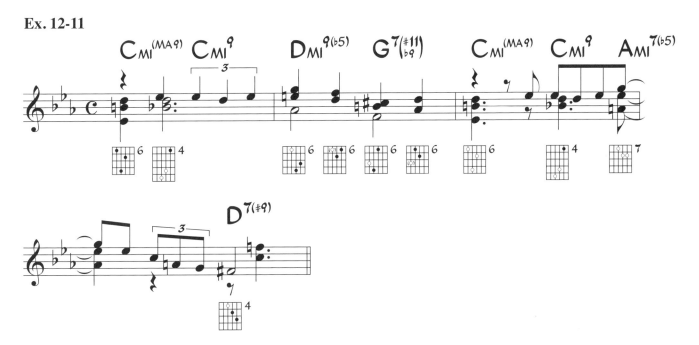

Ex. 12-12 shows the first three measures of Guy Wood's "My One And Only Love." The melody in the first bar is the Cmaj-Amin hexatonic scale, so I'm harmonizing it with two-note secundal structures that climb up the hexatonic scale under the melody. At the beginning of the second bar the climbing 2nds become diatonic to the C major scale, serendipitously landing on the perfect Dm9 voicing. From there countermelodies fill in under the longer melody notes.

Ex. 12-12

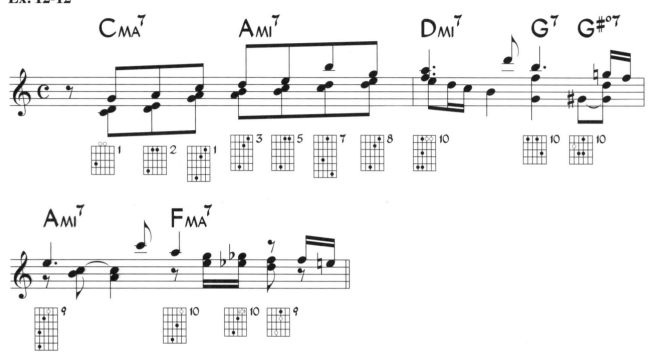

Ex. 12-13 is the first four bars of Gigi Gryce's "Minority," using some ideas inspired by a Bill Evans version.

Ex. 12-13

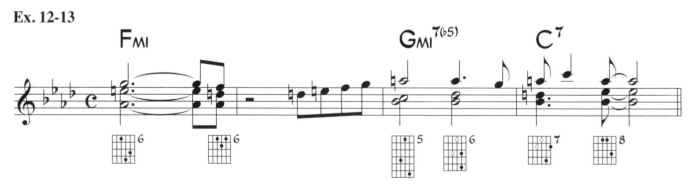

Ex. 12-14 shows the last four bars of "Minority," again Bill Evans-inspired.

Ex. 12-14

Ex. 12-15 is the first four bars of Sam Rivers' "Beatrice."

Ex. 12-15

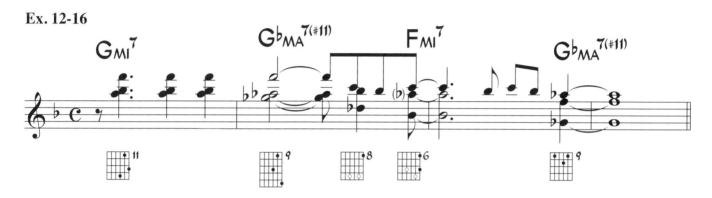

Ex. 12-16 shows the last four bars of Sam Rivers' "Beatrice."

Ex. 12-16

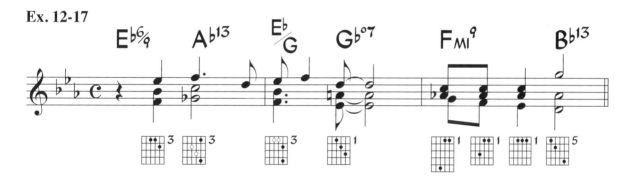

Ex. 12-17 is the first three measures of Burton Lane's "How About You."

Ex. 12-17

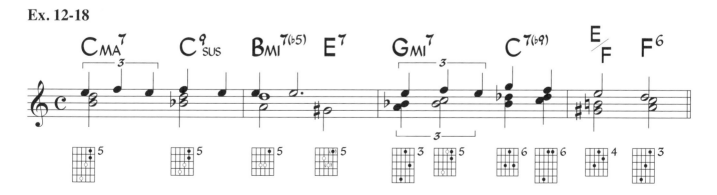

Ex. 12-18 shows bars 9-12 of the Sammy Cahn, Axel Stordahl, and Paul Weston tune "I Should Care."

Ex. 12-18

Ex. 12-19 revisits bars 9-11 of Victor Young's "Stella By Starlight."

Ex. 12-19

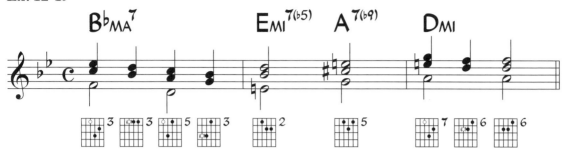

Ex. 12-20 shows the pick-up bar and the first three bars of the A section of "Danny Boy," a great tune for using counter-melodies to create enhanced harmonizations.

Ex. 12-20

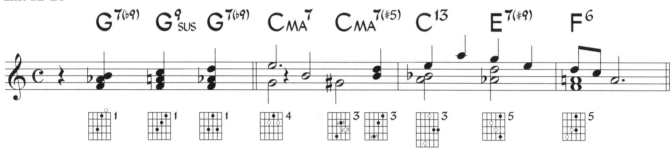

Ex. 12-21 shows the pick-up bar and the first three bars of the B section of "Danny Boy."

Ex. 12-21

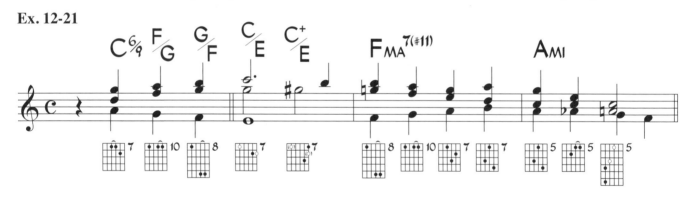

Ex. 12-22 shows the pick-up bar and the first three bars of the last section of "Danny Boy."

Ex. 12-22

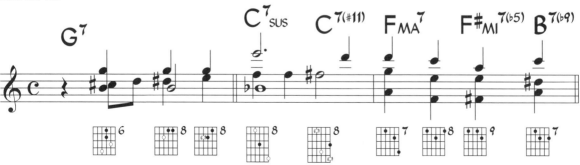

Ex. 12-23 is the last bar of the bridge and first three bars of the last eight of Bob Haggard's "What's New?"

Ex. 12-23

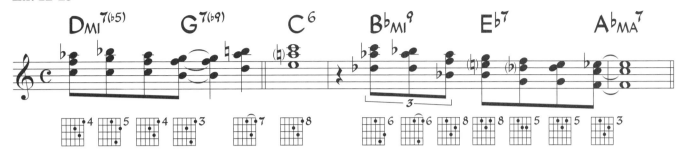

A MELODY IN SIMULATED SHEARING-STYLE VOICINGS

THE FRAGMENT FROM "WHAT'S NEW" IN SIMULATED SHEARING-STYLE

Ex. 12-24 is the last bar of the bridge and first three bars of the last eight of Bob Haggard's "What's New?" in simulated Shearing-style block chords. Notice it's really just Ex. 12-23 with the melody doubled in the octave below.

Ex. 12-24

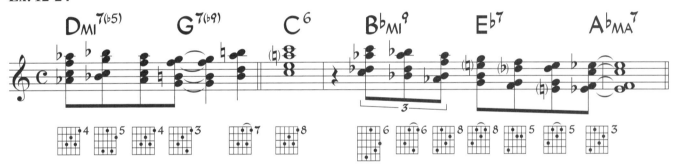

A DIFFERENT SOUND - MELODY ON THE BOTTOM ONLY

I was listening to a recording of Gene Bertoncini playing Jobim tunes (Gene Bertoncini's *Jobim – Someone To Light Up My Life*) with just a percussion accompaniment and marveled at his ability to create more variety in the orchestrations by sometimes placing the melody in the lowest voice. The thought occured to me that a good way to start developing the concept would be to experiment with leaving the top melody voice off of the Shearing-Style voicings since the melody is doubled on the bottom already.

Ex. 12-25 is based on Ex. 12-24 with the melody on the bottom only. Because there's no melody on top the voicings are slightly simplified to enable the melody to stand out more. (See next page.)

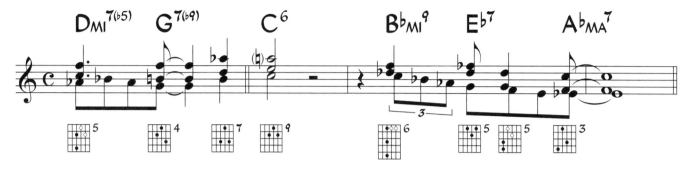

TWO MORE FRAGMENTS

Ex. 12-26 is based on Ex. 10-1, a fragment from "Polkadots And Moonbeams," with simplified voicings and the melody on the bottom only.

Ex. 12-26

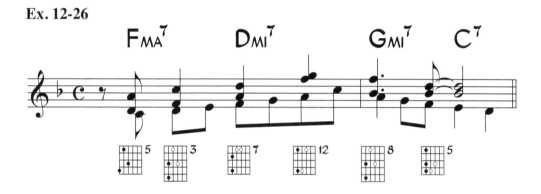

Ex. 12-27 is based on Ex. 10-2, a fragment from "Stella By Starlight," with simplified voicings and the melody on the bottom only.

Ex. 12-27

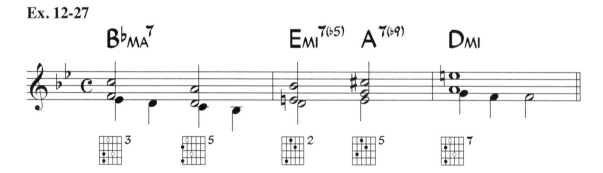

A PARTING THOUGHT

Many of the melody examples in three-note voicings can be expanded by adding another voice or two. Play Ex. 12-28, the first four bars of "Lullaby of the Leaves" revisited. It contains the same three voices as Ex. 12-4 with a fourth voice added. Sometimes the added voice is between the top two voices, sometimes between the bottom two. The result contains slash chords, some drop 2 and drop 3 voicings, and a couple of incidental Shearing chords.

Ex. 12-28

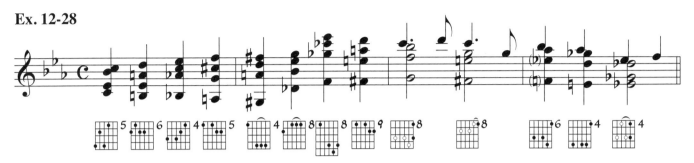

Feel free to experiment with expanding on any of the three-note examples, and try mixing with anything else you like along the way.

I think we've covered enough to give you a lifetime of enjoyable material to work on, so practice hard and have fun.

The New Real Book Series

The Standards Real Book (C, Bb or Eb)

A Beautiful Friendship
A Time For Love
Ain't No Sunshine
Alice In Wonderland
All Of You
Alone Together
At Last
Baltimore Oriole
Bess, You Is My Woman
Bluesette
But Not For Me
Close Enough For Love
Crazy He Calls Me
Dancing In The Dark
Days Of Wine And Roses

Dreamsville
Easy To Love
Embraceable You
Falling In Love With Love
From This Moment On
Give Me The Simple Life
Have You Met Miss Jones?
Hey There
I Can't Get Started
I Concentrate On You
I Cover The Waterfront
I Love You
I Loves You Porgy
I Only Have Eyes For You
I Wish I Knew

I'm A Fool To Want You
Indian Summer
It Ain't Necessarily So
It Never Entered My Mind
It's You Or No One
Just One Of Those Things
Love For Sale
Love Walked In
Lover, Come Back To Me
The Man I Love
Mr. Lucky
My Funny Valentine
My Heart Stood Still
My Man's Gone Now

Old Folks
On A Clear Day
Our Love Is Here To Stay
'Round Midnight
Secret Love
September In The Rain
Serenade In Blue
Shiny Stockings
Since I Fell For You
So In Love
So Nice (Summer Samba)
Some Other Time
Stormy Weather
The Summer Knows

Summer Night
Summertime
Teach Me Tonight
That Sunday, That Summer
The Girl From Ipanema
Then I'll Be Tired Of You
There's No You
Time On My Hands
'Tis Autumn
Where Or When
Who Cares?
With A Song In My Heart
You Go To My Head
And Hundreds More!

The New Real Book - Volume 1 (C, Bb or Eb)

Angel Eyes
Anthropology
Autumn Leaves
Beautiful Love
Bernie's Tune
Blue Bossa
Blue Daniel
But Beautiful
Chain Of Fools
Chelsea Bridge
Compared To What
Darn That Dream
Desafinado
Early Autumn
Eighty One

E.S.P.
Everything Happens To Me
Fall
Feel Like Makin' Love
Footprints
Four
Four On Six
Gee Baby Ain't I Good
To You
Gone With The Wind
Here's That Rainy Day
I Love Lucy
I Mean You
I Should Care
I Thought About You

If I Were A Bell
Imagination
The Island
Jersey Bounce
Joshua
Lady Bird
Like Someone In Love
Line For Lyons
Little Sunflower
Lush Life
Mercy, Mercy, Mercy
The Midnight Sun
Monk's Mood
Moonlight In Vermont
My Shining Hour

Nature Boy
Nefertiti
Nothing Personal
Oleo
Once I Loved
Out Of This World
Pent Up House
Polkadots And Moon-
beams
Portrait Of Tracy
Put It Where You Want It
Robbin's Nest
Ruby, My Dear
Satin Doll
Search For Peace

Shaker Song
Skylark
A Sleepin' Bee
Solar
Speak No Evil
St. Thomas
Street Life
Tenderly
These Foolish Things
This Masquerade
Three Views Of A Secret
Waltz For Debby
Willow Weep For Me
And Many More!

The New Real Book - Volume 2 (C, Bb or Eb)

Afro-Centric
After You've Gone
Along Came Betty
Bessie's Blues
Black Coffee
Blues For Alice
Body And Soul
Bolivia
The Boy Next Door
Bye Bye Blackbird
Cherokee
A Child Is Born
Cold Duck Time
Day By Day

Django
Equinox
Exactly Like You
Falling Grace
Five Hundred Miles High
Freedom Jazz Dance
Giant Steps
Got A Match?
Harlem Nocturne
Hi-Fly
Honeysuckle Rose
I Hadn't Anyone 'Til You
I'll Be Around
I'll Get By

Ill Wind
I'm Glad There Is You
Impressions
In Your Own Sweet Way
It's The Talk Of The Town
Jordu
Killer Joe
Lullaby Of The Leaves
Manha De Carneval
The Masquerade Is Over
Memories Of You
Moment's Notice
Mood Indigo
My Ship

Naima
Nica's Dream
Once In A While
Perdido
Rosetta
Sea Journey
Senor Blues
September Song
Seven Steps To Heaven
Silver's Serenade
So Many Stars
Some Other Blues
Song For My Father
Sophisticated Lady

Spain
Stablemates
Stardust
Sweet And Lovely
That's All
There Is No Greater Love
'Til There Was You
Time Remembered
Turn Out The Stars
Unforgettable
While We're Young
Whisper Not
Will You Still Be Mine?
You're Everything
And Many More!

The New Real Book - Volume 3 (C, Bb, Eb or Bass clef)

Actual Proof
Ain't That Peculiar
Almost Like Being In Love
Another Star
Autumn Serenade
Bird Of Beauty
Black Nile
Blue Moon
Butterfly
Caravan
Ceora
Close Your Eyes
Creepin'
Day Dream

Dolphin Dance
Don't Be That Way
Don't Blame Me
Emily
Everything I Have Is Yours
For All We Know
Freedomland
The Gentle Rain
Get Ready
A Ghost Of A Chance
Heat Wave
How Sweet It Is
I Fall In Love Too Easily
I Got It Bad

I Hear A Rhapsody
If You Could See Me Now
In A Mellow Tone
In A Sentimental Mood
Inner Urge
Invitation
The Jitterbug Waltz
Just Friends
Just You, Just Me
Knock On Wood
The Lamp Is Low
Laura
Let's Stay Together
Lonely Woman

Maiden Voyage
Moon And Sand
Moonglow
My Girl
On Green Dolphin Street
Over The Rainbow
Prelude To A Kiss
Respect
Ruby
The Second Time Around
Serenata
The Shadow Of Your Smile
So Near, So Far
Solitude

Speak Like A Child
Spring Is Here
Stairway To The Stars
Star Eyes
Stars Fell On Alabama
Stompin' At The Savoy
Sweet Lorraine
Taking A Chance On Love
This Is New
Too High
(Used To Be A) Cha Cha
When Lights Are Low
You Must Believe In Spring
And Many More!

The New Real Book Play-Along CDs (For Volume 1)

CD #1 - Jazz Classics - Lady Bird, Bouncin' With Bud, Up Jumped Spring, Monk's Mood, Doors, Very Early, Eighty One, Voyage **& More!**
CD #2 - Choice Standards - Beautiful Love, Darn That Dream, Moonlight In Vermont, Trieste, My Shining Hour, I Should Care **& More!**
CD #3 - Pop-Fusion - Morning Dance, Nothing Personal, La Samba, Hideaway, This Masquerade, Three Views Of A Secret, Rio **& More!**
World-Class Rhythm Sections, featuring Mark Levine, Larry Dunlap, Sky Evergreen, Bob Magnusson, Keith Jones, Vince Lateano & Tom Hayashi

Recent Sher Music Publications

Afro-Caribbean Grooves for Drumset

By Jean-Philippe Fanfant, drummer with Andy narell's band, Sakesho.

Covers grooves from 10 Caribbean nations, arranged for drumset. **CD includes both audio and video files.** $25.

Endorsed by Peter Erskine, Horacio Hernandez, etc.

The Real Easy Book Vol. 3
A SHORT HISTORY OF JAZZ

Published by Sher Music Co. in conjunction with the Stanford Jazz Workshop. Over 200 pages. $25.

History text and tunes from all eras and styles of jazz. Perfect for classroom use. Available in C, Bb, Eb and Bass Clef versions.

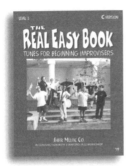

The Real Easy Book Vol. 1
TUNES FOR BEGINNING IMPROVISERS

Published by Sher Music Co. in conjunction with the Stanford Jazz Workshop. $19 list price.

The easiest tunes from Horace Silver, Eddie Harris, Freddie Hubbard, Red Garland, Sonny Rollins, Cedar Walton, Wes Montgomery Cannonball Adderly, etc. Get yourself or your beginning jazz combo sounding good right away with the first fake book ever designed for the beginning improviser. Available in C, Bb, Eb and Bass Clef.

The Real Easy Book Vol. 2
TUNES FOR INTERMEDIATE IMPROVISERS

Published by Sher Music Co. in conjunction with the Stanford Jazz Workshop. Over 240 pages. $29.

The best intermediate-level tunes by: Charlie Parker, John Coltrane, Miles Davis, John Scofield, Sonny Rollins, Horace Silver, Wes Montgomery, Freddie Hubbard, Cal Tjader, Cannonball Adderly, and more! Both volumes feature instructional material tailored for each tune. Perfect for jazz combos! Available in C, Bb, Eb and Bass Clef.

The Jazz Musicians Guide To Creative Practicing

By David Berkman

Finally a book to help musicians use their practice time wisely! Covers tune analysis, breaking hard tunes into easy components, how to swing better, tricks to playing fast bebop lines, and much more! 150+pages, plus CD. $29 list.

"Fun to read and bursting with things to do and ponder." – Bob Mintzer

The Serious Jazz Practice Book By Barry Finnerty

Includes CD - $30 list price. A unique and comprehensive plan for mastering the basic building blocks of the jazz language. It takes the most widely-used scales and chords and gives you step-by-step exercises that dissect them into hundreds of cool, useable patterns.

"The book I've been waiting for!" – Randy Brecker.

"The best book of intervallic studies I've ever seen." – Mark Levine

The All Jazz Real Book

Over 540 pages of tunes as recorded by: Miles, Trane, Bill Evans, Cannonball, Scofield, Brecker, Yellowjackets, Bird, Mulgrew Miller, Kenny Werner, MJQ, McCoy Tyner, Kurt Elling, Brad Mehldau, Don Grolnick, Kenny Garrett, Patitucci, Jerry Bergonzi, Stanley Clarke, Tom Harrell, Herbie Hancock, Horace Silver, Stan Getz, Sonny Rollins, and MORE!

Includes a free CD of many of the melodies (featuring Bob Sheppard & Friends.). $44 list price. Available in C, Bb, Eb

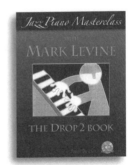

Jazz Piano Masterclass With Mark Levine
"THE DROP 2 BOOK"

The long-awaited book from the author of "The Jazz Piano Book!" A complete study on how to use "drop 2" chord voicings to create jazz piano magic! 68 pages, plus CD of Mark demonstrating each exercise. $19 list.

"Will make you sound like a real jazz piano player in no time." – Jamey Aebersold

Metaphors For The Musician
By Randy Halberstadt

This practical and enlightening book will help any jazz player or vocalist look at music with "new eyes." Designed for any level of player, on any instrument, "Metaphors For The Musician" provides numerous exercises throughout to help the reader turn these concepts into musical reality.

Guaranteed to help you improve your musicianship. 330 pages - $29 list price. Satisfaction guaranteed!

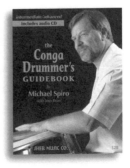

The Conga Drummer's Guidebook By Michael Spiro

Includes CD - $28 list price. The only method book specifically designed for the intermediate to advanced conga drummer. It goes behind the superficial licks and explains how to approach any Afro-Latin rhythm with the right feel, so you can create a groove like the pros!.

"This book is awesome. Michael is completely knowledgable about his subject." – Dave Garibaldi

"A breakthrough book for all students of the conga drum." – Karl Perazzo

Latin Music Books & CDs

The Latin Real Book (C, Bb or Eb)

The only professional-level Latin fake book ever published!
Over 570 pages. Detailed transcriptions exactly as recorded by:

Ray Barretto
Eddie Palmieri
Fania All-Stars
Tito Puente
Ruben Blades
Los Van Van
NG La Banda
Irakere
Celia Cruz

Arsenio Rodriguez
Tito Rodriguez
Orquesta Aragon
Beny Moré
Cal Tjader
Andy Narell
Mario Bauza
Dizzy Gilllespie
Mongo Santamaria

Manny Oquendo
Puerto Rico All-Stars
Issac Delgaldo
Ft. Apache Band
Dave Valentin
Paquito D'Rivera
Clare Fischer
Chick Corea
Sergio Mendes

Ivan Lins
Djavan
Tom Jobim
Toninho Horta
Joao Bosco
Milton Nascimento
Leila Pinheiro
Gal Costa
And Many More!

The Latin Real Book Sampler CD

12 of the greatest Latin Real Book tunes as played by the original artists: Tito Puente, Ray Barretto, Andy Narell, Puerto Rico Allstars, Bacacoto, etc.

$16 list price. Available in U.S.A. only.

Muy Caliente!

Afro-Cuban Play-Along CD and Book
Rebeca Mauleón - Keyboard
Oscar Stagnaro - Bass
Orestes Vilató - Timbales
Carlos Caro - Bongos
Edgardo Cambon - Congas
Over 70 min. of smokin' Latin grooves! Stereo separation so you can eliminate the bass or piano. Play-along with a rhythm section featuring some of the top Afro-Cuban musicians in the world! $18.

Introduction to the Conga Drum - DVD
By Michael Spiro

For beginners, or anyone needing a solid foundation in conga drum technique.

Jorge Alabe – "Mike Spiro is a great conga teacher. People can learn the real conga technique from this DVD."

John Santos – "A great musician/teacher who's earned his stripes"

1 hour, 55 minutes running time. $25.

101 Montunos
by Rebeca Mauleón

The only comprehensive study of Latin piano playing ever published.

- Bi-lingual text (English/Spanish)
- 2 CDs of the author demonstrating each montuno
- Covers over 100 years of Afro-Cuban styles, including the danzón, guaracha, mambo, merengue and songo—from Peruchin to Eddie Palmieri. $28

The True Cuban Bass

By Carlos Del Puerto, (bassist with Irakere) and **Silvio Vergara**, $22.

For acoustic or electric bass; English and Spanish text; Includes CDs of either historic Cuban recordings or Carlos playing each exercise; Many transcriptions of complete bass parts for tunes in different Cuban styles – the roots of Salsa.

The Brazilian Guitar Book
by Nelson Faria, one of Brazil's best new guitarists.

- Over 140 pages of comping patterns, transcriptions and chord melodies for samba, bossa, baiaõ, etc.
- Complete chord voicings written out for each example.
- Comes with a CD of Nelson playing each example.
- The most complete Brazilian guitar method ever published! $28.

Joe Diorio – "Nelson Faria's book is a welcome addition to the guitar literature. I'm sure those who work with this volume wiiill benefit greatly"

The Salsa Guide Book
By Rebeca Mauleón

The only complete method book on salsa ever published! 260 pages. $25.

Carlos Santana – "A true treasure of knowledge and information about Afro-Cuban music."
Mark Levine, author of The Jazz Piano Book. – "This is the book on salsa."
Sonny Bravo, pianist with Tito Puente – "This will be the salsa 'bible' for years to come."
Oscar Hernández, pianist with Rubén Blades – "An excellent and much needed resource."

The Latin Bass Book
A PRACTICAL GUIDE
By Oscar Stagnaro

The only comprehensive book ever published on how to play bass in authentic Afro-Cuban, Brazilian, Caribbean, Latin Jazz & South American styles. $34.

Over 250 pages of transcriptions of Oscar Stagnaro playing each exercise. Learn from the best!

Includes: 3 Play-Along CDs to accompany each exercise, featuring world-class rhythm sections.

Inside The Brazilian Rhythm Section
By Nelson Faria and Cliff Korman

This is the first book/CD package ever published that provides an opportunity for bassists, guitarists, pianists and drummers to interact and play-along with a master Brazilian rhythm section. Perfect for practicing both accompanying and soloing.

$28 list price for book and 2 CDs - including the charts for the CD tracks and sample parts for each instrument, transcribed from the recording. Satisfaction guaranteed!

More Jazz Publications

The Digital Real Book

On the web

Over 850 downloadable tunes from all the Sher Music Co. fakebooks.

See www.shermusic.com for details.

Walking Bassics: The Fundamentals of Jazz Bass Playing

By swinging NY bassist Ed Fuqua

Includes transcriptions of every bass note on accompanying CD and step-by-step method for constructing solid walking bass lines. $22.

Endorsed by Eddie Gomez, Jimmy Haslip, John Goldsby, etc.

The Jazz Theory Book

By Mark Levine, the most comprehensive Jazz Theory book ever published! $38 list price.
- Over 500 pages of text and over 750 musical examples.
- Written in the language of the working jazz musician, this book is easy to read and user-friendly. At the same time, it is the most comprehensive study of jazz harmony and theory ever published.
- Mark Levine has worked with Bobby Hutcherson, Cal Tjader, Joe Henderson, Woody Shaw, and many other jazz greats.

The European Real Book

An amazing collection of some of the greatest jazz compositions ever recorded! Available in C, Bb and Eb. $40
- Over 100 of Europe's best jazz writers.
- 100% accurate, composer-approved charts.
- 400 pages of fresh, exciting sounds from virtually every country in Europe.
- Sher Music's superior legibility and signature calligraphy makes reading the music easy.

Listen to FREE MP3 FILES of many of the songs at www.shermusic.com!

The Jazz Piano Book

By Mark Levine, Concord recording artist and pianist with Cal Tjader. For beginning to advanced pianists. The only truly comprehensive method ever published! Over 300 pages. $32

Richie Beirach – "The best new method book available."
Hal Galper – "This is a must!"
Jamey Aebersold – "This is an invaluable resource for any pianist."
James Williams – "One of the most complete anthologies on jazz piano."

Also available in Spanish! ¡El Libro del Jazz Piano!

Concepts For Bass Soloing

By Chuck Sher and Marc Johnson, (bassist with Bill Evans, etc.) The only book ever published that is specifically designed to improve your soloing! $26
- Includes two CDs of Marc Johnson soloing on each exercise
- Transcriptions of bass solos by: Eddie Gomez, John Patitucci, Scott LaFaro, Jimmy Haslip, etc.

"It's a pleasure to encounter a Bass Method so well conceived and executed." – **Steve Swallow**

The Yellowjackets Songbook

Complete package contains six separate spiral-bound books, one each for:
- Piano/partial score • C melody lead sheet
- Synthesizer/miscellaneous parts
- Bb & Eb Horn melody part • Bass • Drums

Contains 20 great tunes from their entire career. Charts exactly as recorded – approved by the Yellowjackets. World famous Sher Music Co. accuracy and legibility. Over 400 pages, $38 list price.

The Improvisor's Bass Method

By Chuck Sher. A complete method for electric or acoustic bass, plus transcribed solos and bass lines by Mingus, Jaco, Ron Carter, Scott LaFaro, Paul Jackson, Ray Brown, and more! Over 200 pages. $16

International Society of Bassists – "Undoubtedly the finest book of its kind."
Eddie Gomez – "Informative, readily comprehensible and highly imaginative"

The World's Greatest Fake Book

Jazz & Fusion Tunes by: **Coltrane, Mingus, Jaco, Chick Corea, Bird, Herbie Hancock, Bill Evans, McCoy, Beirach, Ornette, Wayne Shorter, Zawinul, AND MANY MORE!** $32

Chick Corea – "Great for any students of jazz.'
Dave Liebman – "The fake book of the 80's."
George Cables – "The most carefully conceived fake book I've ever seen."

The Jazz Solos of Chick Corea

Over 150 pages of Chick's greatest solos; "Spain", "Litha", "Windows", "Sicily", etc. for all instrumentalists, single line transcriptions, not full piano score. $18

Chick Corea – "I don't know anyone I would trust more to correctly transcribe my improvisations."